Feminism

Issues & Arguments

Feminism

Issues & Arguments

Jennifer Saul

OXFORD
UNIVERSITY PRESS

OXFORD
UNIVERSITY PRESS

Great Clarendon Street, Oxford OX2 6DP
United Kingdom

Oxford University Press is a department of the University of Oxford.
It furthers the University's objective of excellence in research, scholarship,
and education by publishing worldwide. Oxford is a registered trade mark of
Oxford University Press in the UK and in certain other countries

© Jennifer Saul 2003

The moral rights of the author have been asserted

First published 2003
Reprinted 2012

British Library Cataloguing in Publication Data
Data available

Library of Congress Cataloging in Publication Data
Data available

ISBN 978-0-19-924947-3

Printed and bound by CPI Group (UK) Ltd, Croydon, CR0 4YY

To my grandmother, Bertha Williams Mather, who ensured that feminism was a part of my life right from the start.

Preface

For several years I have taught feminism to students with (in many cases) no background in feminism or philosophy, and no prior commitment to feminism. I found it extraordinarily difficult to find an appropriate text for this group. Because much feminist philosophy begins from a critique of more traditional philosophy, feminist writing tends to assume a familiarity with the basic philosophical literature. In addition, most textbooks are written for students who are already committed to feminism. This makes it possible for authors to presume a shared base of assumptions that were simply not appropriate for the class I taught. I made an additional decision that rendered my textbook-finding task if anything more difficult: since my students had largely enrolled for a taste of what feminism is, and since feminism in fact does have enormous practical relevance, I decided to orient the class as far as possible around issues that students already cared about or were likely to face at some point in their lives. Rather than teaching differences between liberal and socialist feminism, then, I taught topics like pornography, sexual harassment, and gender differences, using these topics as ways to introduce a variety of perspectives within feminism.

As I taught the course described above, I realized that a book following this approach had the potential to be useful not only as a textbook but also as an introduction to feminism for the curious general reader. The present book is the result of these thoughts. In it, I have attempted to combine both theoretical and practical concerns in a way that makes the material accessible and interesting even for readers who are not already feminists. There are, of course, costs to this approach. The emphasis on accessibility and the refusal to assume prior knowledge or commitments mean that I cannot address feminist issues at as high a level of theoretical sophistication as some might like. However, there are many excellent books already available for those able to assume more background than I do. It also means that some debates that are very important to feminism have had to go largely unexplored here: for example, I do not address the huge and lively literature on the idea that women differ so much from one another that the concept *woman* makes no sense. I do try, however, to incorporate some of the concerns that motivate this literature—differences between women play a role in many chapters, and a particularly important role in some. Another sort of omission involves my focus—with the exception of Chapter 9—on the US and the UK. I have focused on these countries for the sake of brevity and coherence, and because I am far more personally familiar with them than with other countries.

Instead of attempting comprehensiveness in my presentation of feminist issues, I have selected a sampling of issues designed to give some idea of the range of topics that are of feminist concern. On each issue, I have only been able to present a fraction of the feminist views available. Nonetheless, I have tried to offer a range of views on the topics that I discuss, and to take seriously criticisms of those views that I end up advocating. These are thorny issues, and there is much room for debate. I have tried to show the way to productive debate over these often emotionally fraught topics by presenting detailed arguments for multiple views. My hope is that readers will then be well situated to develop their own views on these matters, based on a solid understanding even of those views that they disagree with.

Outline Contents

Detailed Contents

Acknowledgements

Six years ago, Peter Carruthers suggested that I write this book (soon after he decided to replace our first-year political philosophy class with a first-year feminism class). I am grateful to him, and to all the members of Sheffield's philosophy department (academic staff, secretaries, and students), for the encouragement they have given me throughout the writing of this book. They have provided a working environment so ideal that I find it difficult to believe how fortunate I have been.

Many people, both in Sheffield, and elsewhere, have generously read draft chapters and provided extremely useful feedback: Pamela Anderson, Louise Antony, Albert Atkin, Chris Bennett, Thom Brooks, Esa Diaz-Leon, Ray Drainville, Sue Dwyer, Miranda Fricker, Dimitris Galanakis, Chris Hookway, Larry Horn, Rosanna Keefe, Rae Langton, Steve Laurence, Anna Mahtani, Mari Mikkola, Uma Narayan, Susan Okin, Teresa Robertson, Komarine Romdenh-Romluc, Frank Saul, Julie Saul, Anna Sherratt, Tom Simpson, Jon Webber, Leif Wenar, Ian White, Kathryn Wilkinson, and several anonymous referees. I am deeply grateful to all of them. Several others have provided very useful advice on specific points. In particular, I would like to thank Saba Ahmed, Bill Herbert, Lydia Ievins, Patricia Novotny, Joe Saul, Vicki Schultz, and the members of Joan Korenman's excellent interdisciplinary women's studies mailing list, WMST-L. Audiences at the Universities of Crete, Ljubljana, Maribor, and Valencia, Reed College, and the Palm Shores Retirement Center gave me the chance to try out some of the material in this book at an early stage, and I thank them for the excellent and enjoyable discussions they gave it. I would like to thank Julie Yoo and her students at Lafayette College for trying the book out, and for providing much-needed encouragement during the difficult final days of writing. I am grateful to Paul Sludds for suggesting the thought experiment featured in the introduction. Finally, I have learned an enormous amount from years of discussions with my students at Sheffield: they have made feminism extremely enjoyable to teach, and I thank them for it.

My editor, Ruth Anderson, has been a fount of good sense and helpful support throughout this project. I am very grateful to my intrepid research assistant, Mari Mikkola, for her patience, thoroughness, and ability to maintain a sense of the absurd as my requests took her to internet sites that she never really wanted to see.

Finally, I owe particularly deep debts of gratitude to my parents, for supporting me in all my endeavours, including this one; and to my partner, Ray Drainville. Throughout this book, Ray has been my most careful reader and editor, subjecting my ideas and writing to fierce yet friendly scrutiny; over and over again suggesting just the right turn of phrase to get my point across; and insisting that '. . . and another argument' is not an acceptable section heading. Ray also designed the book's cover. I thank him for all of this work, and for supporting me through all the strains of writing this book.

Introduction

Many people today think that feminism was a fine thing in its time but that it has done its job, at least in most Western countries. Western countries have laws forbidding discrimination on the basis of sex. Women can vote, hold jobs, and get educations. Women are entering traditionally male workplaces and professions in ever-increasing numbers. Women did face barriers in the past, and they do face barriers elsewhere in the world, but in the West, according to this line of thought, the battle has been won.

Perhaps part of the belief that feminism is (or should be) a thing of the past comes from an overly restricted understanding of what feminism is. Many people take feminism's goals to have been simply the achievements noted above. If that were the case, then it would indeed be true that feminism has done its job. But most feminists have goals that go well beyond these accomplishments. This is not because they wish to see women elevated above men, as popular caricatures have it, but rather because they believe women still face large and serious problems. This may at first seem puzzling: what problems could there be that have not yet been addressed? Feminists' answers to this question vary enormously, as do their solutions to the problems that they see. This is a key reason why the term 'feminism' evades easy definition. Rather than try to define 'feminism', I aim—in the course of this book—to give the reader a sense of the breadth of issues that concern feminists and the range of views that feminists take on these issues. For the moment, though, I offer two examples that give some indication that there is still work for feminism to do. The examples concern economic and political equality.

First, economic equality: women in the US are 50 per cent more

likely than men to live in poverty (McLanahan and Kelly 1999: 144).
Women in the US with full-time, year-round jobs earn, on average,
only 73 per cent of what their male counterparts earn (National
Committee on Pay Equity 2002). Women in the UK, on average, earn
'24.1% less an hour than men doing an equivalent job' (Toyne 2002)
and are significantly more likely than men to live in poverty
(McLanahan and Kelly 1999: 143). It looks as though there is still work
for feminism to do: women and men are not equal economically, and
the high rate of female poverty is a pressing problem.

Now turn to politics. Not so long ago, the idea of a woman president
in the US or prime minister in the UK was nearly inconceivable. Once
this fact was called to one's attention, it became very difficult to insist
that women and men really were equally situated politically. But
things are no longer like this—Britain has had a female prime minister, and an exceptionally powerful one. A woman president is not
inconceivable. Does this mean, then, that women and men are
equally situated politically, or least close to getting there? I'm not so
sure. Trying to imagine the political positions of the sexes reversed is a
helpful way to see this. This reversal requires more than imagining a
woman president. It requires imagining that both the president and
the vice-president are female, that the presidential and vice-
presidential candidates from the other major party are also female,
and that it seems perfectly plausible for things to continue this way for
some time. The ludicrousness of this scenario serves to illustrate the
extent to which politics is still very, very male. It also helps to show
the invisibility of that which we take for granted. We don't find the
maleness of politics at all odd, surprising, or even noticeable until we
try a thought experiment like this. Once we do this, however, we see
important structural features of the world we live in that we had not
noticed before. Much of this book will concern the ways in which new
concepts, arguments, and questions can alert us to the surprisingna-
ture of many things that we take for granted. (Indeed, this is an
important role for philosophy more generally.)

The two examples I have offered, concerning poverty and politics,
by no means *prove* that there is still work for feminism to do. Indeed,
many people insist that what I've called attention to in these examples
is merely the result of free choices made by men and women living in

a state of equality. According to this line of argument, making discrimination on grounds of sex illegal is enough to bring it about
that women and men are equally situated on a level playing field.
Any differences in where men and women end up, then, must be
due to the free choices that individual men and women happen
to make.

Many feminists, however, think that there is much more to be said.
They maintain that there is much more to power relations between
the sexes than the presence or absence of laws against sex discrimination. In particular, they argue for the significance of matters
traditionally considered private and personal, rather than political—
the structure of families, sexual relationships, appearance-related
concerns, or the words we use. To take just one example: women
generally perform the majority of child-rearing tasks, and most
better-paying and more secure jobs are incompatible with substantial
childcare responsibilities. Unsurprisingly, then, women tend to hold
less well-paid and less secure jobs. One could react to this by saying
that it offers a satisfying explanation for the fact that men are financially better off than women, and one on which nobody needs to be
blamed for sexism. Or, as I will urge in Chapter 1, one could argue that
it shows that the real problems for women go far beyond obvious sorts
of discrimination—and that solving them will require a restructuring
of families and workplaces.

This also serves to highlight something about feminism that many
find surprising: feminism is not just about women. If families change
so that domestic burdens do not fall so heavily on women, they will
in all likelihood be shared more fully with men. But this does not
mean that feminism is about elevating women at the expense of
men. If workplaces make it easier to combine good jobs with childcare, women will be more able to hold good jobs—but men will also
be more able to participate more fully in raising their children. As I
note in Chapter 1, studies show that men would welcome such
changes. This sort of example, then, shows not only the ways in
which men's and women's situations are interlinked, but also the
ways in which improving women's situations can improve men's as
well.

This book highlights nine issues that have been important to feminist discussions. A common theme in our discussion of these issues will be ways in which feminists have shown the political significance of matters not traditionally considered political. These issues range from the very practical (sexual harassment, abortion) to the more theoretical (do women think differently from men, and if they do, should this affect our moral and political theories?). Together, they show the potential of feminism both to transform old debates and to introduce entirely new ones.

1

The Politics of Work and Family

Family life is traditionally considered to be the most intimate and personal of realms, one that is and should be governed by instinct or emotion. In particular, it has been thought that the family has nothing to do with political considerations like justice or injustice. As a result, theorists of justice have generally ignored the family, maintaining that the structure and composition of families is fundamentally a personal and not a political matter. Feminists have shown, however, that this sharp division between the personal and the political cannot be upheld. Families both shape and are shaped by factors that are clearly of political significance. In particular, we shall see, their structures play a key role in impoverishing and disadvantaging women; and their structures are shaped, at least in part, by constraints imposed by laws, workplaces, and the ways that children are educated. Poverty and its causes are clearly matters of vital importance for political theorists; and laws, workplaces, and education have long been considered political matters. The family, then, is inescapably political. The importance to feminism of breaking down the sharp distinction between the public, political realm and the private, familial realm cannot be overestimated. Carole Pateman writes: 'The dichotomy between the private and the public . . . is, ultimately, what the feminist movement is about' (1989: 118).

Because the structure of the family has not been the subject of much attention in political thought, properly appreciating its significance requires new conceptions of key notions like discrimination. This chapter, then, serves to illustrate the way that feminists have reconceived some of the most basic and important political ideas in order to understand the situation of women. We will see that it also serves to illustrate the way that the situation of women is crucially linked to that of men.

My discussion will move back and forth between empirical and philosophical issues. After introducing the traditional understanding of sex discrimination, I will describe some ways that current work-places and divorce courts disadvantage women without committing discrimination as traditionally understood. Then I will turn to explaining a way in which these problems can be understood as discrimination. Next, I will discuss the consequences for traditional political theory of taking family structure and its effects seriously. Finally, I will discuss feminist proposals for challenging the assumptions that underpin the current structures of workplaces and families. At many points along the way, I will consider objections to the views that are my main focus.

Before we begin, it is important to clear up some potential mis-understandings. First, this chapter will focus primarily on mothers. I do this not because they are somehow more important or more central to feminism than other women (they are not), but rather because they provide an especially clear illustration of the sort of problem at issue. However, many of the concerns raised are also of obvious relevance to non-mothers with caregiving responsibilities (such as those who care for elderly relatives).[1] Second, I will often draw on generalizations about women and men: these are statistical generalizations, which are of course not true of all women and men.[2]

---

[1] In discussing division of household labour, I focus on heterosexual couples. Research suggests that gay and lesbian couples have a more equal division of household labour than heterosexual couples (Shelton and John 1996: 309). I also focus on married couples. Some research suggests that cohabiting, unmarried couples have a more equitable division of labour than married couples (Shelton and John 1996: 309). One source of possible confusion in examining the literature discussed in this chapter, however, is that some studies (such as Christopher et al. 2001) use the term 'married' to refer to both married and cohabiting couples.

[2] It is perhaps also worth noting that I focus here on issues of employment. I do not discuss the very important issue of support available to unemployed women. A good cross-cultural discussion of this can be found in Christopher et al. (2001).

Difference and dominance

Difference

The traditional way to understand sex discrimination has been what Catherine MacKinnon calls the 'difference' analysis. According to this analysis, it is discriminatory to treat people differently on grounds of sex, unless sex makes a legitimate difference to the decision being made. This approach defines sex discrimination as the arbitrary or irrational use of sex in the award of benefits or positions. In order to be discriminatory, then, a decision has to be based on sex, and sex must not be a legitimate factor to take into account. So:

1. It is not discriminatory to take sex into account in making a decision if there is a legitimate reason for doing so. One might, for example, be able to make a case that the position of live-in counsellor for a women's dormitory should be female. Basing a hiring decision on sex in such a case would not, then, count as discriminatory.

2. It is not discriminatory to have a selection procedure that in fact results in many more men than women being hired, as long as sex itself is not a factor in the decision procedure. If it were the case, then, that men were in general far better than women at needlework, and one set out to hire the best needleworkers, it would probably turn out that one ended up hiring far more men than women. This would not be discriminatory, as long as ability to do needlework rather than sex was the basis for hiring decisions.

With this understanding in place, we will turn to two examples of ways that MacKinnon and other theorists believe the difference analysis falls short—with regard to job definitions and divorce settlements. In doing so, we will be employing MacKinnon's alternative, the dominance model of discrimination—a model that will be explained in more detail shortly. We will see that apparently gender-neutral assumptions about workers have damaging effects on women.

Job descriptions

In our society as it currently stands, the best-paid and most secure jobs have requirements that are difficult to meet for anyone who is the primary caregiver for small children. This seems to be true in many different areas of employment. The expected working week in both blue-collar and white-collar jobs with good benefits (such as pensions and healthcare)[3] has been increasing steadily (Schor 1991; Williams 2000: 50–1). The best-paid and most secure working-class jobs are generally factory jobs that often require overtime (Williams 2000: 80). White-collar jobs also require long hours, with forty-hour weeks sometimes being considered 'part-time' (Williams 2000: pp. 72–3). In, addition many jobs give workers little choice concerning the time of day that the work must be done. Finally, many jobs require that workers be able to relocate readily when needed.

Jobs with requirements like these simply cannot be done by someone who is the primary caregiver for a young child. The only sort of parent who can fill these jobs is one who has someone else doing the childcare. Employers will, quite legitimately, hire only those workers who can do the jobs for which they are hiring. Since so many good jobs are incompatible with substantial childcare responsibilities, employers will quite reasonably end up hiring workers who are not primary childcare providers.

Women are, statistically, far more likely than men to be primary childcare providers. In addition, women, in general, undertake by far the greater proportion of household labour. Studies on these issues are tremendously complicated. Results vary greatly, depending on techniques used for gathering data. But all studies agree that women do substantially more housework[4] and childcare than men. Many studies report that women do up to 80 per cent of the housework and childcare, and even the most conservative estimates put women's share of this work at around two-thirds (Maushart 2002: 135; Shelton and John 1996: 299; Williams 2000: 2; Kimmel 2000: 128). Since

---

[3] The latter concern is more relevant to the US than the UK. The UK provides nationalized healthcare at taxpayers' expense, while the US does not.

[4] 'Housework' refers not only to chores within the house, but also to domestic duties outside the house, like lawnmowing or shopping.

women so often have these household responsibilities, the selection procedure of hiring only those who can fulfil the responsibilities of the job will have the result that far more men than women get jobs with good pay and benefits.

Under the difference analysis of discrimination, this is not discriminatory. Whether or not a worker can fulfil the responsibilities of a job is an entirely legitimate and reasonable thing for an employer to take into account. An employer may in fact be trying very hard to increase the number of women that she hires. But as long as so few women meet the requirements of jobs being offered, she will end up hiring more men than women.

Women, of course, take job requirements into account when they decide what jobs to seek. Joan Williams cites a study of a factory in which blue-collar workers on the factory floor earned much more money than clerical workers. Despite this disparity, not many women attempted to transfer to the better-paid positions. Why? Because clerical workers were entitled to twenty days of sick or personal leave, while floor workers to only two. Those with significant caregiving responsibilities choose the jobs that allow them to fulfil these responsibilities (Williams 2000: 80). In general, traditionally male jobs are structured around the assumption that their holders do not have significant caregiving responsibilities. This difference between traditionally male and traditionally female jobs helps to bring about an extreme degree of job segregation by sex. According to Williams, 'Nearly 60 percent of women hold jobs in traditional women's work such as clerical, sales, and service occupations, which typically pay half to two-thirds of the wages in blue-collar work' (p. 81).

Due to the incompatibility of better-paid, full-time work with childcare, women who are primary childcare providers often end up in part-time work, or lower-paid full-time work. Single mothers find it even more difficult to work full-time jobs. It is of course unsurprising that part-time workers earn less each year than full-time workers. What may be more surprising, and what is very difficult to justify, is that part-time workers in the United States earn 40 per cent less *each hour that they work* than full-time workers (Crittenden 2001: 97; Williams 2000: 54).

As primary caregivers, women also often take periods of time off from paid work. But in many jobs, both blue-collar and white-collar, advancement depends on seniority, and interruptions in one's work eliminate whatever seniority one might have had (Crittenden 2001: 96; Williams 2000: 79). Women, then, earn less than men because they are unable to fill better-paid jobs, because they work part-time rather than full-time, and because they cannot gain the seniority needed for promotion.[5]

Divorce

While many married mothers are working short hours for low pay with poor promotion prospects, their husbands are working full-time, gaining promotions and seniority, and increasing their earning potential. The difference between men's and women's economic prospects is often magnified still further when women take time off from paid work to care for children. In either case, a key reason that the male partners are able to concentrate successfully upon their careers is that the female partners take on most of the burden of childcare.

When marriages break up (as they so often do), women are severely disadvantaged by the way that courts award settlements. Indeed, divorce has been a key force that drives many women into poverty. At first glance, what courts do in awarding settlements is not discriminatory. They begin from the assumption that the money earned by each spouse is the money that spouse receives from their employer, and on the face of it this is a perfectly gender-neutral assumption. However, its effect is to severely disadvantage women. In addition, it neglects (as we will explore more fully later) the way that the non-earning spouse's family work has contributed to the earning spouse's income. The question posed in most divorce settlements has been: How much of the man's wage should the woman get? Courts generally give women very little. 'Although one study found that 80 percent of women assume they will be able to get alimony if they need it, in fact few women are awarded alimony today (about

---

[5] Undoubtedly, other factors also pay a role. For example, black women are far more likely to live in poverty than white women. Black men are also more likely than white women to live in poverty, though less likely than black women (McLanahan and Kelly 1999: 131). Racism, then, is also clearly an important factor in bringing about many women's poverty.

8 percent) or ever have been' (Williams 2000: 122). Child support is also meagre, and especially so for some of the poorest of women—those on AFDC (the main welfare programme in the US). Demie Kurz notes that such women are only entitled to $50 each month for child support payments.

Federal law dictates that women on AFDC can receive only $50 a month for child support; AFDC takes the rest of the father's payment as a kind of reimbursement for the welfare subsidies mothers and children have received. Thus, the group most in need of child support is denied that support by a federal program, which requires in effect that they pay back the government while they are still in poverty, thus making their attempts to escape poverty more difficult.

(Kurz 1995: 83)

After divorce, most mothers have child custody, and continue to face all the same difficulties in the workplace that come from being a primary caregiver. In addition, they face the additional difficulties that come from raising a family on their own. The combined effect of all this is that, according to the US Census Bureau, 45 per cent of divorced mothers' households are near or below the poverty line.[6] According to Demie Kurz (1995: 77), 39 per cent of divorced mothers' households are *below* the poverty line. Although the situation of divorced mothers is far better than that of never-married mothers, 69 per cent of whose households are at or near or below the poverty line, it is still a dire one (Bureau of the Census 1997). In the United Kingdom, 32 per cent of single mothers are below the poverty line (Christopher et al. 2001: table 1).

Dominance

Dominance and job descriptions

Catherine MacKinnon has offered a different understanding of discrimination, one which she calls the dominance model (MacKinnon 1987). This approach focuses not just on discrimination as traditionally

---

[6] Some research seems to suggest that there have been very recent improvements in the situation of divorced women. See McKeever and Wolfinger (2001).

understood, but more generally on the distribution of power in society, and on ways in which this power distribution is maintained.[7] To see how this works, we'll begin with the issue of job descriptions. The dominance model asks us to look not just at hiring decisions but also at the way key institutions are structured—in this case, it is crucial to look at decisions about what jobs require. The fact is that most jobs were designed with the expectation that the person who filled them would be free of extensive childcare responsibilities. Such a person would either be childless, or—more likely—someone else would be responsible for the childcare. In other words, these jobs were designed for men with wives who did the childcare. 'Day one of taking gender into account was the day the job was structured with the expectation that its occupant would have no childcare responsibilities' (MacKinnon 1987: 37).

The idea behind the dominance conception of discrimination—as applied to job descriptions—is that women may be disadvantaged by the way that positions are defined, even when they are not disadvantaged by discrimination as standardly understood. Indeed, the more positions are defined in a way that makes them difficult for women to fill, the less sex discrimination of the traditional sort will take place. After all, the fewer women who fit the requirements of a job, the less opportunity there is to discriminate on account of sex. Most women will have been ruled out already by the requirements of the job.

The dominance model is not committed to the idea that particular people can always be found who have made discriminatory decisions (though of course it does not deny that this more traditional form of discrimination also takes place). Importantly, the dominance model offers a way to explain how people of goodwill, who may even be deeply committed feminists, can still end up perpetuating a system in which women are seriously disadvantaged. According to the dominance approach, the structure of jobs may be biased against women even if nobody has ever consciously worked toward this goal. The dominance approach allows one to examine the structure of society and its differential effects on men and women. That structure may

---

[7] Deborah Rhode's 'disadvantage framework' works in a similar way (Rhode 1998).

well be one in which women can be said to be 'dominated' even if no discrimination, as commonly understood, is taking place.

Will Kymlicka provides a dramatic illustration of this idea with his description of a hypothetical society in which there is no sex discrimination as standardly understood, but in which women are still dominated by men.

> Consider a society which restricts access to contraception and abortion, which defines paying jobs in such a way as to make them incompatible with childbearing and child-rearing, and which does not provide economic compensation for domestic labor. Women in such a society lack the legal means to guarantee that they will not have children, yet are unable to raise children and work for wages. As a result, they are rendered economically dependent on someone who is a stable income earner (i.e. a man). In order to ensure that they acquire this support, women must become sexually attractive to men. Knowing that this is their likely fate, many girls do not try as hard as boys to acquire employment skills which can only be exercised by those who avoid pregnancy. Where boys pursue personal security by increasing their employment skills, girls pursue security by increasing their attractiveness to men. This, in turn, results in a system of cultural identifications in which masculinity is associated with income-earning, and femininity is defined in terms of sexual and domestic service for men, and the nurturing of children. So men and women enter marriage with different income earning potential, and this disparity widens during marriage, as the man acquires valuable job experience. Since the woman faces greater difficulty supporting herself outside the marriage, she is more dependent on him maintaining the marriage, which allows the man to exercise greater control within it.
>
> (Kymlicka 2002: 382)

In a society like that which Kymlicka describes, women will be disadvantaged in the ways that he outlines even if no individual ever discriminates on the basis of sex. Moreover, the society he outlines is one in which we can imagine women and men ending up in very different roles simply because of women's lack of control over their own reproduction and because of the way that jobs are defined.[8]

---

[8] The issue of women's control over their reproduction is an important one. We will discuss one aspect of it in Chapter 4.

Dominance and divorce

We have seen that divorce courts, using gender-neutral criteria, reach decisions that have the effect of impoverishing millions of women and children. The dominance approach allows us to examine not just the gender-neutrality of the criteria under which decisions are made but the effects and appropriateness of the criteria. On an understanding which focuses on dominance (or, as it is sometimes called, 'disadvantage'), we focus on whether policies under consideration are 'more likely to reduce or reinforce sex-based disparities in political power, social status, and economic security' (Rhode 1998: 351). Once we do this, it becomes clear that current practices are deeply unjust. Our focus here is on post-divorce income allocation.[9]

Not only do current practices play a crucial role in bringing about the impoverishment of women, but they are also based on a blindness to the dynamics of work and family life. In many marriages, husbands are able to earn higher incomes only because wives have taken on a much larger share of the childcare. These women, then, by providing most of the childcare, make an enormous contribution to the family income. However, the only work courts generally recognize as relevant to the family income is that of the partner working outside the home. This, Joan Williams says, is wrong: the childcare provided by mothers is what makes it possible for fathers to earn their higher incomes. It is only by ignoring this work that courts can maintain that fathers are more entitled to the family income than mothers are. Williams puts it very simply: 'Once family work is acknowledged as *work*, a new rationale emerges for income sharing after divorce: An asset produced by two people should be jointly owned by them' (2000: 125).

---

[9] In this section I focus on the work of Joan Williams, although she herself would not use the term 'dominance approach' for the way that she understands these issues. She takes MacKinnon's dominance model to include not just the sort of structural analysis we have engaged in here, but also MacKinnon's very specific claims about the role of sexual domination in the male and female gender identity, and in the subordination of women. (These claims of MacKinnon's are discussed further in Chapters 2 and 3.) While I agree that these claims are part of MacKinnon's overall picture, and indeed play a key role in her account of the precise way in which women are dominated, I do not take them to be essential to the dominance approach. In this I follow Kymlicka (2002).

Power within families

All of this also has effects on power within families. While most people today (at least in Western countries) would deny that husbands should have more power than wives in marriages, this is precisely what happens. One study found that 'in three out of four of the types of couples . . . studied [all types except lesbian couples], . . . the amount of money a person earns—in comparison with a partner's income—establishes relative power' (Okin 1989: 158). Since husbands tend to earn much more than their wives, this means that husbands tend to have more power than wives within marriages. The devastating effects of divorce on women also enhance the power differential, by making women hesitate to leave marriages even when those marriages become abusive: 'Many women, especially full-time housewives with dependent children, have no way of adequately supporting themselves, and are often in practice unable to leave a situation in which they and/or their children are being seriously abused' (p. 152). The problem of dominance, then, not only economically disadvantages women, sometimes reducing them to poverty. It also deprives them of a full say in family decision-making and can make it difficult for them to leave abusive relationships.

Choices

Defenders of the current situation often argue that nothing can or should be done about it, as it results from the free choices of individuals. But we can now see that the situation is far more complicated than this. A mother who needs both to work and to care for her children does not really have much of a choice about what to do: she must find a job which allows her to raise her children, and this will far too often be a poorly paid and insecure job with few benefits. Even the more fortunate are severely constrained in their choices. Williams recounts a conversation she had:

> I was sitting side by side with a woman I had just met at Plastercraft, chatting as our daughters painted Cinderella a gaudy pink. 'I decided to quit my job and stay home,' she told me. 'But it was my choice; I have no

regrets.' I asked her whether she would not really prefer to continue working as a lawyer, with shorter hours of work. She replied wistfully: 'Of course, that's what I really want'.

(Williams 2000: 271)

Rather than simply asking whether the current situation results from individual choices, we can ask whether these choices are limited in ways that they should not be. As economist Ann Bookman puts it,

[W]hat exactly are 'voluntary' part-time workers choosing? Are they choosing to work without health insurance or pensions? Are they choosing to have few opportunities for job advancement? . . . I don't think so.

(quoted in Williams 2000: 6)

The current situation, then, is one in which women are impoverished both by the structure of workplaces and by divorce courts ignoring the way in which childcare contributes to the family wage. In addition, they are more likely to end up powerless within their relationships, and even trapped in abusive situations. Okin writes,

[Women] are rendered vulnerable by the actual division of labour within almost all current marriages. They are disadvantaged at work by the fact that the world of wage work . . . is still largely structured around the assumption that 'workers' have wives at home. They are rendered far more vulnerable if they become the primary caretakers of children, and their vulnerability peaks if their marriages dissolve and they become single parents.

(Okin 1989: 139)

Dominance, the family, and gender

Politics and the family

So far, our focus has been on ways in which workplaces and divorce courts disadvantage those with substantial caregiving responsibilities. Since such people are primarily women, these are ways in which women are disadvantaged. In order to understand the situation properly, then, we must turn to the structure of families. As I noted earlier, the presumption that families are cordoned off from the political realm has led political theorists to largely ignore this issue. Feminists argue that this inattentiveness to the family has been a mistake (see e.g. Okin 1979; 1989; Pateman 1988; 1989). The structure of the family has enormous effects on one's prospects in life. We have seen that traditional family structure plays a significant part in impoverishing women. Political theorists are very concerned with matters that affect one's life chances in such dramatic ways: much attention, for example, has been devoted to the effects of the economic circumstances into which one is born, and to finding ways to counteract these effects. So, it would seem, the same sort of attention should be devoted to the way that sex affects one's life chances, and to finding ways of avoiding or counteracting these effects.

Some feminists have argued that attending to these issues within traditional political theories is impossible; and it is indeed true that attempting to deal with them reveals problems in many traditional theories. However, a growing number of feminists are arguing that these theories are not beyond repair, and that they can even be useful resources for feminist arguments. A specific example will help us here. Susan Moller Okin (1989) discusses women and the family with respect to John Rawls's *Theory of Justice* (1971).[10] According to Rawls, the best way to determine what is required for a just society is to ask what principles would be agreed on by parties behind the 'Veil of Ignorance'. Such parties would know basic facts about human life and history, but would not know anything about *themselves* specifically (hence the 'Veil of Ignorance'). In particular, they would not know their own economic position, class, race, intelligence, health, sex,[11] or views on what constitutes a good life. Because of this, they would need to consider the possibility that they could end up in any position in society. This means that since each is ignorant of what sort of person they might turn out to be, each will work to ensure the best result

---

[10] In addition to Okin, others who have argued for the feminist usefulness of Rawls's theory include Karen Green (1986), Will Kymlicka (2002), Janet Radcliffe Richards (1980), and Rawls himself (1999).

[11] Rawls did not initially include sex as one of the traits unknown to those behind the Veil of Ignorance. In response to feminist criticisms he has made it clear that sex is to be included on the list (Okin 1989: 91).

for all members of society.[12] Imagining what one would agree to behind the Veil of Ignorance, then, allows self-interest to motivate fairness.

Rawls does not pay much attention to what people behind the Veil of Ignorance would think about men's and women's roles in society. Okin argues, however, that those behind the Veil would care a great deal about these matters. In particular, they would know that the standard gender-structured family has played a key role in rendering women much poorer than men. They would have to consider the possibility of ending up a divorced woman from a traditional marriage, able to earn very little money, responsible for several children, and receiving little or no help from her ex-husband; or of being a never-married mother, without affordable childcare, struggling to earn money and raise a family on her own. Okin argues that they would want to do everything in their power to avoid these possibilities, and that—in particular—they would want to bring about an end to the linkage between sex and roles in the family. Not knowing what sort of person they might be, they would not want social forces pressuring them into a particular role simply on the basis of their sex. Even more importantly, they would not want to find themselves forced, on the basis of their sex, into a role that consigns them to a high risk of poverty, an inability to escape abuse, or a lack of decision-making power over key issues in their lives.

Okin also makes use of a specific principle to which Rawls says parties behind the Veil of Ignorance would agree: that any inequalities which do exist in society must be attached to positions or offices which are open to all. Rawls is careful in specifying what he means by this. He contrasts his preferred notion of *equality of fair opportunity* with what he calls *formal equality of opportunity*. All that is required by the latter is that the positions in society be legally open to all. Equality of fair opportunity, on the other hand, requires not only this, but also that all should have 'a fair chance to attain them' (Rawls 1971: 73). Rawls explains this further by suggesting that 'those who are at the

---

[12] Rawls argues that they will be especially concerned with the situation of the worst off in society.

THE POLITICS OF WORK AND FAMILY | 19

same level of talent and ability, and have the same willingness to use them, should have the same prospects of success regardless of their initial place in the social system' (Ibid.: 73). Okin argues that Rawls's principle, understood in terms of equality of opportunity, would rule out the way that our current society perpetuates a sex-linked division of family responsibilities.[13] As things currently stand, the expectation that women will be the primary caregivers makes it difficult for women to pursue many occupations and does a great deal to prevent men from becoming primary caregivers. Positions in our society, then, are not truly open to all.

The roles men and women are generally allocated on the basis of their sex are known as gender roles. Traditionally, feminists have distinguished the *biological* categories of male and female sex from the *social* categories of men's and women's gender roles. This distinction allows us to acknowledge the possibility that one who is biologically male might live as a woman, by occupying a female gender role. Its main point, though, has been to allow feminists to argue that even if the facts of biology are fixed—dividing us into male and female—this need not fix the facts of social roles. This highlights the possibility of changing the social roles of men and women, either by rendering them more similar to each other or by inventing entirely new ones (or in some other ways).

The distinction between sex and gender has in recent years become increasingly controversial due to arguments that neither sex nor gender is as clear-cut as has been thought (see e.g. Spelman 1988; Butler 1990; Fausto-Sterling 1992; Stoljar 1995; Nicholson 1998). However, this important controversy is not relevant to the discussion here, as Okin is relying only on the relatively uncontroversial claim that women are generally expected to be the primary caregivers. Although the roles that men and women play in the family vary widely and importantly across cultures and economic groups, it is uncontroversial that women are in general far more likely than men to be the primary

---

[13] Understood in terms of formal equality of opportunity, it would not require this: the absence of discrimination, as understood by the difference analysis, would be sufficient.

caregivers for children and other dependants, and also that they are likely to undertake the majority of household tasks.[14]

Perpetuation of gender roles

Okin believes that the current allocation of roles in the family by sex is due to the way in which we are socialized into gender roles, and to government and workplace policies which serve to reinforce the association between women and caregiving, and to pressure couples into traditional roles. It is very difficult to establish claims like these conclusively, and there is a huge literature on the way these forces—especially socialization—work. Here, the most I can do is offer a few pieces of suggestive evidence that provide some support for Okin's claims regarding the perpetuation of gender roles.

Socialization

In countries like Britain and America, few children today are explicitly told that housework and childcare are women's work. Nonetheless, they may get more subtle messages that guide them into thinking of themselves in gendered ways, and that influence the lives they end up leading. Here I will just give two examples.

Infant socialization

Most parents today insist that that they are not teaching their children that girls and boys are different, and indeed that they treat their female and male children in the same way. Any differences, they maintain, result from the children's own personalities, uninfluenced by them. Studies show, however, that—whatever their

---

[14] This is not to say, however, that there are not important differences related even to this issue. For example, some studies seem to show that black men's share of household labour is closer to equal than other men's: according to Michael Kimmel, 'in more than one-fourth of all black families, men do more than 40 percent of the housework' (Kimmel 2000: 129). Nonetheless, it is still true that, *in general*, women in black families do most of the household labour. Studies also show that families in which mothers and fathers work different shifts (primarily working-class) come closer to an equal division of labour (Kimmel 2000: 129). Again, however, it is still *generally* true that women in working-class families do most of the household labour.

self-descriptions—parents treat even newborn girls and boys very differently from each other. Although female and male newborns are nearly indistinguishable from each other in behaviour or physiology, mere hours after birth parents will describe their girls as 'tiny, soft, and delicate' and their boys as 'strong, alert, and coordinated' (Renzetti and Curran 1992: 32). These stereotyped perceptions seem to affect parents' interaction with their newborns: parents are more likely to engage in boisterous physical play with baby boys than baby girls. It is clear that parents' behaviour is not simply responsive to the nature of their babies' personalities, and it is hard to imagine that it does not influence their babies' development. (For more on these issues, see Kimmel 2000: 122–6.)

Watching parents

Gender roles are in an important sense self-perpetuating. Today's children, like previous generations, have grown up in households in which mothers, whether or not they also work outside the home, undertake the bulk of domestic labour. These practices come to seem normal, and they affect children's expectations for their own lives. Studies have shown that the division of labour between parents has a significant effect on the amount of household work that children do. This effect is more complex than one might expect. In the most traditional families—in which mothers do not work outside the home— adolescent boys and girls do equal amounts of housework, but this housework is strongly divided along gender lines. (Boys might mow the lawn while girls clean.) In families in which both mothers and fathers work full-time outside the home but mothers do twice as much housework as fathers, however, girls do four times as much housework as boys. One key lesson children seem to learn from their parents, then, is a general principle about how much work males and females should do. Where the division of labour is equal (in terms of quantity) but strongly gendered, children learn to divide tasks in an equal but strongly gendered way. Where the division is both unequal and strongly gendered, children not only learn but magnify the unequal division according to gender (Okin 1994a: 36).

Workplace policies

Workplace policies also serve to reinforce the traditional division of labour. Consider, for example, parental leave policies. It is much easier for women than for men to obtain leave to care for babies and young children. In the US, leave time for fathers is a relatively recent innovation. The Family and Medical Leave Act of 1993 mandated that both men and women were entitled to up to twelve weeks' unpaid leave to care for relatives. However, as it is unpaid, many workers are unable to take it up. In addition, employees must have worked a minimum number of hours in the previous year to be entitled to the leave, and not all employers are covered by the law.[15] Maternity leave of four to six weeks, when it is available, may be either paid or unpaid, depending on employers' policies.[16] In the UK, women are currently entitled to twenty-six weeks of paid maternity leave (Department of Trade and Industry 2002a), and fathers have just become entitled to two weeks' paid paternity leave upon the birth or adoption of a child (Department of Trade and Industry 2002b). Both parents are entitled to thirteen weeks of unpaid parental leave (Department of Trade and Industry 2002c).[17]

Mothers, then, are by far the most able to take care of new babies during the first several weeks or months of life. Even if fathers want to be equal parents, they are often not able to be. This sets patterns that can be hard to break. In addition, the differing nature of maternity and paternity leave entitlements sends a clear message that child-rearing is women's work. Such messages can be difficult to resist.

Against ending gender roles

In this section, I consider two objections to Okin's argument that we need to end the linkage between sex and roles in the family and workplace. The arguments I consider here are based on ones that I

[15] See US Department of Labor, 'Compliance Assistance: Family and Medical Leave Act', at http://www.dol.gov/esa/whd/fmla/. Consulted 5 Nov. 2002.

[16] See 'Maternity Leave', at http://www.babycenter.com/refcap/pregnancy/pregnantatwork/449.html. Consulted 2 July 2002.

[17] In Apr. 2003 paid maternity leave will be extended to 26 weeks. See Department of Trade and Industry (2002c).

frequently hear from my students. The first holds that there is no need to end the linkage between sex and family roles, because for the student-age generation today there is no longer any such linkage. The second maintains that it is a mistake even to try to end this linkage because it is due to biology and therefore cannot be altered.

Gender roles are obsolete

Some of my students argue that, although previous generations grew up with rigidly fixed ideas about gender roles in the family, they did not. Hence, problems will resolve themselves as their generation takes the place of previous ones. Women and men who are in their teens and early twenties now are free of gendered expectations: they no longer believe that childcare is women's work. The current economic disparities will be brought to an end by new generations that do not see roles within the family as linked to sex.

Unfortunately, I suspect that many of these optimistic students are wrong. Although we cannot say for sure how those who have not yet had children will (or will not) divide up the tasks of childcare, we can examine what has become of past generations that made the same claims. When we do this, it becomes clear that gender roles are overwhelmingly powerful, even for those who do not consciously endorse them. It is particularly telling, it seems to me, to examine what happened to Naomi Wolf. By the time Wolf had her first child, she was already a best-selling feminist author. Wolf was determined not to be bound by traditional roles, and had an exceptionally well-established career of her own. Her husband was a man who had married a best-selling feminist author—unlikely to be a devout believer in traditional roles. Their friends also believed in dividing childcare equally. Both Wolf and her friends were sufficiently well off for one to expect them to be in a particularly good position to arrange their lives to suit their desires. And yet, Wolf writes,

> All around me, it seemed, the baby's birth was cleaving couple after couple—once equals in roles and expectations—along the lines of the old traditional gender roles. That was certainly what I experienced when my husband went back to work and I found myself with a tiny baby, staring out the kitchen window into the backyards of the suburbs . . . The baby's

arrival acted as a crack, then a fissure, then an earthquake, that wrenched open the shiny patina of egalitarianism in the marriages of virtually every couple I knew.

(Wolf 2001: 191)

Wolf and her friends thought that their commitments to gender equality would ensure that they did not fall into traditional gender roles, but they were wrong. Sociologists have found that beliefs about gender equality do not have the sorts of effects on division of household labour that one might expect. Although most studies show that the *proportion* of housework and childcare done by men who believe in gender equality is higher than the proportion done by men who have more traditional beliefs, this higher proportion seems to be almost completely due to a decrease in the amount of household labour done by women. Men who believe in gender equality do not actually seem to do much more work around the house (see Kimmel 2000: 128–9; Shelton and John 1996: 306). According to Michael Kimmel, the most dramatic effect of men's beliefs in gender equality is a tendency to overestimate the share of household work that they do (Kimmel 2000: 128–9).

These uneven divisions of household labour are often perceived as fair by both men and women. This might make some sense if the division of labour within the household were determined by the division of labour outside the house—that is, if the number of hours spent on housework increased when the number of hours working outside the home decreased. In fact, however, the number of hours a man works outside the home seems to make no difference to the number of hours of domestic labour he does: men do not devote any more time to housework when their demands at work outside the home decrease (Maushart 2002: 102).

One way that couples avoid seeing their situations as unfair is to compare each partner's lifestyle not with the other partner, but with previous generations. Women tell themselves that their husbands do much more work around the house than their fathers did. Men tell themselves a similar story (Manshart 2002: 114). The effect of this is that men who make small career sacrifices (relative to those of their wives) to spend time with their children will be viewed as doing an enormous amount; and women who make considerable career sacrifices may still be viewed as neglectful of their children. Thus, unequal divisions of labour come to be seen as equitable. But how do these unequal divisions of labour take hold?

A partial answer may be that people don't *decide* to live their lives this way, but simply find themselves doing so, for reasons they don't really understand. Susan Maushart, already a politically active feminist when she married, simply found herself feeling she should do all the cooking as soon as she was married (p. 21). It is worth remembering that most of us have grown up in families in which the mother did the majority of housework and childcare. It is very difficult to see environments like those we have grown up in as anything but normal. This means that it may be very difficult to notice when gendered divisions of labour are taking hold.

One way of realizing how strong our gendered expectations are is to reflect on how natural it seems for a woman to defend her husband by saying 'He does his share—he helps with the baby whenever I ask him to'; and how strange it would be for a man to defend his wife by saying, 'She does her share—she helps with the baby whenever I ask her to'. This shows something about our expectations, and about just how strong they are. The world has indeed changed a lot—we don't consciously believe that women should bear primary responsibility for childcare, and we may even not consciously believe that women do in general still bear this responsibility. But at some other level, at least some of these assumptions linger.

In all likelihood then, my students are wrong when say they will divide up tasks equally. It is not that they lack commitment to this ideal. I have no doubt that they believe in it, and that they intend to live by it. However, experience of the past has shown that such beliefs and intentions are not enough to bring about the realization of the ideal. Whatever factors intervene, they are powerful enough (at least much of the time) to prevent even the most committed feminists from actually living out their plans of dividing housework and childcare equally.

The objection from nature

Another response to Okin's calls for changes to family structure relies on claims about what is natural. According to this sort of explanation, women do more childcare than men because women are naturally either better suited or more inclined to this sort of work and men are either naturally better suited or more inclined to work outside the home. Women have evolved to be child-rearers and men have not, so the current division of tasks is inevitable. Moreover, since women are simply better at child-rearing tasks, it would be a grave mistake to try to change the current division of labour.

Women's natural abilities and desires

One commonly cited bit of evidence for the idea that women are naturally suited to child-rearing is cross-cultural uniformity: in every culture, women are the primary caregivers for children and other dependent loved ones. So, one might think, women must be especially well suited to these tasks. However, this uniformity can be explained without positing that women have such special abilities. The fact that only women can give birth and breastfeed is sufficient to explain why they are responsible for the early care of infants, and the habits formed during these early years (in many pre-technological societies, breastfeeding lasts longer) can explain why the responsibility continues. Although it is no longer the case that only women *can* care for babies—due to technological advances—a long history of women as child-rearers would doubtless bring about cultures in which women are *expected* to raise children. Thus, uniformity of female childcare can easily be explained without recourse to claims of natural differences between women and men.

It is difficult to argue successfully that women have a greater natural desire to engage in childcare than men do. The problem with any argument based on current women's and girls' desires is simply that women and girls grow up in a culture in which women are in fact expected to do more childcare than men. This means that it will always be very difficult to know that any childcare desires are natural rather than the result of cultural conditioning.

Similar problems arise with efforts to argue that women are naturally more skilled at childcare and housework than men. It is surely right that women are better at certain tasks involved in raising children. An obvious (perhaps too obvious) example is breastfeeding. Men will (presumably) never match women's breastfeeding abilities. However, this ability doesn't matter as much as it might seem: it is relevant only to a very early portion of a child's life. Moreover, modern technology makes it possible for mothers' breast milk to be stored and given to infants by fathers. However, women also tend to have greater skills at a wide variety of household tasks—women are indeed generally better at cleaning, cooking, and caring for children than men are. There is, however, an easy explanation for this: women have more practice at these tasks. The fact that women do them better does not show that women are *naturally* better suited to them.

In order to argue that women are naturally better suited to the tasks involved in mothering, one needs to turn to skills that men and women would be equally likely (or unlikely) to have been taught. It is difficult to find clear cases of skills of this sort that are relevant to childcare, and that differ between women and men. One oft-cited example is the skill of recognizing one's infant, a few hours after birth, by smell alone (Buss 1999: 213; Moir and Moir 1998: 272). Apparently, women are much better at this task than men are. It is difficult, though, to see how this shows that women are better suited than men to rearing children. As Helen Todd asks, 'Should mothers everywhere be frightened to allow their babies out with only their father in case he loses them amongst a host of identical babies and is unable to retrieve them by smell alone?' (Todd 2001: 11).

Ann and Bill Moir suggest that one of the most important traits women have is an ability to tolerate dull and repetitive tasks. They argue that women are more able to cope with boredom than men are, thus making them better suited than men to cope with a life of child-rearing.

Men get bored more easily. His biology has equipped him with sensation-seeking qualities that build empires and take him to the moon, but also make him shy away from dull tasks . . . Domestic chores are simply not exciting enough a challenge to turn on his frontal cortex, and so he is liable to burn the shirt as his mind strays in search of something to relieve his boredom.

(Moir and Moir 1998: 251–2)

Many whose lives have been devoted to child-rearing and housework might baulk at the description of these activities as boring: while there is a great deal of repetition in certain tasks, surely the development of a child is anything but dull. Moreover, Moir and Moir's explanation would only make sense if all men were empire-builders or astronauts. But most men's jobs are not like this. If Moir and Moir's claims about men's ability to tolerate repetition were right, we should expect to find that men were incompetent at traditionally male jobs such as assembly-line work.

Arguments from what is natural

In addition to the problems noted above, it is also worth reflecting more generally on the form that the argument from nature takes. Really, it seems to me, there are two arguments at work. One argument claims that if women are naturally better suited and more inclined than men to childcare, it would be a *mistake* to try to change current domestic arrangements. The other argument claims that if women are naturally better suited and more inclined than men to childcare, it is *pointless* to try to change current domestic arrangements—as they are inevitable.

Both arguments are fatally flawed. One key reason is that natural inclination and ability are not the only sorts of inclination and ability that we have. My inclination to use an Apple Macintosh is not natural, nor is my ability to do so. But I certainly have both the inclination and the ability. The fact that they are not natural does nothing to lessen their roles in my working life.

To see why this matters, pretend for the moment that we have established that women are naturally more inclined and better suited to childcare than men. Now, bearing in mind that not all inclinations and abilities are natural ones, pretend also that men become far better at childcare and far more interested in doing it than women if we just give them the right three-page brochure to read. If this were the case, current domestic arrangements would not be inevitable, and it is far from obvious that we should want to preserve them. Obviously, this example is a fanciful one. But it shows that inferences from what is natural to what is inevitable or desirable are far from straightforward.[18] This idea will play an important role in the next section.

Hrdy

Many feminists entirely reject claims that women and men have evolved to have different desires or abilities. Moreover, feminists have offered strong critiques of the methods of evolutionary science, particularly when it comes to claims about human psychology and abilities (see e.g. Bleier 1984; Fausto-Sterling 1992). If these critiques are accepted, we may instantly have reason to reject claims from evolutionary science that female childcare is inevitable. However, it is also important to note that we do not need to accept these critiques in order to reject such claims. Sarah Blaffer Hrdy, a feminist evolutionary theorist, believes that caring for children does indeed come more naturally to women than to men, but rejects the idea that this means it is inevitable or even desirable for women to do more childcare than men.

Hrdy holds that women possess stronger natural caregiving instincts toward infants and children than men do. But, she argues, citing evidence from both humans and animals, men also have such nurturing impulses. For both women and men, a key force in activating caregiving impulses is spending time with babies and small children (Hrdy 1999: 209–13). If men do this, their nurturing instincts become just as strong as women's. This suggests that if men were given encouragement to spend time with children, and if workplaces facilitated this, the apparent disparity between men's and women's desires to prioritize child-rearing would disappear.

Now turn to skill-based arguments. The skills needed to raise children in a hunter/gatherer culture (that is, at the time modern humans evolved) are very different from the skills needed by today's parents. So even if women did evolve to be especially skilled at tasks involved in childcare, this wouldn't mean they would be especially good at childcare today. Moreover, Hrdy also points out that the skills needed to keep oneself and one's offspring alive under the harsh

---

[18] For more on arguments from nature, see Antony (1998).

conditions early humans faced would be quite varied: a mother would need, for example, to acquire food under difficult circumstances, and compete successfully with others for resources. Women, then, have evolved not only to care for children but to do many other tasks— even if we assume (controversially) that women evolved to raise children. Women's evolved abilities—whatever they may be—do not translate easily into any particular role in contemporary society.

Hrdy's view on differences between the sexes fits rather well with Okin's demands for changes. The division of labour by sex impoverishes women in large numbers. Moreover, the current system not only pushes women into childcare roles but pushes men out of them. The injustice of this is most obvious in the case of men's paltry entitlements to parental leave, but also present in the other pressures reinforcing traditional roles. Williams writes that 'nearly half of men between eighteen and twenty-four surveyed expressed interest in staying home with their children' (Williams 2000: 59). If Hrdy is right, a more equitable system would result in men's child-rearing desires being just as strong as women's. Given that men *already* want to spend increasing amounts of time on childcare, it is deeply unjust to have a system that deprives them of their chance to do this.

There seems to be no support for the very strong claim that women are so much better suited to child-rearing than men are that we should embrace current divisions of labour as inevitable or desirable. It is important to note, though, that even if we accepted this claim, it would *still* be worth attempting to do something about the problems we have discussed. It would still be appropriate to criticize a system which consigns so many women to poverty simply because they have followed their natural talents or desires by prioritizing their children.

Fighting dominance

I am firmly convinced that if women had been fully involved in the running of society from the start they would have *found* a way of arranging work and children to fit each other. Men have had no such motivation, and we see the result.

(Richards 1980: 113–14)

The dominance analysis has shown us that the gendered division of household labour, the ways jobs are structured, and the way that income is allocated upon divorce all combine to impoverish women, both relative to men and—in all too many cases—in absolute terms. In this section, I will look at several approaches to changing the current situation. The first response is simply that women should put their children in childcare—no other changes are needed. Next we will look at problems with current versions of 'family-friendly' policies. After this, we shall look at further suggestions for improvement, many of which will be fairly obvious once the weaknesses of earlier approaches are clearly seen. The most important element of this discussion, however, will be the way that these policy suggestions follow naturally from abandoning key assumptions behind the current system.

Daycare as solution

The most well-known feminists of the 1960s and 1970s, like Betty Friedan, focused on the importance of women moving into the labour force. They did *not* focus much on reorganizing the workplace, and some downplayed or even denigrated the work involved in child-rearing. They fought for women to be allowed into workplaces on the same terms as men, without much effort to change these terms. As a result, feminism of this era is commonly associated with the idea that women should simply delegate all childcare to daycare centres or to paid in-home childcare providers.[19]

This proposal is highly problematic, for many reasons. First, most mothers do not want simply to place their children in childcare in order to work long hours, and they should not have to do this in order to have decent jobs. The only way for a worker to hold many jobs, as they are currently designed, is indeed to delegate the care of children to someone else. But this, I have argued, shows that something is wrong with current workplace structures and assumptions.

[19] This view of 1960s and 1970s feminism is somewhat oversimplified: writers like Sheila Rowbotham argued—albeit very briefly—for restructuring work and breaking down gender roles, which would presumably mean increasing men's participation in domestic labour (Rowbotham 1973: 122).

Next, the childcare solution only works (if it works at all) if one has the money to pay for enormous amounts of childcare.[20] It is, then, far from universal in its application. In particular, it offers nothing to the women impoverished under the current system. However, many wealthier couples have adopted this solution. In a revealing detail that shows how undervalued caregiving is, the women hired to care for children—either at home or in childcare centres—are paid extremely low wages (Crittenden 2001: chs. 11 and 12). Many of these women—especially those who provide in-home childcare—are illegal immigrants,[21] and lack the protection afforded to other workers. They are separated from their own children in order to earn extremely low pay from employers who in many cases deny them even the most basic benefits. (For more on the working conditions of home-based childcare workers, see Tronto 2002.) This solution does nothing for the women who suffer most, and even increases their suffering.[22]

How could feminists who endorsed this proposal think that they were solving the problem? It seems obvious now that this is a proposal that only helps those who are relatively privileged in the first place. One explanation is that those who proposed this solution were themselves overwhelmingly white and middle-class.[23] They simply failed to look beyond their own situations—or, if they did look beyond them, they failed to see very clearly. (This sort of blindness due to one's own social situation is discussed in more detail in Chapter 8.) The result was that the circumstances of the most disadvantaged women—those who are poor and/or non-white—were ignored in favour of a focus on middle-class white women.

---

[20] Or if childcare is publicly funded, which looks unlikely to happen in the US for the foreseeable future, and only slightly less unlikely in the UK.

[21] According to Ann Crittenden, a key reason for this is that in America childcare workers are classified as unskilled, and are therefore denied visas that would readily be available if they were classified as skilled. Since not many Americans want to work in childcare, many childcare workers are illegal immigrants (Crittenden 2001: ch. 12).

[22] For an argument that hiring of childcare workers within the home is always wrong, see Tronto (2002). This argument does not extend to placing children in childcare centres.

[23] It is important to note that not all feminists of this period were white and middle-class, though prominent ones associated with this solution were. For more on these issues, see hooks 1982, 'Black Women and Feminism', 159–96.

We see this blindness also in the fact that the problem with which Friedan concerned herself was that of how women could lead fulfilling lives. She demonstrated many ways in which confinement to the life of a housewife could be deeply unfulfilling, and argued powerfully that this should not be the only option for women. However, she neglected the fact that many women of her time were already working outside the home for very low wages, and did not see work as a path to fulfilment, but rather as their only way to survive. bell hooks writes,

> Had attention been focused on women who were already working and who were exploited as cheap surplus labor in American society, it would have de-romanticized the middle class white woman's quest for 'meaningful' employment. While it does not in any way diminish the importance of women resisting sexist oppression by entering the labor force, work has not been a liberating force for masses of American women.
>
> (hooks 1982: 146)

Friedan's excessively rosy picture of the work environment prevented her from undertaking the sort of detailed analysis of its problems that would be needed in order to deal with many of the most important problems women face.

More generally, childcare as a solution does nothing to address the problems we have examined in this chapter. These crucially involve anachronistic workplace assumptions and failures of courts to recognize the work of caring for a family. Instead, the childcare solution asks women to join men in acting as what Williams calls 'ideal workers'—that is, workers who are largely free of domestic responsibilities. Neither men nor women are well served by a solution that fails to address this assumption. Overall, nearly 80 per cent of people surveyed (both male and female) said that they would prefer 'a career path that would offer slower advancement in return for being able to schedule their own full-time hours and give more attention to their families' (Williams 2000: 55). Men and women both, then, would prefer a world in which workplaces were not structured around 'the ideal worker'.

Failing to change the structure of workplaces, and failing to change divorce settlements, also leaves in place society's deep undervaluing of caregiving work. The childcare solution suggests that those who can afford it should simply delegate such work to others. Those who cannot afford, or do not want, to delegate childcare are left at risk of joining the ranks of the poor—or being forced into deeper poverty. But caregiving work is some of the most vital work that there is. We all begin our lives helpless and vulnerable, in need of constant care. Many of us will also be debilitated at later points in our life, and need someone to take care of us. Without people performing these duties, humanity would, quite literally, come to an end. We should value this work properly, by ensuring that those who take it on are not impoverished by it.

'Family-friendly' policies

Many companies now offer 'family-friendly' policies designed to make it easier to combine paid employment and parenting. Nonetheless, they fail to properly question the 'ideal worker' model.

Parental leave

We have already seen that many workers are offered no parental leave at all, and still fewer are offered paid parental leave. When paid leave is offered, men's entitlements are tiny relative to women's, or (quite often) nonexistent. The frequent lack of parental leave altogether is based on the anachronistic assumption that workers are free of childcare responsibilities, and helps to force those with child-care responsibilities out of many jobs. The huge difference in men's and women's entitlements cannot be explained solely by the fact that women, and not men, give birth. It is also based on the assumption that mothers, and not fathers, will do the work of caring for infants— an assumption that both mothers and fathers increasingly object to. The fact that mothers are given greater leave entitlements serves to perpetuate the traditional division of labour by sex. In addition, it may contribute to discrimination (even as traditionally understood) against women in the workforce. The UK's Industrial Society's report *Mothers versus Men* argues that these policies serve to make discrimination against women very appealing to employers. If mothers are entitled to generous leave packages to which fathers are not entitled, women workers are simply costlier (Summerskill 2000: 4).

Part-time work and flexibility

As we have seen, part-time work is the only option available to many mothers who want or need to work. It is usually extremely poorly paid, and rarely carries with it key benefits such as pensions or healthcare. Moreover, opportunities for advancement and job security tend to be slim or nonexistent.

More and more employers today offer some kind of flexibility to their employees. Typical examples include allowing rearrangement of schedules to suit employees' needs (say, by working longer hours on four days and having an extra day off); allowing employees to work from home on some days; or allowing employees to reduce their schedules. These innovations sounds like an excellent thing, and to some degree they are. But there are problems. First, even companies that officially allow employees these options often make it clear that those who make use of them will not be taken seriously as workers. Arlie Russell Hochschild writes of a company that brought her in to determine why employees were not making use of family-friendly policies. She found managers saying, 'My policy on flextime is that there is no flextime' (Hochschild 1997: 32); and a corporate culture that expressed itself (among other ways) in a handbook that included the lines: 'Time spent on the job is an indication of commitment. Work more hours' (p. 19). Joan Williams notes that in some companies any worker who so much as expresses interest in part-time work is immediately and permanently barred from advancement (Williams 2000: 73). Next, even more importantly, flexibility is not equally available to all workers: it is far more likely to be offered to the best-paid of the workforce. According to Betty Holcomb, 38.4 per cent of managers and other professionals have flexible time options, but only 18.5 of other workers do. She suggests that even companies which claim to offer flexible time to all of their workforce in practice allow it only for those in high-level positions (Holcomb 2000).

Both part-time work and flexibility—components of the 'mommy tracks' that became popular in the 1990s—fail to challenge the idea that workers should be free of childcare responsibilities. Although they may make it possible for those with such responsibilities to hold jobs they would not otherwise be able to hold, they—at best—prevent such people from advancing in their careers and earning wages commensurate with the work they do. All too often, they fail to do even this, leaving caregivers unable to earn a decent living or to receive vital benefits like health insurance and pensions.

A new model of work and family

Proposals

If we abandon the assumption that the ideal worker should be free of domestic responsibilities, we get a very different picture of how work-places should function. (The proposals I discuss here derive largely from Williams 2000 and Okin 1989.)[24] If all workers are assumed to have substantial domestic responsibilities, then no workers should be penalized for spending time on childcare. Flexible time arrangements should be available, and those who opt for flexible time should not be penalized. Free childcare should be available (either government or employer-sponsored) either at or near workplaces. Parental leave should be available on equal terms to both parents (with the exception of leave directly related to pregnancy),[25] and those who take parental leave should not be penalized for doing so. Part-time workers should receive benefits (either from the state or from employers), and be allowed advancement opportunities. Proponents of these sugges-tions do not suggest that such workers should be allowed to advance at the same rate as full-time ones, of course, but instead that their

[24] To a large extent, the proposals in this paragraph focus on employers rather than governments. This is because a key topic is that of making it possible for caregivers to obtain good jobs. This requires changes to workplaces, and therefore requires at least a partial focus on employers. While childcare and benefits (such as health insurance) could be financed not by employers but by governments (as is the case in many European countries), this alone would not solve the problem we are considering here. However, merely making good jobs available is also arguably not sufficient to end women's poverty; decent and affordable trans-portation and housing are also needed, and this probably has to be done by governments.

[25] There has been controversy over exactly how feminists should approach the need for pregnancy-related benefits. The controversy revolves around whether one whose goal is equality can acknowledge women's need for benefits that men do not need. Okin and Deborah Rhode have argued that this is possible, in ways that invoke notions closely akin to what this chapter has discussed under the term 'dominance' (see Okin 1979: 323–5; Rhode 1998: 344–62).

advancement should be linked to what they accomplish rather than simply blocked because they have worked part-time. These policies should be available to all workers, rather than only to the highest-paid employees who need help least. Finally, Williams suggests that work-weeks should be shortened, and mandatory overtime abolished. This demand coincides with a growing movement which protests long hours, seeking to reduce working hours for the sake of health, as well as to allow workers more time with their families and more time for other pursuits (Williams 2000: 61).

Workplace policies that disadvantage women by disadvantaging primary childcare providers are beginning to be recognized as discriminatory. This represents a major success for the dominance understanding of discrimination. In the UK, for example, a court recently determined that a policy requiring rotating shifts had the effect of discriminating against women (Moore 2002). Williams (2000) maps out suggestions for convincing US courts to recognize such policies as discriminatory. Recognizing such policies as discriminatory represents important progress toward increasing the compatibility of work and childcare.

It is also important that those who prioritize caring for others over paid work should not be denied healthcare and pensions—as is often the case in the US, where these benefits are linked to employment. In the UK, healthcare is provided to all citizens, but older women still fall into poverty as pensions are linked to earnings (Hughes 2002). Taking seriously the importance of domestic labour requires decent pensions and healthcare for those who engage in it.

If we pay proper attention to the contribution domestic labour makes to household income, we get a new picture of how income from paid labour should be viewed. Where one spouse earns substantially more because the other spouse is working in paid labour only part-time or not at all, divorce courts should view the wage-earning spouse's income as a joint product of both spouses' work. Rather than asking how to divide up the income of the 'working' partner, courts should instead face the importantly different—and more accurate—question of how to divide up the income jointly earned by both partners. (For a more detailed discussion of how this might work, see Williams 2000; Okin 1989.)

Okin argues that joint entitlement to jointly earned income should be recognized even earlier. She suggests that in cases where one spouse works only at domestic labour within the home, the other spouse's employer should issue two equal pay cheques: one to each partner. Although in many cases this would not matter, income differences often lead to power imbalances, with (generally) the man wielding more power. Okin's proposal would offer clear recognition of domestic labour's importance to family income, and would also potentially give greater financial power to women within marriages. It might seem that to do this would be to interfere inappropriately in family life. But Okin argues that her proposal involves no more interference than is present already. In each case, employers are deciding who should be given possession of an income that is jointly earned. Under the current situation, employers give this income to the partner who works directly for them. Under Okin's proposal, they would give the income to both partners. Each alternative affects family life equally. The difference is that Okin's involves recognizing the contribution that stay-at-home partners (generally women) make.

Objections

Impracticality

It is often thought that the workplace reforms discussed above are extremely impractical: companies cannot afford to offer the sorts of policies that would be needed if they abandoned the idea that ideal workers are free of domestic responsibilities, and governments (especially the US government) would never mandate such policies, let alone help to fund them. Both of these claims, however, can be cast into doubt.

Joan Williams discusses several companies that now actively encourage flexible-time and part-time work, provide full benefits to workers who take up these options, allow such workers to be promoted, and offer on-site daycare. These companies have found that such policies allow them to retain valued staff, save money that would have been spent on retraining if staff had left, and reduce absenteeism rates. In short, they have found that such policies save them money and increase productivity. So policies of the sort discussed above may *help*, rather than hinder, businesses. This does not show that such policies would always be feasible. In particular, it is probably clearer that these policies are financially beneficial to companies for highly trained workers than for less highly trained ones—and confining the policy to highly trained workers would do little to alleviate female poverty. However, examples like these do cast doubt on the idea that such policies are obviously unfeasible.

The US government—generally far less generous in terms of social policy than European countries—not only could, but did, implement many proposals of the sort discussed here. During the Second World War, women were needed to take on men's jobs while men were away at war. Edgar Kaiser, director of Oregon Shipyards, strongly believed that mothers needed access to a huge range of services in order to enable them to do this. He convinced the Maritime Commission to work with him to set up neighbourhood centres that included a wide range of high-quality services—including meals, healthcare, and twenty-four-hour childcare. Unfortunately, these centres have since been closed down and largely forgotten. It is important to remember that this was done at a time when one would expect social services to be cut back: all effort, and all possible funds, needed to go only to the war and essential services. Yet, even at this time, these centres were funded. Why? For Kaiser, it made good business sense— he wanted productive workers and low absenteeism rates, and this was the way to get it. More generally, women's ability to combine work outside the home with caring for their families was, for this brief time, considered vital to the nation's interest.[26]

Discrimination against non-parents
Although the policies suggested above make good sense when we consider the perspective of parents, they may seem more troubling when we consider the perspective of workers who do not have children. If parents are entitled to reduced work-weeks, flexible time, and good promotion prospects despite working fewer hours, and non-parents are entitled to none of these benefits, non-parents surely have

---

[26] The Kaiser centres are discussed by Crawford (1995).

cause to complain. If non-parents are not permitted flexible time, for example, there is a case to be made that they are being discriminated against: they are being denied a benefit on the basis of being childless. The problem becomes even more striking when we consider that caregiving work includes not just childcare, but care for sick and elderly friends and family—non-parents are just as likely to have such duties as parents. This work is significant: according to a recent study, 20 per cent of the poorest workers spend thirty or more hours each week providing care for elderly relatives (Rahmanou 2001). There is surely no moral justification for urging flexibility when it comes to childcare and not for other sorts of care.

Importantly, however, the proposals suggested need not—and should not—be offered only to parents. Shorter workweeks, flexible time, and non-marginalized part-time work should be available to all workers. If they are manageable for parents, they are manageable for others. Williams urges that employers should ask, not 'Why do you need it?', but 'Will it work?' (Williams 2000: 98). If policies like these are workable, then there is no reason why they could not offer every-one ways of combining work with other goals that they have in life, whether or not these are caregiving ones.

The family

Proposals like those described above would help to improve the situation of those with substantial caregiving responsibilities: they would no longer be barred from decent pay, job advancement, health insurance, and pensions, and they would no longer face such a risk of falling into poverty. These proposals would also make it easier for men to involve themselves more fully in family life, and to take on greater childcare responsibilities. But it is not at all clear how far these proposals would go toward ending the gendered division of domestic labour. In particular, if socialization plays an important role in maintaining the current division, these proposals would not eliminate it.

For this reason, Okin believes that schools need to take measures to counteract gendered socialization. They should avoid teaching materials that perpetuate gender roles (children's books, for example, which show women cooking and men being doctors), and they should educate both boys and girls in the challenges of combining household labour and work outside the home. In addition, they should teach girls not to assume that child-rearing is their main destiny, and teach boys not to assume that someone else will care for their children. Much progress has already been made in this direction: as Michael Kimmel notes, women and girls in children's books are less likely than they were in the 1970s to be depicted as 'helpless domestic helpmeets' (Kimmel 2000: 156). But, as Kimmel also notes, there has been little change in depictions of men and boys. As in real life, women and girls are working both within and outside the home. But—also as in real life—men are not doing much caregiving work. This shows there is still much to be done.

Does the family really need reform?

Much of Okin's argument for the importance of changing family structure depends on the way in which current structures serve to impoverish women. But if reforms like those that she and Williams propose are instituted and succeed in their aims, being a primary caregiver for young children will not have such dire effects on one's economic prospects. Some of the motivation, then, for changing family structure would disappear. So, one might argue, workplace and divorce reforms are enough. If we make sure that traditional gender roles in the family don't impoverish women, what is there to complain about?

One can respond to this objection by noting that it only addresses part of Okin's argument. Okin's concerns are not only economic, but also concern free choice of occupation and role in life. Sex-based pressures can make it difficult for a woman who has no interest in child-rearing to choose a life that will make her happy—or for a man who would like to devote himself to full-time childcare to do so. If the various roles in life are to be truly and fully open to all, they need to stop being linked to sex.

This response, however, is problematic. Even if one eliminates gender socialization, there will still be forces of socialization—like, for example, Okin's suggested educational policies. Human beings are, and always will be, complicated products of biological and social forces. Jean Grimshaw rightly objects to the idea that there is a ' "real" or "natural" self which, if simply "left alone", would spontaneously or autonomously produce its "real" needs or desires' (1986: 135), and it sometimes seems that this idea is behind the thought that socialization reduces our freedom. *If* (and this is a big 'if') the enormous economic and power-related effects of traditional gender roles were eliminated, it would not be enough to argue that socialization into gender roles reduces free choice of occupation—all socialization has the effect of making some courses of life easier to pursue than others. (Okin's proposed educational reforms, for example, would socialize children into believing that they should not pursue a life of delegating caregiving to others.) One would need to argue that there is still something especially problematic about gender socialization. This is a more difficult task. Many feminists hail the role of mothering as an especially valuable and fulfilling one (see e.g. Ruddick 1989). If it is so valuable and fulfilling, what would be wrong with socializing women into caregiving roles in a world in which caregiving was no longer linked to poverty, and could viably be combined with other work?

The answer to the problem above, I think, is that socializing *women alone* into caregiving roles would be a very mysterious sort of thing to support. Since caregiving work *is* extremely valuable and fulfilling, surely it would be best to raise both boys and girls to value and pursue it—no justification can be given for treating one sex only as the caregiving one. Okin's proposals are designed to end a system by which girls alone are socialized into caregiving.

Why keep the family?

The next objection suggests that the proposals we have discussed don't go nearly far enough. Okin is concerned with trying to make monogamous heterosexual families fairer places. But maybe, this objection suggests, that's the wrong thing to do. The monogamous heterosexual family has been crucially involved in a lot of injustice, as we have seen. So why try to keep it? One should, at the very least, not *assume* that this sort of family is worth preserving.[27] Perhaps feminists should abandon the project of trying to improve monogamous heterosexual families and instead devote themselves to proposing

---

[27] For an interesting argument to this effect, see Munoz-Dardé (1999).

alternatives: communal child-rearing, multi-parent families, lesbian and gay parents. Or maybe feminists should even oppose procreation.[28] These considerations, however, do not count against the proposals we have discussed.[29] The reason is that many, many women are currently in, or want to be in, monogamous heterosexual families. It is important to make these families fairer, and to try to ensure that they do not have disastrous effects on the women in them. It is also vitally important to help those in alternative family arrangements, and it is worthwhile to work to imagine as yet undreamt-of alternatives. But these facts do nothing to diminish the importance of helping women who, right now, are impoverished by—or risk impoverishment by— the typical structure of current monogamous heterosexual families.

SUGGESTIONS FOR FURTHER READING

Note: In every chapter, I provide italicized notes on some of the reading. In particular, I try to indicate where readers seeking UK rather than US information should look.

Structures of families and workplaces

Crittenden, A., *The Price of Motherhood*. New York: Henry Holt, 2001.
Fredman, S., *Women and the Law*. Oxford: Clarendon Press, 1997. (*Especially good for UK information.*)
Okin, S. M., *Justice, Gender, and the Family*. New York: Basic Books, 1989.
Williams, J., *Unbending Gender: Why Family and Work Conflict and What to Do About It*. Oxford: Oxford University Press, 2000.

Discrimination

Bartlett, K., and Harris, A., *Gender and Law*. New York: Aspen, 1998.
Fredman, S. *Women and the Law*. Oxford: Clarendon Press, 1997. (*Especially good for UK information.*)

[28] See e.g. Valeska (1983), who argues that (at the time of her writing), those without children have an obligation not to have children, and instead to assist in the raising of children in their communities.
[29] And they are not necessarily meant to do so. For example, the appropriateness of reforms like those proposed by Okin is simply not Munoz-Dardé's topic.

Kymlicka, W., *Contemporary Political Philosophy*, 2nd edn. New York: Oxford University Press, 2002.

MacKinnon, C., 'Difference and Dominance', in *Feminism Unmodified*. Cambridge, Mass.: Harvard University Press, 1987.

Rhode, D., 'The Politics of Paradigms: Gender Difference and Gender Disadvantage', in A. Phillips (ed.), *Feminism and Politics*. Oxford: Oxford University Press, 1998.

Williams, J., *Unbending Gender: Why Family and Work Conflict and What to Do About It*. Oxford: Oxford University Press, 2000.

Feminist discussions of Rawls

Exdell, J., 'Feminism, Fundamentalism, and Liberal Legitimacy', *Canadian Journal of Philosophy* 24(3) (1994): 441–64.

Green, K., 'Rawls, Women and the Priority of Liberty', *Australasian Journal of Philosophy*, supplement to vol. 64 (1986): 26–36.

Okin, S. M., *Justice, Gender, and the Family*. New York: Basic Books, 1989, chapter 5.

—— 'Political Liberalism, Justice, and Gender', *Ethics* 105 (1994): 23–43.

Rawls, J., *A Theory of Justice*. Cambridge, Mass.: Harvard University Press, 1971.

—— *Political Liberalism*. New York: Columbia University Press, 1993.

—— *The Law of Peoples*. Cambridge, Mass.: Harvard University Press, 1999.

Women's 'nature'

Antony, L., ' "Human Nature" and Its Role in Feminist Theory', in J. Kourany (ed.), *Philosophy in a Feminist Voice*. Princeton, NJ: Princeton University Press, 1998.

Bleier, R., *Science and Gender: A Critique of Biology and Its Theories on Women*. New York: Pergamon, 1984.

Fausto-Sterling, A., *Myths of Gender: Biological Theories about Women and Men*. New York: Basic Books, 1992.

Hrdy, S. B., *Mother Nature*. London: Chatto & Windus, 1999.

Kimmel, M., *The Gendered Society*. New York: Oxford University Press, 2000.

Renzetti, C., and Curran, D., 'Gender Socialisation', in J. A. Kourany, J. P. Sterba, and R. Tong, *Feminist Philosophies*. London: Prentice-Hall, 1992.

Tauris, C. *The Mismeasure of Woman*. New York: Touchstone, 1992.

2

Sexual Harassment

Prior to the legal recognition of sexual harassment in the 1970s, it was considered to be only a personal matter if an employer demanded sex of an employee and fired her for refusing (Crouch 2001). Courts would not get involved. It was considered regrettable, perhaps even immoral, but simply not of legal concern. Most people undoubtedly think it is a good thing that today such conduct would be recognized as sexual harassment, and as very much a matter for the courts.[1] No employee should have to submit to sexual demands as a condition of employment. Putting someone in this position is now labelled 'quid pro quo sexual harassment'.

Once such behaviour was recognized as harassment, a new question arose for the courts: could there be other, similar sorts of behaviour that no employee should have to tolerate? Take, for example, the behaviour that women employees faced at Stroh's Brewery in the US in 1991:

> They were told that women could not hold certain jobs and that they should go home and get 'women's jobs'. They were referred to . . . as 'bitch' and 'squaw' [. . .] One woman was 'grabbed . . . on the rear end', a male coworker 'displayed his pubic hair [to a second woman] and grabbed [her] head and pushed it down to his crotch', a male coworker drove a forklift toward another woman [. . .] several other women had their machines sabotaged and their tires slashed or deflated [. . .] In addition, the women were subjected to a barrage of sexual comments, graffiti, and pin-ups.
>
> (Schultz 1998: 1695: I have abbreviated the list.)

---

[1] Or, in the UK, industrial tribunals. For convenience, I will often write simply of 'courts'.

This harassment drove many women employees away. By the time it occurred, courts had already recognized a new category of sexual harassment, 'hostile environment sexual harassment.' It has now become widely accepted that behaviour of the sort that the women of Stroh's were subjected to is sexual harassment, and that it is both unacceptable and illegal. Most would think it is right that the women of Stroh's sued for hostile environment sexual harassment, and that they won.

When we consider these cases, the legal recognition of sexual harassment seems clearly a good thing. Indeed, it is often seen as one of the great successes of recent feminism. And yet, much of what we hear these days about sexual harassment law is critical of it—and many of these criticisms seem very worrying. Some claim that the recognition of sexual harassment has led to a prohibition on all romantic, sexual, and possibly even friendly interactions in the workplace. Some claim that sexual harassment law infantilizes women, by treating them as delicate souls who need to be protected from all sexual behaviour and language. But these criticisms are countered by those who claim that sexual harassment law is not like this at all: that it does not prohibit romantic or even sexual behaviour in the workplace; and that it does not provide special protection for women.

Unsurprisingly, given these competing claims, many are worried by a feeling that they do not truly understand what sexual harassment is. What is going on? The answer, in my view, is that we have not yet fully made up our minds exactly which behaviour should count as sexual harassment. And this is just what should be expected from a concept so new: before feminists began to work for legal recognition of sexual harassment, there was no sense that behaviours of the sort described above were of the same sort, and no term for this sort of behaviour. Although of course sexual harassment took place, it was not thought of in this way (Crouch 2001).

In this chapter, I examine some disputes over the nature of sexual harassment, and attempt to draw out the points of contention that give rise to these disputes. The chapter will accordingly be divided into three sections, addressing three key questions: (1) Does the recognition of sexual harassment treat women as frail and in need of special protection? (2) How severe does behaviour have to be to qualify as sexual harassment? (3) To what extent does sexual harassment law single out sexual behaviour? Although I favour certain solutions to these questions over others, my main goal will be to argue that we need to settle on some answers—but also that our current lack of agreement should not be cause for despair.

Women as frail, in need of protection

Some have argued that sexual harassment law helps to perpetuate the idea that women are helpless victims in need of special protection. In particular, it is often thought to perpetuate the idea that women need to be protected from any mention of sex or any sexual behaviour. But, as we shall see, sexual harassment law does not single out women for special attention: either men or women can commit sexual harassment, and either men or women can be victims of sexual harassment. Courts' decisions have accorded with this. So it is hard to see how sexual harassment law could be seen as contributing to the notion that women require special protection. What, then, is the source of this worry? Its source, it seems to me, lies in the fact that there is indeed a connection between sexual harassment law and concern over the treatment of women in particular. The nature of this connection, however, is more complicated than proponents of this worry take it to be; and it turns out not to be the sort of connection that can justify their concerns.

The worry

Writers like Camille Paglia (2001), Daphne Patai (2001), Ellen Frankel Paul (2001), and Katie Roiphe (2001) argue that sexual harassment laws encourage both women and men to think of women as in need of protection from things like sexual speech. This, they suggest, not only perpetuates damaging stereotypes about women but also encourages women to think of themselves as frail rather than strong. They point out, rightly, that women do not always need protection from sexual speech or even insults.

The perpetrators should either be endured, ignored, rebuked, or avoided, as circumstances and personal inclination dictate ... women should 'lighten up,' and even dispense a few risqué barbs of their own, a sure way of taking the fun out of it for male boors.

(Paul 2001: 249)

Writers like these suggest that feminists should want women to be strong and assertive, rather than urging them to turn to others for protection against offensive sexual behaviour. They hold that sexual harassment laws and regulations help to perpetuate the view that women are in need of special protection from exposure to sexual words and behaviour. The idea behind these complaints is that sexual harassment legislation is of a piece with an 1897 Michigan law prohibiting swearing in front of women and children, but not in front of men. Under this law, a man who was canoeing, fell in a river, and swore was charged in 1998 with swearing within earshot of women.[2] Few feminists would defend a law like this, which is clearly based on an outdated, paternalistic view of women as delicate creatures who could be harmed by overhearing foul language.

Feminist opponents of sexual harassment laws take such laws to be just as condescending as the Michigan law on swearing. They hold that it is far from feminist to view women as in need of such protection, and to cause women who might otherwise be strong and assertive to view themselves in this way.

Instead of learning that men have no right to do these terrible things to us, we should be learning to deal with individuals with strength and confidence. If someone bothers us, we should be able to put him in his place without crying into our pillow or screaming for help or counseling.

(Roiphe 2001: 255)

Opponents of sexual harassment law insist that recognition of sexual harassment as an offence means denying that women are capable of asserting themselves and fighting back against the occasional offensive comment.

---

[2] For more information, see http://www.aclu.org/FreeSpeech/FreeSpeech. cfm?ID=10087&c=42. Consulted 28 Oct. 2002. The law has now been found unconstitutional.

But sexual harassment law is not like this. The most widely accepted definitions at work in US sexual harassment law are those offered by the federal government. (British law is similar, so I take US law as a representative example.) There are in fact separate guidelines for workplace and educational harassment, but I have drawn on these separate guidelines and slightly simplified language to arrive at the versions below.[3]

Quid pro quo sexual harassment: This occurs when a person in a position of authority demands sexual favours in return for hiring, promotion, good grades, or the like; alternatively, it occurs when such a person retaliates (or threatens retaliation) in the form of firing, poor grades or the like, against someone who refuses sexual advances. The demands need not be explicit.

Hostile environment sexual harassment: This is verbal or physical conduct of a sexual nature (including unwelcome sexual advances) which has the purpose or effect of unreasonably interfering with an individual's work performance or creating an intimidating, hostile, or offensive working environment.

Sexual harassment law is not concerned merely with occasional offensive comments. Such behaviour would not unreasonably interfere with an individual's work environment. Instead, the law concerns itself with comments and behaviour that rise to the level of creating an intimidating, hostile, or offensive working environment; or with demands of sexual favours on pain of firing. Generally, it is thought that the behaviour in question has to be severe or pervasive in order to qualify as sexual harassment. Confronted with such behaviour, witty comebacks and put-downs like those suggested by Paul would be of little avail. They are simply not a very viable response to harassment that comes from a person with power over one: and it is hard to imagine that the women of Stroh's would have accomplished much by responding to their harassers with jokes and

[3] These definitions are based on those given in 'Guidelines on Discrimination Because of Sex: Sexual Harassment', Equal Employment Opportunity Commission Code of Federal Regulations, Title 29, Section 1604.11; US Department of Education, Office of Civil Rights, Sexual Harassment Guidance.

put-downs.[4] One does not need to be frail and delicate to require protection in such situations.

Nor are women especially protected by sexual harassment law. Under sexual harassment law, both women and men can be victims of sexual harassment, and both can be perpetrators. There is, in fact, no sex differentiation in the definitions given above. Sexual harassment law, then, is not committed to a view of women as in need of special protection from every stray sexual comment. (1) It does not give any special protections to women; and (2) it is only concerned with behaviour that is severe. The criticism above, then, is not a legitimate criticism of sexual harassment law.

Explaining the source of the worry

The idea that sexual harassment law is tied to a conception of women as frail and in need of special protection from sexual comments may be based on a misunderstanding of the origins of sexual harassment law. Sexual harassment law does originate in concerns specifically about women, and it is still of special importance to women. Indeed, this fact is vital for understanding why it is that sexual harassment is considered to be a feminist issue—why it is that feminists should be especially concerned with this particular sort of problematic workplace behaviour.

There are many reasons that feminists have taken a special interest in sexual harassment. Women have been victims of sexual harassment more often than men.[5] Moreover, sexually harassing behaviour has been used as a way of keeping women out of traditionally male environments (see e.g. Crouch 2001; MacKinnon 1979; Schultz 1998). Sexual harassment has caused women to quit their jobs, accept less well-paid jobs, and sometimes leave the workplace altogether. It has played an important role in holding women back. It has created

---

[4] Nonetheless, some concern over institutional sexual harassment codes may be justified. These codes, as we will see in the next section, do have the potential to treat more minor incidents as sexual harassment.

[5] The percentage of sexual harassment claims filed by men has been increasing, but complaints from women are still far more common. In 2001, 13.7 per cent of claims came from men (Talbot 2002).

obstacles for women that men have rarely had to face in the work-place. Some feminists have argued that the reason women have been victims of sexual harassment so much more often than men is that women are stereotypically viewed as sex objects with little other worth (Farley 1978). This, they argue, serves to make sexual harassment seem like acceptable behaviour. Sexual harassment can also contribute to perpetuating a view of women as sex objects.

All the above are reasons for viewing sexual harassment as particularly important to women. They also form starting points for the idea that sexual harassment is a form of sex discrimination. This is very important, as the reason sexual harassment is illegal is that it is considered sex discrimination. Neither the US nor the UK has laws specifically against sexual harassment. (The widely cited definitions referred to earlier are from government guidance documents.) Instead, courts have ruled that sexual harassment constitutes sex discrimination, and that for this reason it is illegal. Looking at ways to see sexual harassment as discriminatory, then, will serve two purposes: it will help us to see why one might think that sexual harassment law gives special protection to women; and it will help us to understand the nature of the legal prohibition against sexual harassment.

The dominance approach[6]

The dominance approach to *sexual harassment* (which has not been widely adopted legally) is a version of the dominance approach to *discrimination* discussed in Chapter 1. It starts from the idea that, as Catharine MacKinnon put it, 'discrimination consists in the systematic disadvantagement of social groups' (1979: 116). To understand discrimination against women, then, one needs to understand ways in which women are systematically disadvantaged relative to men. 'A rule or practice is discriminatory, in the [dominance] approach, if it participates in the systemic social deprivation of one sex because of its sex' (p. 117). The dominance approach to sexual harassment argues

---

6 I am using the term 'dominance' to make obvious the connections to the dominance approach to discrimination discussed in Chapter 1. In MacKinnon's early writings on sexual harassment, she used the word 'inequality' rather than 'dominance'.

that sexual harassment is a practice that contributes to systematically disadvantaging women, and that it is therefore discriminatory.

How is sexual harassment taken to disadvantage women? Since women are victims of sexual harassment more than men, women are disadvantaged by suffering its harms. These harms may include being forced to tolerate unacceptable working conditions, being threatened and coerced into having sex, and being fired or paid less for not having sex. According to MacKinnon and others, sexual harassment has, in addition, played a crucial role in keeping women subordinate to men. It has caused women more than men to be forced out of employment, or to give up otherwise desirable jobs. In particular, she argues that an important way men have safeguarded traditionally male occupations for themselves has been to make them unattractive to women. A primary (though by no means the only) way of doing this was via sexual harassment. To make this more vivid, consider the state of the law at the time that MacKinnon and others began fighting for sexual harassment legislation. At this time, there was no legal recourse for women who were faced with a choice of sex with their employers or being forced out of their jobs. And this was a choice that faced women far more often than men. Women in an environment like Stroh's would have had no legally legitimate complaint regarding the way that they were treated. And yet this treatment clearly did make it more difficult to carry out their jobs than it was for men. Many women found that the only way to deal with the problem was to leave, as neither workplace policies nor laws protected them against sexual harassment. Here is a description of the harassment that caused a secretary/receptionist, Nancy Fillhauser, to leave her job in the early 1970s:

She said he was constantly remarking concerning his wishes to have sexual contact with her, and that she reacted in such a way as to certainly inform him that such intentions were not welcome. When she would walk by him, he would occasionally pat her behind. He would make comments to his friends about her figure or legs whenever she wore a dress, implying that she was a loose woman and would do anything with anyone. The claimant asserted that the employer attempted to arrange a liaison with one of his friends for a price. On another occasion, she said one of his friends came to the office and made a comment about the weather being cold, and the employer said that the claimant could keep him warm.

(MacKinnon 1979: 42).

Because there were no complaints procedures to deal with this behaviour, Fillhauser quit her job.[7] Since the sort of behaviour she faced happened to women far more often than men, women were facing burdens in the workplace that men were not. Under the dominance approach, this general, society-wide disadvantage to being a woman is what is wrong with sexual harassment: it places barriers in the way of women's achievement that are not placed in the way of men's, and it is an important force in preventing women's advancement.

For MacKinnon, sexual harassment is also vital to maintaining a system in which men are dominant and women subordinate. For MacKinnon, the key to this subordination is sexuality—men are sexually dominant and women are sexually submissive.[8] Sexual harassment involves the introduction of a sexual dynamic to workplaces and educational institutions. Since sex (according to MacKinnon) plays a vital role in perpetuating the subordination of women to men, this helps to perpetuate male dominance in workplaces and educational institutions. Thus, sexual harassment can be seen as a particularly central way of disadvantaging women. This, then, is an important reason why she takes it to be discrimination under the dominance approach.

Under the dominance approach, sexual harassment is conceived of as (exclusively) discrimination by men against women. The effect of this is that analogous behaviour with the sexes reversed does not count as sexual harassment under this approach. So, for example, a female professor who offers a male student a high grade in return for sex will not count as sexually harassing him, because sexual harassment is solely a form of male discrimination against women. A predominantly female environment in which males are subjected to

---

[7] A dispute then arose over whether Fillhauser would be eligible for unemployment benefits. The description of Fillhauser's employer's behaviour comes from these proceedings. She was at first denied unemployment benefits, then eventually allowed them (see MacKinnon 1979: 80–1).

[8] For more on MacKinnon's views on sexuality, see Chapter 3 below.

constant comments on their bodies, pornographic images of naked men, etc. will also fail to count as sexually harassing (for the same reason). Similarly, those who engage in apparently sexually harassing behaviour against members of their own sex (either male or female) will also fail to count as sexually harassing.

The dominance approach to sexual harassment, then, does treat women and men differently: under this approach, only women can be victims of sexual harassment, and only men can be perpetrators. Does this offer a way to argue that law on sexual harassment treats women as in need of special protection?

The first problem with this idea is that the dominance approach does *not* view women as fragile creatures who are incapable of coping with sexual comments and behaviour. The reason this approach focuses on sexual harassment of women by men is not because it sees women as inherently delicate, but rather because of its view of the power dynamics in society. On this view, the reason that women are in particular need of protection against sexual harassment is, as we have seen, that the sexual harassment of women plays a key role in maintaining women's subordination to men. This has nothing to do with the idea that women's innocence should be protected against all things sexual: instead, the concern is with the wrong of dominance. Under the dominance approach, women would indeed be granted protections that men are not. However, defenders of the dominance approach would claim that such protections are wholly appropriate, because women are still generally in subordinate positions to men both in the workplace and in the home; and because women are subjected to sexual violence far more than men are. It is women's sexual subordination to men that requires women to be given protections that men do not need.

The second problem is that the dominance approach to sexual harassment has not been much adopted legally (Crouch 2001: 47). Even if the dominance approach *did* rest on the idea of women as fragile and in need of special protection, the *law* could not be said to rest on such an idea. Instead, sexual harassment has been seen as sex discrimination under two other conceptions of sex discrimination: the difference approach and the stereotype approach.

SEXUAL HARASSMENT | 55

The difference approach

The difference approach is also due to MacKinnon, although she has rejected it in favour of the dominance approach. This approach is based on the most straightforward understanding of discrimination law: that sex discrimination occurs when men and women are treated differently in employment or education on the basis of their sex, and when there is no legitimate reason for taking sex into account.[9] Under this approach, sexual harassment is discrimination because its recipients—male or female—would not be treated in the way that they are if they were of the opposite sex. Both men and women can count as sexually harassed, and both men and women can count as sexually harassing. A heterosexual male employer who forces women employees to have sex with him would not do this if they were male. A heterosexual female employer who demands sex from her male employees would not make these demands if the employees were female. Each, therefore, has discriminated against their employees on the basis of their sex. Similarly, lesbian and gay employers who demand sex of same-sex employees would not do so with opposite-sex employees. This approach, then, in no way gives women any protections that are not also given to men.

The stereotype approach

This approach begins from the idea that it is discriminatory to behave toward people in a way that is based on sex stereotypes. It is discriminatory, for example, to demand that women conform to a female stereotype, and to penalize them for not doing so. Such behaviour involves treating one sex in a way that the other would not be treated.

There are a number of ways to see sexual harassment as based on sex stereotypes. One important way is to view sexual harassment of women as based on a stereotype of women as 'sexual fair game' and 'passive, willing recipients of their male superiors' (Crouch 2001: 42). It is easy to see quid pro quo harassment as based on such a stereotype, although somewhat harder to see hostile environment sexual harassment in this way. However, hostile environment

---

9 We discussed the difference approach to discrimination in Chapter 1 as well.

harassment directed at women is often caused by the view that women are unsuitable for the sort of work they are trying to do. Schultz (1998) has argued that such behaviour is based on stereotypes about women's competence. She notes that stereotypes about men may also come into play: certain jobs are viewed as masculine, and the idea that women can do these jobs may be upsetting to men whose view of themselves can depend to a great degree on the supposed masculinity of their jobs. A woman pipefitter described her experiences:

> Some of the men would take the tools out of my hands. You see it is just very hard for them to work with me because they're really into proving their masculinity and being tough. And when a woman comes on a job that can work, can get something done as fast and efficiently, as well, as they can, it really affects them. Somehow if a woman can do it, it ain't that masculine, not that tough.
>
> (Schroedel 1986: 20–21, quoted in Schultz 1998: 1691)

Harassment of men by women may also be seen as based on stereotypes. For example, hostile environment harassment of a man in a predominantly female workplace may well be based on stereotypes about his competence or suitability for the work. It is more difficult to understand how quid pro quo harassment may be based on stereotypes about men, as it is not stereotypical to view men as passive recipients of female advances—although one might argue, at least in certain cases, that such behaviour is based on a stereotype of men as always interested in sex and always receptive to sexual advances.

The stereotype approach has also been used as a way of recognizing harassment of those who do not conform adequately to stereotypes of their sex (Schultz 1998). Thus, men who are harassed for not being masculine enough or women who are harassed for not being feminine enough may, under this approach, be seen as sexually harassed. They could be seen as harassed even if they are harassed by members of their own sex, and even if sexual desire played no role in the harassment. This line of reasoning could allow courts to recognize harassment on the basis of sexual orientation (or perceived sexual orientation) as a form of sexual harassment (Schultz 1998.) Those who are harassed for not being heterosexual can at least sometimes be understood as harassed for not conforming adequately to the stereotypes of their sex. After all, being sexually attracted to women goes against the stereotype of femininity.

Neither the stereotype approach nor the difference approach validates the idea that sexual harassment law gives women forms of protection that are not given to men. As we have seen, each approach very clearly has the resources to recognize harassment of either men or women, by either men or women. Viewing sexual harassment as discrimination, then, does not mean viewing men and women as differently situated with respect to sexual harassment.

Comparing approaches

We have now reviewed three ways of understanding sexual harassment as sex discrimination. In what follows, I argue that the difference and sex stereotype approaches, although not without their own problems, are preferable to the dominance approach.

Problems for the dominance approach

We have already discussed one problem for the dominance approach: its failure to recognize the possibility of sexual harassment other than men harassing women. For proponents of the dominance approach, this is not a problem. They insist that this merely constitutes proper recognition of the fact that women and men are differently situated in society (Crossthwaite and Priest 1996; MacKinnon 1979). However, for those who feel that sexual harassment is possible with other configurations of harasser and harassed, this will not be convincing.

Another problem is Catharine MacKinnon's view that sexuality is *the* crucial factor in women's subordination to men—which she takes to be universal or near-universal. This seems too simple, both as an understanding of inequalities between women and men, and as an understanding of sexuality. It seems too simple as an understanding of inequality because so many other forces seem to play important roles. For example, the dynamics of workplace and family life described in the previous chapter seem vital to understanding why women are so much poorer than men. But this is quite a separate matter from sexual domination and subordination. MacKinnon's picture seems too simple as an understanding of sexuality, because it fails to acknowledge the huge variety that exists in sexual relationships. In too many cases, it will indeed be true that male dominance and female subordination are central to a sexual relationship, and to a relationship more generally. But not all sexuality is like this. Finally, MacKinnon's is simply too crude a picture of the dynamics of power and oppression: race, class, and sexual orientation all affect which people hold power over which others, and what form that power will take. To assume that interactions between a white woman and a black man can be understood as simply a matter of male sexual dominance fails to do justice to these complexities (Harris 1993).

It is worth noting, however, that one might adopt a dominance view of sexual harassment while denying MacKinnon's views on sexuality. One might maintain that sexual *harassment* is a vital force in subordinating women to men, without insisting that *all* (or even most) sexual interactions are such a force. A proponent of such an approach would still presumably need to be willing to accept that only men can be perpetrators of sexual harassment and only women can be victims.

Problems for the difference approach

Despite initial appearances, the difference approach does not, in fact, succeed in categorizing all analogous behaviours in the same way. In particular, cases where both sexes are targeted for harassment may fail to count as sexual harassment under this approach. To see this, consider the case of a bisexual employer who demands sex from both her male and her female employees and fires them if they do not comply. If the employer were heterosexual and demanded sex from only her male employees, her behaviour would be sexual harassment; similarly, if she were homosexual and demanded sex only from her female employees, her behaviour would be sexual harassment. But, according to the difference approach, because she is bisexual and demands sex from *both* male and female employees, her behaviour cannot be sexually harassing—neither her male nor her female employees are in a position to say that had they been of the opposite sex the harassment would not have taken place. One 'equal opportunity harassing' case is that of *Holman* v. *Indiana* (2000):

A husband and wife working for the state's Department of Transportation charged that the same supervisor sexually harassed them both. He asked the wife to go to bed with him and gave her negative job evaluations when she rejected him. But he was also accused of 'grabbing the husband's head while asking for sexual favors', then getting back at him for not complying by opening his locker and throwing away his belongings.

(Talbot 2002)

This case was judged not to be one of sexual harassment because both a man and a woman were victims of the behaviour in question. Clearly, this is an unacceptable outcome. Nobody wants to be committed to the view that two wrongs make a right, and this view seems to be committed to it: demanding sex from just women is wrong, and demanding sex from just men is wrong, but demanding sex from both women and men is not wrong.[10]

Those who have framed and initially applied the difference approach, of course, did not intend to protect 'equal opportunity harassers' from charges of sexual harassment. That they did not consider this potential problem seems to have been an oversight, due to the fact that they were focusing primarily on cases of men harassing women.

Problems for the stereotype approach

The stereotype approach, like the difference approach, may cover fewer cases of sexual harassment than it at first appears. Imagine, for example, an employer obsessed with a particular employee, who demands sexual favours of him simply because she is obsessed with him as an individual and eager to have sex with him. Unless it can be shown that her behaviour is based on a stereotype of men, it does not count as sex discrimination under the stereotype approach and therefore does not count as sexual harassment. But this behaviour certainly *seems* like sexual harassment, whatever its basis. An additional problem, then, with the stereotype approach is that one could defend oneself against a harassment charge by claiming that one's behaviour

---

[10] It is important to note that this problem may also arise for hostile environment sexual harassment. An environment in which both men and women are subjected to abuse will not count as a sexually harassing one on the difference approach.

was motivated by an obsession with a particular individual rather than a stereotype.

Each of these approaches to understanding sexual harassment faces some problems. Only one of them, however—the dominance approach—could in any way be seen as giving women protections not given to men. Even if the dominance approach were clearly the best and universally adopted, however, we have seen that it is questionable whether it could be considered to treat women as fragile innocents. Moreover, the dominance approach has not been widely adopted and it faces many problems. Other approaches—such as the difference and stereotype approaches—seem likely to do a better job of capturing the wide range of behaviours that seem as though they should be categorized together as sexual harassment. These approaches have also been more successful legally. There is no reason, then, to suppose that recognition of sexual harassment requires a belief that women are delicate souls in need of protection from all things sexual.

Severity

Many people worry that sexual harassment law is making minor interpersonal misunderstandings the stuff of lawsuits. They worry that any pursuit of romance or even friendship in the office, or any mildly off-colour joke, runs the risk of being considered sexual harassment; and that any attempt to liven up a dull lecture with a bit of humour, or any friendly behaviour toward a student, may get a professor fired. Workplaces and classrooms, on this line of thought, are becoming cold, tightly controlled places where people must interact in stiff and regimented ways, without showing a trace of humanity—and sexual harassment law is to blame.

Yet others maintain that sexual harassment law could not possibly have these effects (Zalesne 1999a; 1999b). Courts have consistently found that behaviour has to be severe and pervasive to count as sexual harassment, and an occasional joke or misguided friendly gesture simply isn't severe enough for sexual harassment. Indeed, courts have been criticized for their deep reluctance to recognize behaviour as sufficiently severe to qualify as harassment. To take just one example:

in a 1990 case, a technician abused a thermal protection inspector by holding a knife to her throat, pushing her into a filing cabinet, threatening to bang her head into the ground, and grabbing 'her pelvic area and breasts' (*Weinsheimer* v. *Rockwell International Corp.*, discussed in Schultz 1998: 1731). The court found that she could not have found this treatment unacceptable because 'she had used "abusive and vulgar language" in speaking to her boyfriend on the telephone at work'. Verdicts like this certainly do not sound like over-regulation of innocent behaviour, to put it mildly. How, then, could it be that so many people think that sexual harassment law is stifling harmless interactions between people?

Media misrepresentations

Defenders of sexual harassment law argue that the media has misrepresented a few cases of sexual harassment accusations, and thereby fed the perception that sexual harassment law is out of control, over-regulating human behaviour to the point where normal interactions are impossible.

Many authors have discussed the case of Donald Silva, an English professor who was suspended from the University of New Hampshire. According to most reports of the case (e.g. Bernstein 2001), he was suspended for lectures in which he used or discussed sexual analogies, for making some inept but not horrendous jokes outside class, and for giving a student a spelling test which included sexual sentences (a different student, reported as overhearing, was offended). However, the full details of the case are different: they also include offering a student an undeserved 'A' for a class, making many women uncomfortable by standing or leaning too close to them, backing one woman up against a table, and asking for students' home addresses and phone numbers. The spelling test incident, fully fleshed out (as it generally was not in popular reports) was this: A female student was waiting to see Silva while he was administering a spelling test to a male student. Silva invited her to come in and wait, and made eye contact with her (rather than the student he was testing) as he said, 'It may or may not be appropriate for a student to earn her "A" by sleeping with her professor' (Clark 2001: 198). With these additional allegations, the complaint against Silva looks more serious. It no longer looks so clear that the university was blindly acting to protect women against all sexual comments, or to stamp out all sexual expression.

Other well-publicized cases have been similarly misreported. A nice example comes from the Stroh's Brewery case discussed earlier: the media chose to focus almost exclusively on one complaint alone. This was the complaint that the Stroh's advertising campaign featuring 'the Swedish Bikini Team' served to perpetuate a view of women as sex objects (Schultz 1998). There were, as we saw at the start of this chapter, many other complaints that were much clearer instances of harassment. Focusing on the advertisement, and ignoring so many other aspects of the case, gave a false impression regarding the quantity and severity of behaviour needed for a successful sexual harassment complaint.

Finally, the status of many sexual harassment claims is often not made sufficiently clear. The decisions of employers and universities regarding what constitutes sexual harassment are reported as though they closely follow the law on sexual harassment, despite the fact that—as we shall see—the law is often very different from institutional policies. In addition, much more attention is given to claims of sexual harassments than to eventual verdicts. For example, a great deal of attention was given to Paula Jones's allegations against President Clinton. These seemed to many too minor to constitute sexual harassment, thus feeding the idea that sexual harassment law has 'gone too far'. There was little attention, however, given to the judge's decision that Jones's allegations, even if true, were indeed too minor to constitute sexual harassment (Zalesne 1999b).[11]

Institutional policies

As intimated above, institutional sexual harassment policies tend to cast their net much more widely than courts do in deciding what counts as sexual harassment. (As we will see, they do this to avoid costly lawsuits.) The relationship between these policies and the law

---

[11] For more such cases of misreporting, see Zalesne (1999b).

on sexual harassment is a complex and contested one. We will approach it by examining Mane Hajdin's worries about the notion of sexual harassment. Hajdin raises the concern that many institutional sexual harassment regulations, by forbidding any unwelcome sexual behaviour or comments, effectively rule out all sexual behaviour and comments in the workplace (Hajdin and LeMoncheck 1997). He takes this to be an unacceptable restriction, and claims that it is an inevitable consequence of sexual harassment law. Accordingly, he argues that there should be no laws against sexual harassment.[12]

Hajdin's argument begins from the fact that institutional definitions of sexual harassment—set out in internal sexual harassment policies—often forbid all unwelcome sexual conduct or conversation. Hajdin's worry is that it can be very difficult to know *in advance* whether a particular sexual overture will be unwelcome or not. Imagine, he suggests, that you want to avoid committing sexual harassment by avoiding any unwelcome sexual advances, but you find yourself attracted to a co-worker and would like to make the first move. How do you know whether this will be acceptable or not? Some people, after all, for personal or religious reasons, would find any sexual advance unwelcome. Others might simply find any sexual advance *from you* unwelcome. You might think that you could find out whether such a sexual advance would be welcome or not by asking. But imagine yourself asking, 'Would it be alright if I made a sexual advance?' The very act of asking this question is, in itself, a kind of sexual overture—which might itself be unwelcome, just like a more conventional sexual overture. Needless to say, the problem cannot be solved by asking, 'Would it be all right if I asked whether it would be all right for me to make a sexual advance?' This is no less recognizably a sexual advance (although it is, admittedly, a much stranger one). Thus, he claims, one can never know in advance whether a sexual advance is unwelcome. As a result, one who wants to avoid committing sexual harassment will be unable to ever make a romantic overture in the workplace. A parallel argument applies to

---

[12] While he agrees that many of the behaviours considered sexual harassment are wrong, and that some of them should be illegal, he does not think there should be laws specifically against sexual harassment.

sexual jokes in the workplace: learning that someone does not find sexual jokes unwelcome is not enough to establish that they will not find *your* joke unwelcome. The only way to find that out is to describe the joke so fully that anyone likely to be offended will be offended even by the description. Thus, the only rational course of action is to refrain from all sexual jokes.

One might object that Hajdin seems to somewhat underestimate the social abilities and repertoires of people interacting in a workplace. There are many ways to indicate interest, or lack of interest, in a sexual or romantic relationship, and people regularly make use of them. It seems too strong, then, to say that fear of committing sexual harassment would put an end to all relationships that begin in a workplace. Similar considerations apply to concerns about joke-telling. On the other hand, subtle cues are often misunderstood. Fear of such misinterpretation may well deter cautious people from making advances or telling jokes, and people who are poor at reading social cues might well unwittingly make unwelcome advances or tell unwelcome jokes. So the fact that there are subtle social cues available doesn't fully solve the problem Hajdin poses.

The relationship between worries like this one and the law is not an obvious one. As noted earlier, courts have consistently found that sexual behaviour that is found unwelcome by its recipients is not automatically sexual harassment. To count as quid pro quo harassment, a sexual advance has to be accompanied by such behaviour as threats of firing or poor grades, or promises of promotion or good grades. To count as hostile environment harassment, behaviour has to be sufficiently severe or pervasive to create an environment that reasonable people would find intolerable. Suppose, then, that you want to ask a co-worker out on a date. As long as you don't make employment-related threats or promises as a part of your romantic overture, you can rest assured that you are not committing quid pro quo harassment. Suppose you want to tell an off-colour joke. A single joke is extremely unlikely to create such an offensive working environment that a reasonable person would find it intolerable. (The sort of joke that could do this, if any, would surely be easily recognizable as offensive.)

Hajdin is right, however, that many institutional sexual harassment policies define 'sexual harassment' in such a way that much more minor behaviour qualifies, and indeed in such a way that mere unwelcomeness is sufficient for sexual harassment.[13] Thus, while you would not legally have committed sexual harassment merely by making an unwelcome advance, you might well have done so according to your institution's definition. The law, then, is importantly different from many institutional sexual harassment policies. Hajdin argues that such institutional policies are an inevitable consequence of laws against sexual harassment. One reason for institutions to have codes like these, which prohibit behaviour that is not, legally speaking, sexual harassment, is that they want to completely avoid the creation of a hostile working environment. Suppose you work for a company in an entry-level position. If one co-worker says, 'You have nice legs' in the course of clumsily asking you out on a date, this is unprofessional, but unlikely to be judged by a court to have created a sufficiently offensive work environment to count as sexual harassment. But if every one of thirty co-workers comments on some portion of your anatomy, the environment becomes a very different one. It is entirely possible that this large a collection of actions that are not, individually, sufficient for sexual harassment, will—taken as a whole—legally constitute sexual harassment. It is reasonable, then, for employers to prohibit actions that individually are not sexual harassment: if enough of them occurred there would be sexual harassment, and the employer wants to avoid sexual harassment lawsuits. An employer can only do this, Hajdin argues, by ruling out many individual behaviours that would not in themselves constitute sexual harassment. Due to this quite rational behaviour on the employer's part, Hajdin's worry is a real one. There *are* sexual harassment codes, many of them, that prohibit any unwelcome sexual advances. More generally, there are many sexual harassment codes that prohibit behaviour that, legally speaking, is not sexual harassment. According to Hajdin, such harassment codes are inevitable as long as sexual harassment is illegal.

Hajdin's inevitability claim, however, seems wrong. Let us grant that employers will inevitably have an interest in restricting behaviours that, individually, do not rise to the level of sexual

---

[13] For more on this, see the discussion in Schultz (forthcoming).

harassment. It by no means follows that they must call this behaviour 'sexual harassment', and treat it as severely as they would sexual harassment. Instead, they might produce a list of behaviours that *can* contribute to creating a sexually harassing environment, and make employees aware of the potential problems that could arise. They could even discourage these behaviours without calling them 'sexual harassment' and without treating them as severely as they do sexual harassment. They could confine their use of the term 'sexual harassment', and the more severe penalties, to behaviour that actually creates an unacceptable working environment. Doing this requires more thought and sensitivity than is involved in merely prohibiting all unwelcome sexual behaviour. But this may well be a price worth paying.

If this is possible, however, one might well wonder why it has not more often been done. The answer, it seems to me, is that there really is a great deal of confusion over what exactly sexual harassment is. Take, for example, the information on the British Equal Opportunity Commission's (EOC) website. In a section regarding the law on sexual harassment, this site explains that 'behaviour must be unwanted, unreasonable, and offensive to the recipient'. Thus, mere unwelcomeness is not enough for sexual harassment: behaviour must also be unreasonable and offensive. However, in a section offering guidance to employers, sexual harassment is defined as 'unwelcome physical, verbal or non-verbal conduct of a sexual nature', and emphasizes that 'the essential characteristic of sexual harassment is that it is unwanted by the recipient'.[14] When the body empowered to enforce anti-discrimination legislation gives such conflicting messages regarding the nature of sexual harassment, is it any wonder that there is confusion? And is it any wonder that institutions fearing lawsuits adopt the more expansive understanding of sexual harassment?[15]

There is, then, a serious problem, but not the one that Hajdin describes. It is not inevitable that employers will define 'sexual

[14] EOC, 'Sexual Harassment: What the Law Says' and 'Dealing with Sexual Harassment', at www.eoc.org.uk

[15] Vicki Schultz has documented a similar tendency in the US: those advising employers frequently use an understanding of sexual harassment on which unwelcomeness is sufficient for sexual harassment (see Schultz, forthcoming).

harassment' so broadly that any unwelcome behaviour qualifies. However, it probably is inevitable that they will do so as long as so much lack of clarity surrounds the notion of sexual harassment. We—and the bodies advising on sexual harassment law—need to agree upon whether mere unwelcomeness or offensiveness is sufficient for an action to count as sexual harassment, and to stick clearly by this decision. This of course raises the issue of what we should decide. Courts have been very clear on this—mere unwelcomeness is not enough for sexual harassment—but we *might* want to disagree with the courts. However, it seems to me that it would be a mistake to disagree on this issue. As long as people have different backgrounds, different beliefs, and different modes of interacting with each other, some unwelcome interaction is inevitable. Making merely unwelcome behaviour illegal would indeed create an environment of fear and tension in workplaces or on campuses.[16] Moreover, merely unwelcome behaviour that is neither severe nor pervasive is simply not that serious a matter. It does not seem like something with which the law should concern itself. On the other hand, unwelcome behaviour that is so severe and pervasive that it creates an unreasonable environment is a very serious matter, and one in which the law should involve itself. Categorizing these two sorts of behaviour together, as would be done by a sexual harassment law that did not restrict its attention to severe or pervasive behaviour, can only serve to trivialize the serious cases. In fact, even the current situation has already led to such trivialization. We can see this in claims (with which we began this section) that victims should respond to sexual harassment with witty comebacks, or by learning to tolerate an occasional joke. Those who focus only on the relatively minor behaviours that can be dealt with effectively through such means will fail to appreciate the importance of dealing properly with severe and pervasive behaviours that create an unacceptable environment. Expanding the law to cover more minor behaviours, then, would clearly be a move in

---

[16] Universities may be especially problematic: work and home are difficult to divide for students living in dormitories; and 17-year-olds away from home for the first time, thrown together with people of different backgrounds, are likely to engage in unintentionally unwelcome behaviour simply out of inexperience.

the wrong direction. Instead, sexual harassment policies and guidance on sexual harassment need to be brought into line with the law.

Non-sexual behaviour as sexual harassment

Another unclear area is the issue of whether behaviour[17] that is not itself sexual can qualify as sexual harassment. Take the case of a female employee in an otherwise all-male workplace, who is subjected to constant sex*ist* insults. Does it matter whether or not these insults are sex*ual* in character? If only sexual behaviour can qualify as sexual harassment, then it does make a difference: the woman will not be able to bring a sexual harassment complaint if the insults are not sexual in content. But if non-sexual behaviour may also qualify, then the woman will be able to bring a sexual harassment complaint either way.

The legal situation is notably murky on this issue. Although a few courts have recognized non-sexual behaviour as sexual harassment,[18] many have not. And guidance-giving bodies offer conflicting advice. The US Equal Employment Opportunity Commission (EEOC) website[19] offers a definition of 'sexual harassment' (much like that discussed earlier) under which only sexual behaviour qualifies. But it also notes, much later in the same document, that non-sexual behaviour may count as sexual harassment ('Policy Guidance on Current Issues of Sexual Harassment'). The British Equal Opportunity Commission website, in its section on the law, allows that both sexual and non-sexual behaviour may qualify as sexual harassment ('Sexual harassment: What the Law Says'). But in its section on advice for employers, it restricts its definition to sexual behaviour ('Dealing with Sexual Harassment').

Vicki Schultz has argued that the focus on sexual behaviour has led courts to refuse to recognize genuine and serious cases of sexual harassment. The problem, in these cases, has been that non-sexual

---

[17] I am including linguistic behaviour as a kind of behaviour.
[18] For example, this was recognized in *McKinney* v. *Dole*, discussed in Schultz (1998: 1732–3).
[19] www.eeoc.gov

components of a pattern of harassing behaviour are ignored. To begin to see the effect that distinguishing sexual and non-sexual behaviour in this way might have, consider again the Stroh's employees' behaviour described at the start of this chapter. The elements that might count as sexual harassment are grabbing on the rear end, displaying pubic hair, pushing a woman's head into a man's crotch, sexual comments, graffiti, and pin-ups. Telling women that they should go home and get women's jobs is irrelevant to a sexual harassment complaint, as is sabotaging women's machines or slashing their tyres. This is a bit counter-intuitive, since it seems clear that all of these actions *together* combined to create a hostile environment for the women workers. Looking at only the sexual actions or only the non-sexual actions fails to tell the whole story of the hostile environment that was created. In this case, the sexual actions alone were taken to be sufficient for sexual harassment. But not all cases have been like this.

In some cases, the sexual aspects of the harassment alone have not been seen as creating an unreasonably hostile environment. One example is that of *Reynolds* v. *Atlantic City Convention Center*, from 1991. Margaret Reynolds, an electrician, alleged that she had been sexually harassed upon being named subforeman for a contract at the Atlantic City Convention Center in the US.

> The harassment did not take the form of sexual advances or other sexually oriented conduct. Instead, it consisted of conduct that challenged Reynolds's authority and right to be subforeman. The men refused to work for her and stood around laughing while she unloaded heavy boxes. They engaged in a work stoppage—some even quit their jobs—so as not to submit to the authority of a woman. She . . . was 'harassed constantly with verbal abuse and obscene gestures' . . . When a client exhibitor demanded that Reynolds and the other female electrician be removed from the floor during the Miss America pageant—apparently the incongruity between the images of the pageant contestants and the tradeswomen was too much for the exhibitor—Reynolds and her colleague were replaced by a male co-worker. At the end of the pageant, the convention center's director fired the whole crew and hired all but [Reynolds] and a few others back the next day, with a man as the new subforeman.

> (Schultz 1998: 1722)

The court decided that only the obscene gestures and words had the potential to qualify as sexual harassment, because only they were sexual in nature. It found the rest of the behaviour to be irrelevant. According to the court,

> While her male co-workers may have refused to work for her because she was a woman, such refusal is not 'verbal or physical conduct as sexual nature' and so does not figure into the calculus of a sexually offensive working environment.

Since the few actions that were left as candidates for sexually harassing behaviour were not, on their own, very severe, the court found that no hostile environment existed.

Schultz offers many other examples of courts refusing to recognize harassment that does not consist of sexual behaviour as sexual harassment (Schultz 1998). She also provides many examples of harassment codes that single out sexual behaviour, including a large number that treat any sexual behaviour as problematic (Schultz forthcoming). There is, then, at least a significant tendency to assign sexual behaviour a special importance in delineating the nature of sexual harassment.

One historical reason for the focus on sexual behaviour may be that quid pro quo sexual harassment was the first sort to be recognized legally. After all, quid pro quo harassment concerns demands for sex. But it is unclear that the focus on sexual behaviour should be maintained when we turn to hostile environment harassment. If what is wrong with this harassment is its potential to create a hostile environment on grounds of sex, then why should it matter whether that environment is created through sexual behaviour or through other behaviour?

Schultz has argued that it is a mistake for sexual harassment law and policies to focus on sexual behaviour (Schultz 1998; 2001; forthcoming).[20] In addition to the worries raised above, she notes that sexual harassment law was developed on the model of racial

---

[20] F. M. Christensen also holds the focus on sex to be a mistake, and believes that the willingness to legislate against sexual harassment stems from anti-sex sentiment in America, and from the belief that women are in need of special protection (see Christensen 1994: 1–17). See also Crouch (2001: 169).

harassment law (Schultz 2001: 273). Under racial harassment law, racist behaviour and comments are taken to have the potential to create an environment so hostile that it is discriminatory on the basis of race. The obvious analogue in the case of sex discrimination would be environments that contain so much sexist behaviour that they create an atmosphere that is discriminatory on the basis of sex. But many understandings of sexual harassment focus not on sex*ist* behaviour but on sex*ual* behaviour. Why should this be?

For those who accept Catharine MacKinnon's dominance view of sexual harassment, the emphasis on sexual behaviour makes perfect sense. On this view, as we have seen, sexual behaviour plays a special role in subordinating women to men. Introduction of such behaviour into the workplace, then, is especially damaging to women's prospects for equality at work. Those who are unconvinced by this view, however, will not be convinced by this justification for singling out sexual conduct for special attention.

Those who accept either the difference or stereotype approaches to sex discrimination and sexual harassment, however, would find it more difficult to justify a focus on sexual behaviour. It is hard to see how a proponent of the difference approach could deny that a person might be singled out for harassment due to their sex without that harassment itself being of a sexual nature. Indeed, sexist insults would seem clear examples of harassment on the basis of sex, whether or not they were sexual in nature. Similarly, it seems that proponents of the stereotype approach should acknowledge that a person's harassment might be due to a sex stereotype without that harassment involving any sexual conduct. Since sex stereotypes involve many features other than sexual ones (for example, 'Women are bad at science', or 'Men are big and strong'), we would expect harassment caused by such stereotypes to include both sexual and non-sexual conduct.

There does not, then, seem to be a good reason for singling out sexual conduct as particularly suspect. If there is no such good reason, then there should be wider recognition of the ways in which non-sexual conduct may contribute to creating a sexually harassing environment. In any case, we need a clearer agreement over whether non-sexual conduct may count as sexual harassment.

When bodies like the EOC and EEOC give such conflicting signals on points like this, it is no wonder that many people feel they do not understand what sexual harassment is. Sexual harassment is a very serious matter, and it is important that we work to eliminate it. But this cannot be successfully done until we agree upon a clear understanding of what it is. The fact that we lack this now is unsurprising. Sexual harassment is a new concept. We should not throw up our hands in despair and abandon the fight against it. Rather, we should acknowledge the definitional problems that exist, think carefully about what matters to us, and work to arrive at a clear and agreed-upon definition.

SUGGESTIONS FOR FURTHER READING

Overview of issues concerning sexual harassment

Crouch, M., *Thinking about Sexual Harassment: A Guide for the Perplexed*. Oxford: Oxford University Press, 2001. (*Includes discussion of various countries' sexual harassment laws.*)

LeMoncheck, L., and Sterba, J. P. (eds.), *Sexual Harassment: Issues and Answers*. Oxford: Oxford University Press, 2001.

The dominance approach to sexual harassment

Crossthwaite, J., and Priest, G., 'The Definition of Sexual Harassment', *Australasian Journal of Philosophy* 74 (1) (1996): 66–82.

Crouch, M., *Thinking about Sexual Harassment: A Guide for the Perplexed*. Oxford: Oxford University Press, 2001, ch. 3.

MacKinnon, C., *The Sexual Harassment of Working Women*. New Haven, Conn.: Yale University Press, 1979.

Difference approach to sexual harassment

Crouch, M., *Thinking about Sexual Harassment: A Guide for the Perplexed*. Oxford: Oxford University Press, 2001, ch. 3.

MacKinnon, C., *The Sexual Harassment of Working Women*. New Haven, Conn.: Yale University Press, 1979.

Stereotype approach to sexual harassment

Crouch, M., *Thinking about Sexual Harassment: A Guide for the Perplexed*, Oxford: Oxford University Press, 2001, ch. 3.

Levitsky, S., 'Closing the "Bisexual Defense" Loophole in Title VII Sexual Harassment Cases', in LeMoncheck and Sterba, *Sexual Harassment: Issues and Answers*. Oxford: Oxford University Press, 2001, 214–28. (*Links stereotype approach to dominance approach.*)

Schultz, V., 'Reconceptualizing Sexual Harassment', *Yale Law Journal* 107 (1998): 1696–1805.

Worries about sexual harassment laws and regulations (and responses to these worries)

Hajdin, M., and LeMoncheck, L., *Sexual Harassment: A Debate*, Lanham, Md.: Rowman & Littlefield, 1997.

Schultz, V., 'Reconceptualizing Sexual Harassment', *Yale Law Journal* 107 (1998): 1696–1805.

—— 'Sex is the Least of it: Let's Focus Harassment Law on Work, Not Sex', in LeMoncheck and Sterba, *Sexual Harassment: Issues and Answers*. Oxford: Oxford University Press, 2001, 269–73.

—— 'The Sanitized Workplace', forthcoming.

Zalesne, D., 'Sexual Harassment Law: Has it Gone Too Far, or Has the Media?', *Temple Political and Civil Rights Law Review* 8(2) (1999), 351–76.

—— 'Workplace Paranoia: Media Propaganda', *Women's International Net* 21 (1999).

3

Pornography

> In pornography there it is, in one place, all of the abuses that women had to struggle so long even to begin to articulate, all the *unspeakable* abuse: the rape, the battery, the sexual harassment, the prostitution, and the sexual abuse of children. Only in the pornography that is called something else: sex, sex, sex, sex, and sex, respectively. Pornography sexualizes rape, battery, sexual harassment, prostitution, and child sexual abuse; it thereby celebrates, promotes, authorizes, and legitimizes them. More generally, it eroticizes the dominance and submission that is the dynamic common to them all. It makes hierarchy sexy and calls that 'the truth about sex' or just a mirror of reality. Through this process pornography constructs what a woman is as what men want from sex. This is what the pornography means.
>
> Catharine MacKinnon (1987: 171)

> Pornography benefits women, both personally and politically.
>
> Wendy McElroy (1995: vii)

As the quotes above illustrate, some feminists oppose and some feminists defend pornography. But even feminists who oppose pornography are not a monolithic group—some want to use legal means to restrict or eliminate pornography, while others strongly oppose this idea. And feminist defenders of pornography include both those who enthusiastically endorse it, like McElroy, and those who simply disagree with particular criticisms that have been made of it. In this chapter, I explore several very different feminist positions on two key issues regarding pornography: what, if anything, is wrong with it; and what, if anything, should be done about it. In the course of this discussion, I show some important relationships between the arguments made on various sides, and I attempt to isolate some questions whose answers could help to resolve the debate.

The case against pornography

Rejecting obscenity standards

The traditional way to understand pornography is as obscenity. Under US law, a work is obscene if a reasonable person applying community standards would find that it, taken as a whole, appeals solely to the prurient interest (lacks 'serious literary, artistic, or political significance'), and depicts sexual activity in an offensive way (Dwyer 1995: 242, 245). In the UK, obscene works are those whose effect is to 'tend to deprave and corrupt'. Juries are instructed to understand 'deprave and corrupt' in terms of 'the current standards of ordinary decent people' (Itzin 1992: 402–3). Important assumptions behind obscenity law, then, include the ideas that there is something wrong with appealing only to sexual interests (US), and that ordinary community standards should be upheld (US and UK).

Feminists who are opposed to pornography entirely reject the idea of approaching it on the traditional model of obscenity. First, they often consider it *good* to violate community standards. After all, part of feminism's project is to challenge traditional ways of thinking about women. Many feminists also take this to require changing the way that people think about sex—and this may involve violating accepted community standards. Moreover, they differ from obscenity opponents in that they see nothing wrong with material that is solely of sexual interest. Feminists who are opposed to pornography, then, oppose it for very different reasons from those who oppose obscenity. Their opposition is based on the view that it is deeply linked to violence, especially sexual violence, against women—and to women's subordination more generally.

Defining 'pornography'

Feminist opponents of pornography reject not only the traditional view of what is wrong with pornography, but also the traditional view of what pornography is. Roughly, they oppose material involving degradation or abuse of women in a sexual context.[1] While there is no settled agreement on a feminist definition of 'pornography', there is agreement that degradation and abuse are the key factors. Much of the discussion takes as its starting place Catharine MacKinnon and Andrea Dworkin's definition of pornography, and we will do so as well. According to this definition, pornography is:

[t]he graphic sexually explicit subordination of women through pictures and/or words that also includes one or more of the following: (a) women are presented dehumanised as sexual objects, things, or commodities; or (b) women are presented as sexual objects who enjoy humiliation or pain; or (c) women are presented as sexual objects experiencing sexual pleasure in rape, incest, or other sexual assault; or (d) women are presented as sexual objects tied up or cut up or mutilated or bruised or physically hurt; or (e) women are presented in postures or positions of sexual submission, servility, or display; or (f) women's body parts—including but not limited to vaginas, breasts, or buttocks—are exhibited such that women are reduced to those parts; or (g) women are presented being penetrated by objects or animals; or (h) women are presented in scenarios of degradation, injury, torture; shown as filthy or inferior; bleeding, bruised, or hurt in a context that makes these conditions sexual.

(MacKinnon 1993: 121–2, n. 32)

MacKinnon also notes that 'the use of "men, children, or transsexuals in the place of women" is also pornography' (p. 122, n. 32); and that 'erotica, defined by distinction as not this, might be sexually explicit materials premised on equality' (MacKinnon 1987: 176).

The focus of this definition is on sexually explicit material that is subordinating or dehumanizing to women. Importantly, it is not just

---

[1] While the focus is mostly on women—because (as we'll see) there are reasons to suppose that pornography plays a special role in subordinating women—feminists who oppose pornography generally want their concerns to be extended to material that treats others in degrading and abusive ways as well.

overt violence that may count as subordinating or dehumanizing. Presenting women as sex objects or in postures of display[2] can also render a work pornographic. And this is very important to feminist opponents of pornography: while they are especially horrified by depictions of violent abuse, they hold that it is also extremely damaging to depict women as always eager to satisfy men's sexual desires, even if the women are not the victims of violence.[3] This, they believe, perpetuates the idea that women's role is to serve men, and the idea that women want, sexually, only to please men. In turn, these ideas help to legitimize rape and to perpetuate the idea of women as inferior.

It is important to emphasize just how much anti-pornography feminists' definitions of 'pornography' differ from the standard understanding of obscenity. Some sexually explicit material will count as obscenity under standard definitions but not as pornography under feminist definitions. Imagine, for example, a sexually explicit depiction of egalitarian, loving lesbian sex. Imagine also that this depiction has as its sole purpose producing sexual arousal, and that it has no interest other than this. In a community in which lesbian sex is considered offensive, this would be judged offensive and against community standards. Moreover, it has no interest other than that of producing sexual arousal. Under standard definitions of 'obscenity', then, it might well count as obscene. It might not, however, count as pornography under feminists' understandings. As long as the sex depicted is egalitarian, and there is no dehumanization, subordination, or the like, it will not be pornography.

Similarly, works that might count as pornography under feminist definitions would not count as obscenity under more standard ones. Consider, for example, a film involving an approvingly presented[4]

---

[2] There are some problems in establishing exactly what terms like these refer to. I discuss these problems in more detail later.

[3] Sometimes, the term 'violence' is extended to cover these sorts of depictions as well. For ease of comprehension, however, I prefer to use it in a more standard way.

[4] Some feminist definitions of 'pornography', such as Longino's and Russell's, require that the offensive depictions of women be presented in such a way as to endorse them. They add this requirement to avoid counting, for example, anti-pornography activists' discussions of pornography as pornography (Longino 1995; Russell 1993).

sexually explicit depiction of a woman displaying herself as a sex object, shown in a community where such depictions are considered acceptable and embedded in a larger narrative which makes some small unrelated political points—say, about the wrongness of gun control. This work, as I have set up the example, does not violate community standards. Moreover, it does have interest other than that of producing sexual arousal—indeed, one of the points of the film is to convince people that gun control is wrong.[5] This would not, then, count as obscenity under standard tests. However, it is a sexually explicit depiction of a woman displaying herself as a sex object. This means that it is very likely to count as pornography under most feminist definitions.

Feminists who oppose pornography are well aware that their definitions are very different from standard ones, both in law and in commonplace understandings of pornography. It is no objection, then, to argue that their definitions involve making false claims about pornography—that pornography does not always subordinate or dehumanize women. For if we adopt MacKinnon's definition, pornography will by definition involve subordination and dehumanization. Things that are ordinarily considered pornography but which do not involve the subordination of women are simply not pornography for MacKinnon. She has chosen to use the word 'pornography' in a way that is very different from the standard usage, and she fully accepts all the consequences of this choice.

It is perhaps worth noting, however, that feminists opposed to pornography believe that their definitions of 'pornography' will include the vast majority of things commonly considered to be pornography. This claim, however, is entirely separate from their definitions, and from arguments against pornography as they define it. MacKinnon, for example, could be wrong about how much pornography as standardly understood remains pornography under her definition while still being right about how we should view those materials that stand as pornography under her definition.

---

[5] As we will see shortly, speech that makes political points is often taken to be especially deserving of protection.

Arguments against pornography

I will begin by presenting arguments against pornography, reserving criticism of them for a later section. It is worth mentioning again that one may object to pornography without believing that there should be any laws against it. This section concerns *only* reasons that feminists have given for thinking that there is something wrong with pornography. It is perfectly possible to accept all of these arguments while insisting that pornographers not only do, but should, have every legal right to produce pornography. If this seems strange, it is worth considering the fact that we do not really believe there should be laws against everything we think is wrong: most of us think, for example, that promise-breaking is wrong, but we don't think it would be a good idea for all promise-breaking to be legally prosecutable.

Introducing the arguments

Feminists opposed to pornography must argue that their reasons for opposing it are so strong as to overcome the widespread presumption in favour of freedom of expression. It is worth a brief examination of this presumption.

In the United States, freedom of expression receives special protection from the First Amendment to the Constitution. The First Amendment reads, in part, 'Congress shall make no law . . . abridging the freedom of speech, or of the press . . .' 'Speech' is generally interpreted to include all forms of expression, including those, like photographs or films, that we wouldn't ordinarily call 'speech'. Although the United Kingdom has no written constitution, it also has a strong presumption in favour of free speech (though not so strong as the presumption at work in the United States). The main reason for valuing speech so highly is that it is considered to be essential for the proper functioning of a democracy. A key source for this idea is John Stuart Mill's *On Liberty*. In it, he argued that it is vital for citizens to be able to express themselves freely, especially though not exclusively concerning political matters, so that all ideas can be debated and discussed. It is only in this way that we would be likely to work out the truth in difficult matters. Further, he argued that one person's expression should only be restricted for the sake of preventing harm to another.[6] Feminists who oppose pornography do so for a variety of related reasons. Various opponents of pornography claim some or all of the following to be true.

1. Pornography is not just expression, as there are real sexual acts taking place, and sometimes (always or nearly always, according to some), these are acts of rape and violence. (See e.g. MacKinnon 1987; 1989; 1993; Dworkin 1981; Itzin 1992; Russell 1993.)

2. Pornography harms women, by causing (or helping to cause) violence, especially sexual violence, against women. This is argued for on the basis of rapists' testimony, psychological evidence, and women's reactions to pornography. (See e.g. MacKinnon 1987; 1992; 1993; Dworkin 1981; Itzin 1992; Russell 1993.)

3. Pornography plays a key role in shaping men and women, teaching that maleness is about sexual domination and femaleness about sexual submission. This power dynamic then works to subordinate women to men in many other areas of life (MacKinnon 1987; 1992; 1993).

4. Pornography is *itself* an act of subordination and silencing of women. This is another reason that it is not just expression (MacKinnon 1987; 1992; 1993; Langton 1993; Hornsby 1995; 2000).

5. Countries that legislate against hate speech should also legislate against pornography (Forna 1992).

Pornography is real

It is undeniable that many pornographic films and photographs are not just depictions of sex. While murder mystery movies are not films of actual murders taking place, pornographic movies *are* films of actual sex taking place. Moreover, some of the women filmed are not participating willingly—that is, they are being raped on film. Linda Marchiano (aka 'Linda Lovelace'), star of *Deep Throat*, has written a

[6] For an argument that Mill himself would support feminists' arguments against pornography, see Dyzenhaus (1992: 534–51).

book, *Ordeal,* describing how she was imprisoned, tortured, and forced to make this notorious film (Lovelace 1980). The movie *Deep Throat,* MacKinnon argues, is not just expression but a series of actual rapes taking place. Moreover, every time it is shown, people get pleasure from Marchiano being raped. Clearly, there is more to pornography like *Deep Throat* than just expression.

Pornography helps to cause violence (especially sexual violence) against women

A key argument for feminist opponents of pornography is that pornography encourages violence against women, especially sexual violence and rape. Opponents like MacKinnon claim that it does this by depicting women as always interested in sex, particularly in giving pleasure to men; as enjoying being overpowered, tied up, or hit; and as enjoying sex even after they have said 'no' or struggled and resisted. Men who learn about sex through watching pornography, then, will treat women as existing solely for their sexual desires, and will not hesitate to assault women and force sex on them. Because pornography is a key vehicle by which men and boys learn about sex, then, MacKinnon argues, pornography leads to rape and violence against women.

> [In pornography, women] desperately want to be bound, battered, tortured, humiliated, and killed. Or, to be fair to the soft core, merely taken and used. This is erotic to the male point of view. Subjection itself, with self-determination ecstatically relinquished, is the content of women's sexual desire and desirability. Women are there to be violated and possessed, men to violate and possess us, either on screen or by camera or pen on behalf of the consumer . . . [pornography] institutionalizes the sexuality of male supremacy, fusing the eroticization of dominance and submission with the social construction of male and female . . . Men treat women as who they see women as being. Pornography constructs who that is.
>
> (MacKinnon 1987: 172)

To show that pornography does all this is no easy matter. Some arguments are based on psychological studies, and some on the use made of pornography by rapists and murderers. However, many feminist opponents of pornography take the most important argument to come simply from women's reactions to viewing pornography.

Women's reactions

According to many feminist opponents of pornography, pornography's dangers are simply apparent to women when they encounter it. Catharine MacKinnon maintains that the experimental evidence only shows us what women have always known.[7] Roz Schwartz, for example, viewed pornography while serving on a jury in an obscenity trial.

> On a purely gut level, I felt threatened by these books. I felt threatened because they are degrading not only to women but to men as well. Men who read these books, who are only capable of enjoying sex vicariously through this medium, are degraded. The degradation of human beings makes for fertile ground for fascism to take root. This, I think, is the most important thing that emerged for me. I understood on a visceral level what felt like a wide intellectual leap, the connection between pornography and fascism, the ultimate degradation of human beings.
>
> (Schwartz 1988: 14)

Before her experience of serving on this jury, Schwartz was opposed to efforts to restrict pornography. After her experience, she concluded that pornography—at least pornography like that which she saw— needed to be censored. Many anti-pornography feminists believe that pornography's nature is obvious and manifest to women once they see it. This is why much writing on the subject contains very explicit descriptions of pornography, and anti-pornography activists' speeches involve slide-shows of pornography. However, for those who are not convinced by this, they also offer other evidence.

Rapists' and murderers' use of pornography

Many men who have raped and murdered women have been users of pornography. Some have talked about pornography while committing their crimes, some have treated their victims in ways that they saw depicted in pornography, and some even say that pornography has made them commit rape and murderer (MacKinnon 1987: 184–6;

---

[7] Indeed, she is bothered that some seem to need confirmation from experimental evidence: 'You know, it is fairly frustrating that it takes studies by men in laboratories to predict that viewing pornography makes men be sexually more violent and makes them believe we are sexual things, before women are believed when we say that this does happen' (MacKinnon 1987: 202).

1993: 18; Silbert 1989: 223). Opponents of pornography take these facts to be clear indications of the harm that is done to women by pornography.

Psychological research

It is difficult to demonstrate conclusively whether or not pornography causes violence against women. There has been an enormous amount of psychological research on links between pornography and sexual violence, and not all the findings are consistent with one another. I will not attempt to summarize this literature. Instead, I will cite a few of the most disturbing findings that seem to show a linkage between pornography and attitudes toward women and rape. Experimenters have found that exposure to pornography renders subjects more likely to accept rape myths, such as 'A woman doesn't mean "no" until she slaps you' (Donnerstein et al. 1987: 75–6). It also makes subjects more likely to view rape victims as unworthy of sympathy, and more leniently inclined toward rapists (see e.g. Einsedel 1992: 254). In addition, men rate themselves as more likely to commit rape if they could get away with it (Weaver 1992: 298). Finally, subjects viewing films involving rape show a decreased ability to recognize rape as rape (Everywoman 1988: 21). These changes occur both with violent pornography and with non-violent pornography that depicts women as 'sexually insatiable and socially nondiscriminating' (Zillman 1989: 137). With violent pornography, the effects seem to occur only if victims are shown as enjoying the violence (Weaver 1992: 293). At least one study has found that stronger effects are produced by non-violent pornography than by violent pornography (Zillman 1989: 137).

All of this is very disturbing. It suggests that pornography indeed has serious effects on the way that women are viewed. In particular, the evidence suggesting that it makes people view rape as more acceptable lends support to the sorts of claim MacKinnon makes about the force of pornography. The fact that even non-violent pornography has this effect supports her suggestion that depictions of women as always wanting sex make it more difficult for men to understand that rape is bad.

Pornography and inequality in all realms of life

MacKinnon holds that the effects of pornography go well beyond the sexual arena. She thinks it teaches men to view women as inferior, naturally submissive, subordinate, and existing solely for men's use. If this is right, it would indeed have effects beyond the sexual realm. Viewing a co-worker, a potential employee, or a student in this way could certainly affect one's dealings with her. And this is precisely what MacKinnon maintains. In order to claim such widespread effects of pornography, she does not need to argue that all men view pornography. If many men do, and they influence the views of others, it can still make sense to say that pornography has the sweeping effects that MacKinnon suggests. Similar reasoning also allows her to maintain that women's self-conceptions are strongly affected by pornography, whether or not they have seen much of it. Pornography, for MacKinnon, not only trains men to be dominators of women, but (whether directly or indirectly) trains women to be subordinate to men.

MacKinnon, then, considers pornography to be a key force in perpetuating the subordination of women to men in every sphere of life.[8]

---

[8] In fact, MacKinnon's claims are even stronger than this. She takes gender roles—the social roles associated with the biological sexes of male and female—to be sustained by pornography. For her, 'masculinity' is to be defined in terms of sexual domination of women and 'femininity' is to be defined in terms of sexual subordination to men. Pornography, for MacKinnon, is the key force that puts in place and perpetuates these understandings of masculinity and femininity. For more detail on her conception of gender, see MacKinnon (1989: 141–2; Haslanger 1993; 2000). Lesbians and gay men may seem to pose problems for this understanding, since, intuitively, lesbians are women who are not (generally) sexually involved with, let alone sexually subordinated by, men; similarly, gay men are men who are not (generally) sexually involved with, let alone sexual dominators of, women. MacKinnon insists that this does not undermine her claims: she argues that where there is dominance and submission in lesbian or gay sex, there are the gender roles of male and female. Moreover, she thinks that all of us, whatever our sexual preferences, have had our sexual identity constructed by pornography, so sex for all of us has come crucially to involve inequality. One may also object that MacKinnon's view of gender is simply far too simplistic—it fails to accommodate the ways that race, social class, religion, sexual preference, and the like may have an impact on what it means to be a woman or a man. (For more on the importance of such factors to gender, see Spelman 1988.) It is important to note, however, that MacKinnon's views on gender are not essential to the arguments discussed in the text above.

The fact that pornography, according to MacKinnon, causes men to view women as inferior explains not just the prevalence of rape and violence against women but also why, for example, poverty is overwhelmingly female. MacKinnon is sometimes criticized for focusing excessively on pornography and sexuality, to the detriment of issues like female poverty. But she would claim that this criticism is misguided: she believes that sexuality, and particularly pornography, is the root cause of power imbalances between men and women. This means that her way of fighting female poverty *is* to fight pornography.

Subordination and silencing

Subordination

Catharine MacKinnon's claims about pornography are not just causal ones; that is, she doesn't just argue that pornography *causes* men to view women as inferior, or that it *causes* them to engage in behaviour that subordinates women. She also claims that pornography is *itself* the subordination of women. As we saw earlier, she defines pornography as 'the graphic, sexually explicit subordination of women'. This aspect of MacKinnon's view has widely been seen as incoherent: although films, books, or magazines might *depict* the subordination of women, or *cause* the subordination of women, they surely cannot *be* the subordination of women.

Rae Langton has done much to explain how we might make sense of MacKinnon's claim that pornography is the subordination of women (Langton 1993: 293–330).[9] First, she notes, with MacKinnon, the importance of J. L. Austin's observation (in a very different context) that some speech is an act (Austin 1962). For example, saying to your trained attack dog, 'Kill' is indeed saying something: it is speech. But it is also an act of ordering your dog to kill, and can therefore be understood as an act of murder. Less horrifyingly, perhaps, uttering the words 'I do' can be an act of marrying. These are words, but they also constitute an act. Langton argues that some utterances of words—some speech acts—are acts of subordination. As an example, she considers the legislation in South Africa that brought apartheid

---

[9] It is worth noting, however, that Langton does not take these arguments on their own to dictate any one course of action with regard to pornography.

into being. As legislation, this consisted of words: it was speech. But, as Langton notes, it was also an act of subordinating blacks to whites. Langton argues that pornography, if MacKinnon is right, ranks women as inferior and legitimizes violence and discrimination against them. If this is so, then, she argues, it subordinates women.

Silencing

MacKinnon also argues that pornography needs to be eliminated for the sake of freedom of speech. This seems paradoxical. But her reason for this is that she takes pornography not just to subordinate women but also to silence them. In order to give women the ability to speak— that is, to allow them free speech—MacKinnon thinks it is necessary to do something about the speech of pornographers. She takes her proposals, then, to be ways of supporting free speech rather than opposing it.

In order to explain how pornography might silence women, Langton follows Austin (1962) in distinguishing three kinds of act that one may perform in speaking. A *locutionary* act is simply the uttering of words with a particular content. A *perlocutionary* act is the uttering of words with a certain content in order to produce a particular effect. An *illocutionary* act is in many ways the most interesting sort of act. This is the act that is done *in* uttering the words. To see how these distinctions work, consider an example. Suppose George W. Bush appears on TV and utters the words 'I hereby resign'. His locutionary act is simply that of uttering the words 'I hereby resign'. This act may have many perlocutionary effects. The perlocutionary acts might include making Democrats happy, making Republicans nervous, shocking the world, and selling lots of newspapers. There is just one illocutionary act, however, and this is the act simply of resigning the presidency of the United States. Like many other acts, not just anyone can perform it. No matter how I try, I cannot resign the presidency of the United States by uttering the words 'I hereby resign', because I am not the president of the United States (nor can I resign on Bush's behalf).

Langton suggests that there are types of silencing corresponding to these types of speech act. In locutionary silencing, a person is prevented from speaking at all; in illocutionary silencing, a person is prevented from carrying out the illocutionary act that she intends; and in perlocutionary silencing, a person's speech act is prevented from having its intended perlocutionary effects. Let's take the speech act of voting as our example. A person would be locutionarily silenced with respect to voting if she were prevented from casting her vote at all—by roadblocks, for example. She would be illocutionarily silenced if she were allowed to vote but her vote did not count as the vote it was meant to be—although she made the correct mark, the counting machine failed to register the vote. Finally, she would be perlocutionarily silenced if she voted, her vote was counted, but it failed to achieve its intended effect: the other candidate was elected.

Langton holds that pornography brings about both perlocutionary and illocutionary silencing of women. Consider again the studies we looked at earlier, which showed that men who viewed pornography rated themselves as more likely to commit rape if they could get away with it. This kind of effect can result in the perlocutionary silencing of women (although, as Langton notes, this is too mild a name for rape). This occurs when a woman refuses to have sex with a man, but the man is not persuaded by her refusal and he rapes her. Here she has succeeded in uttering the word 'no'—her intended locutionary act. Moreover, she has succeeded in her intended illocutionary act— refusing. But this refusal has not had the desired effect. She has been perlocutionarily silenced.

It might also happen, though, that a woman says 'no' and a man simply doesn't *understand* that she is refusing. When this happens, according to Langton, the woman is illocutionarily silenced. Langton argues that one cannot refuse unless one is understood as refusing. The illocutionary act of refusal becomes impossible if one's attempted refusal cannot be understood, and this is a form of silencing. Pornography brings this about, according to Langton and MacKinnon, by intimating that women *always* want sex, that women enjoy being overpowered, and that women don't really mean 'no' when they say no. Some evidence supports this claim—we saw that viewing pornography increased acceptance of myths like 'a woman doesn't really mean "no" until she slaps you' and decreased subjects' ability to recognize rape as rape. If Langton's and MacKinnon's arguments are right, pornography does indeed silence women; and it silences women in a particularly hideous way. Pornography's silencing of women, according to Langton, is crucially implicated in bringing about rape.[10]

Langton argues that pornography may silence women in other ways as well. In particular, she argues that women's ability to protest (especially to protest pornography) has been silenced by pornography. In support of this she discusses *Ordeal*, Marchiano's autobiography describing how she was raped, tortured, and forced to perform in pornography. This book is now marketed in pornography catalogues as sexually exciting material. With her book, Marchiano attempted to protest, but she was not understood as protesting. Instead, however she tried to protest, her speech was seen as simply more pornography. Langton claims that this is a case of pornography silencing a woman by making it impossible for her to perform the illocutionary act of protesting.

According to this line of argument, pornography convinces men that women like sexual violence and that sexual violence is sexy, and this means women's objections to pornography and to sexual violence will not be taken seriously. In addition, pornography has the power to define what sex is. If violence is understood as sex, it will be more difficult to protest against the violence in pornography: sex is considered natural and good, so it cannot be questioned. These failures may be illocutionary or perlocutionary: if men see it as impossible that one might protest sex as it occurs in pornography, they will not understand women as protesting, which will mean that women cannot carry out the illocutionary act of protesting. If men simply do not care what protesting women say, this is perlocutionary silencing: women *can* protest, but their protests do not have their intended effects.

Pornography may silence women's protests on other matters as well—if pornography convinces men that women are inferior and their views not worthy of consideration, they will not take what women say seriously. Again, this may be illocutionary or perlocutionary

---

[10] One might worry that if, according to Langton, women are *unable* to refuse sex, rape becomes impossible. This would certainly be an undesirable result for Langton. It seems to me, however, that this is a mistake: if consensual sex is understood as requiring not just the absence of refusal but also the presence of consent, then rape takes place whenever one party fails to consent, regardless of whether they succeed in refusing. For more on these issues, see Jacobson (1995).

silencing: illocutionary if men fail to understand that women are attempting to protest, and perlocutionary if the protests (while understood) simply cannot have the desired effects.[11]

Pornography as hate speech

In the United Kingdom, a different feminist argument for restricting pornography is available. The UK has laws against incitement to racial hatred. Feminists have argued that it makes no sense to have laws against race-based hate speech while not having laws against sex-based hate speech. In arguing for such a law, Aminatta Forna writes:

> Pornographic images of women bound, gagged, raped or sodomized; women subjected to humiliation and torture for the readers' pleasure, and shown to enjoy what is being done to them; women posed in a sexually demeaning way—these must be recognized as doing the same harm as pictures or words which treat black people in a similarly subordinate or violent way. If those pictures were of blacks, Asians or Jews, they would be recognized as constituting an incitement to racial hatred.
>
> (Forna 1992: 111)

In the US, speech advocating hatred against particular groups is generally protected as political speech. Attempts at laws banning hate speech are generally struck down as unconstitutional, so this sort of argument is unlikely to be effective. In the UK, however, it has much greater potential.[12]

Proposed laws

Most people assume that feminists who are opposed to pornography advocate censorship. That is, they assume that these feminists would support a policy of banning the publication and distribution of pornography. However, most of the campaigns against pornography in the US and UK have advocated a different sort of law, one proposed by

---

[11] For discussion of whether or not freedom of speech should be understood as protecting one's ability to carry out illocutionary and perlocutionary speech acts, see Jacobson (1995).

[12] For concerns regarding UK racial hate speech laws, their implementation, and anti-pornography proposals modelled on them, see Osman (1988).

MacKinnon and Dworkin. Their proposed law would allow women who have been harmed by pornography to sue the makers and distributors of it. If they can prove that they were harmed, they can win damages.

This proposal is a form of civil rights legislation, because pornography, according to MacKinnon and Dworkin, is a sort of sex discrimination. They hold that it is sex discrimination because, they believe, it makes a key contribution to the *dominance* of women in society: it subordinates women to men.[13] This does not mean that they think only women are ever harmed by pornography. Sometimes, 'men, children or transsexuals' are used 'in the place of women' in pornography, and sometimes such people are harmed by pornography (MacKinnon 1992: 466). In such cases, these people would also be able to sue for damages.

MacKinnon and Dworkin believe that there are important advantages to the sort of law that they suggest. First, their proposed law makes it very clear that what is wrong with pornography is the way that it harms women. If one cannot prove that some particular work of pornography has caused harm, its makers and distributors cannot be successfully sued. Next, the law is not a form of censorship; it is merely a recognition that one way people can be harmed is via pornography. Those who make and distribute pornography are free to go on doing so, but the law gives them an incentive to be sure that what they make and distribute does not harm women. Finally, the law gives *women* the power to fight pornography, rather than putting this power in the hands of the state.

Against restricting pornography

Feminists have disagreed with the arguments above in a wide variety of ways, not all of which can really be construed as defences of pornography. While some argue that pornography is beneficial to women, others merely deny some of the claimed harms, while still others disagree only with the idea of legislating against pornography.

---

[13] See Chapter 1 for a discussion of the dominance conception of discrimination, and Chapter 2 for its application to sexual harassment.

Opposition to legislating against pornography

Some arguments against anti-pornography legislation do not at all depend on defending pornography, its content, or effects. It is perfectly possible to agree with all the criticisms that have been made of pornography and still to maintain that it should not be legally restricted. We will begin with some quite general objections to legislation against pornography. We will see that some of these objections do not actually apply to the sorts of law MacKinnon and Dworkin propose. Others, however, do.

General opposition to restrictions on speech

Open debate as best policy

We have discussed this idea already, but it is worth revisiting. Many feminists, like many non-feminists, simply oppose all restrictions on speech. One important argument against restrictions on speech is that it is dangerous for governments to enter into the business of policing speech. According to this line of thought, free and open debate is vital for the functioning of a democracy, and if some views cannot be expressed, the debate is not as free and open as it would otherwise be. The right way for those who oppose pornography to deal with it, then, is to speak out against it. Those who believe that pornography perpetuates damaging myths about women should say so; or boycott it and its supporters; or build a movement for new and better, less sexist sexually explicit materials. Pornography and its effects, according to this line, can be fought openly in the free marketplace of ideas, rather than by suppressing pornography. Proponents argue that this is the most effective way to fight pornography:

> As feminists we have a responsibility to be critical of those images we find sexist, racist, or exploitative and to counter them in the most effective way there is, not by seeking to get them banned, but by initiating a much more wide-ranging debate about sex, by lobbying for better sex education in schools, by creating more informed, tolerant and responsible social attitudes to the expression of sexuality, and by supporting those who are creating an alternative body of sexual images for women.
>
> (Feminists Against Censorship 1991: 14–15)

This line of argument on its own, however, is ineffective against the case built by anti-pornography feminists. MacKinnon and Langton have argued that pornography silences women's ability to protest, especially to protest pornography. If this is right, it renders the women unable to participate in free and open debate. For this reason, Langton and MacKinnon suggest, pornography cannot be fought with more speech: women are silenced as long as pornography exists. On this view, those who argue against restricting pornography on the grounds of valuing debate seem to be committed to the idea that pornographers' speech is more important than women's speech. Much depends, then, on whether or not women are silenced by pornography. We shall return to this issue shortly.

Who decides?

Another key objection to restrictions on speech is the inherent danger of giving governments power to decide which views can and cannot be expressed. There is no guarantee that governments will suppress the 'right' bits of expression. In fact, when governments have been given the right to restrict sexual speech in the past, they have been most likely to censor speech that feminists would not want censored—contraception and safe sex information, and positive discussions of gay and lesbian sexuality (see Nielson 1988; Califia 1994). Protecting access to such materials is a feminist priority, and campaigns that risk restricting access to these materials undermine this aim.

   This line of thought gains added force from a recent bit of history. In 1992, the Canadian Supreme Court laid down a new interpretation of 'obscenity'. Under this new understanding, obscenity is now a matter of 'the harm it inflicts, particularly harm to women' (Scales 2000: 324). The emphasis is now on material, violent or non-violent, that is 'degrading and dehumanizing'. This new understanding of obscenity is clearly influenced by a *feminist* conception of what is wrong with pornography, and seeks to ban materials that affect women in the ways that MacKinnon describes. Unfortunately, however, enforcers of the law have not shared MacKinnon's views on which materials are degrading, dehumanizing, and harmful to women. As a result, MacKinnon's and Dworkin's own works have been seized at the

Canadian border (Strossen 1995: 159). Canadian customs officials appear, in addition, to have specifically targeted gay and lesbian works: straight pornography and *The Joy of Sex* have been allowed to circulate, but gay and lesbian pornography and *The Joy of Gay Sex* have been banned or detained at the border (Califia 1994: 108–9). Clearly, the feminists who support the new Canadian understanding of obscenity would disagree with the view that the works of MacKinnon and Dworkin are degrading and dehumanizing to women, and with the view that gay and lesbian material is more dangerous than heterosexual material.[14] However, they are not the ones enforcing Canadian obscenity law. Many think the Canadian example shows that any attempts to restrict pornography will result in unintended and undesirable consequences, due to the fact that those enforcing the law will probably not be anti-pornography feminists.[15]

This concern helps to bring out what some have said is a deep and important flaw in MacKinnon's definition (even though her definition was not precisely the one used in the Canadian judgment). The flaw is that, despite the definition's length and level of detail, there is still room for a great deal of disagreement over whether a particular work satisfies the definition. What counts as a posture of display—a pose in an anatomy textbook? In a safe sex handbook illiustration? What is a scenario of degradation? A homophobic law enforcement official might consider any lesbian or gay sex to be degrading. The problem is that we have no guarantees about who will be interpreting the terms in MacKinnon's definition.

> Who knows what exactly is meant by *subordination, sexual submission*, or *degradation*? Feminists use these terms differently from fundamentalists, who believe that lesbianism, work outside the home, abortion, and extramarital sex degrade women.
>
> (Califia 1994: 124)

---

14 Nonetheless, they would not necessarily disagree with all the decisions made by Canadian customs officials. In particular, they might agree with the decision to ban certain pieces of lesbian sadomasochistic writing. See Scales (2000: 330); Dworkin, cited in Califia (1994: 108).

15 See e.g. Strossen (1995); Califia (1994); McElroy (1995). For an interesting defence of the Canadian Supreme Court's decision despite opposition to some of its consequences, see Scales (2000).

Objections to MacKinnon's civil rights ordinance

It is important to note that the Canadian law on obscenity, even with its new understanding of 'obscenity', does not work in the way that MacKinnon's proposed law would. Rather than allowing individuals who have been harmed by pornography to sue, Canadian law simply places restrictions on certain materials. In Canada, pornography is a matter for criminal rather than civil law. The consequences of such a law arguably differ, then, from those that would follow from a law more like the one MacKinnon has proposed. Under the latter, to win damages against a pornographer or distributor a woman would need to show that she has been harmed by pornography. MacKinnon would presumably hold that no one would be able to successfully prove that they had been harmed by her writings or Dworkin's, or by lesbian safe sex manuals. In addition, the general objection to government restrictions on speech cannot apply to a law like that which MacKinnon proposes: her law would give governments no such power. MacKinnon's proposed law, then, is arguably far less likely than the Canadian law to result in the wrong sorts of material being affected.

Nadine Strossen, however, argues that precisely the opposite is the case (Strossen 1995: 59–82). First, she notes (as we have) that many of the terms in MacKinnon's definition are open to a wide variety of interpretations. Next, she points out that it is impossible to predict who might claim to be harmed by what material, or whether or not they could convince a jury of it. There have been murderers who claim to have been inspired by the Bible, *The Brothers Karamazov*, and *Roots*, she notes. No one would expect, prima facie, that these works would cause harm, but arguably on occasion they do. So what should one do, Strossen asks, if one owns a bookstore, and wants to avoid being sued? Since many of the terms in MacKinnon's definition are open to interpretation, and since we can't predict what claims of harm might be made or proven, the only sure way to avoid being sued under such a law is to avoid selling any materials that are sexually explicit. The reason for this is that 'sexually explicit' is one of the few terms in the definition with a fairly well agreed-upon meaning. If some work is not sexually explicit, we know that it cannot be pornography. The American Booksellers' Association has said that this act of self-defence—of not stocking potentially objectionable material—is precisely what their members would be forced to do (Strossen 1995: 68). If bookstores refuse to order sexually explicit materials in order to avoid being sued, pornography as defined by feminists is only one thing that would be affected. Gay, lesbian, and heterosexual safe sex manuals, fiction, and erotica, and perhaps even the works of Dworkin and MacKinnon, would all become very hard to find. Strossen argues, then, that this sort of law would do far more to stifle speech than an outright ban. An outright ban would mean that the government prevented certain materials from ever coming to bookstores, but a law like MacKinnon's leaves matters up to booksellers. Far from being a milder form of restriction, this law is likely to have much more sweeping effects than standard censorship.

Feminist arguments that women are silenced by pornography make possible a response to this worry. If pornography silences women, then speech is already being severely restricted. We have a choice, then, between allowing the silencing of women to continue and risking the suppression of some works as described above. The actual silencing of women seems far more worrying than the mere possibility that some works will have difficulty gaining distribution. Again, then, a great deal turns on the idea that pornography silences women.

Responses to arguments against pornography

In the previous section, we looked at worries that one might have regarding anti-pornography *legislation*, even if one accepted feminist arguments against pornography. One might agree completely with Catharine MacKinnon, for example, concerning the nature of pornography and the role it plays in perpetuating inequality, while still maintaining that it should not be legislated against—for some or all of the reasons given above. Now we turn to reasons for doubting feminist arguments against pornography.

Women's reactions

Feminists who argue against pornography on the basis of women's reactions are on somewhat shaky ground. First, there is a problem with claiming that a subjective feeling of certainty about something is a guide to the truth. Many people in a wide variety of times and places have felt certain that the world is flat, that slavery is acceptable, or that kings are appointed by God, to give a few examples. Since we would not want to take *these* feelings of certainty to indicate the truth, we should be unwilling to rest arguments against pornography on feelings of subjective certainty.

In addition, women actually have a wide variety of reactions to pornography. Many women say that they enjoy pornography, and that it makes a positive contribution to their sex lives. Lisa Palac, a feminist who opposed pornography until she sat through her first pornographic film, writes,

> Before I watched porn, my erotic imagination was groggy. I didn't know what a sexual fantasy was; I hadn't really had them ... Pornography dangled sexual fantasy in front of me. It made me aware that my sexual imagination wasn't limited to the heat of the moment or sensual reminiscence. I could think about *anything*. I could use *anything*—books, magazines, videos—for erotic inspiration.

> (Palac 1995: 245)

Palac found pornography to be empowering. And she did so despite having previously opposed it on feminist grounds.

Any argument that begins from the idea that women's reactions indicate the truth about pornography is forced to contend with the fact that these reactions vary. While one can explain away the reactions of women like Palac by insisting that they have had their sexuality shaped by pornography, it is more difficult to do this consistently while insisting that other women's reactions are good guides to the truth. Women's responses to pornography, then, cannot provide straightforward support for MacKinnon's views.

Real acts

Those who disagree with feminist arguments against pornography do not deny the very real and terrible harm that has been done to some of those involved in the making of it. They agree that women like Linda Marchiano have been raped, assaulted, and coerced and that such offences should be prosecuted to the fullest extent of the law. However, MacKinnon uses Marchiano's case as a part of her argument against pornography *in general*, and this is a questionable move. The fact that some people in a particular industry have suffered terrible abuse is no argument against that industry in general. After all, MacKinnon's own work on sexual harassment and rape in the workplace shows that terrible abuse occurs in many industries.

MacKinnon sometimes *seems* to hold that any woman involved in the production of pornography must have been coerced, and this view is often attributed to her.[16] If this claim were accurate it would indeed give reason for condemning the industry as a whole. However, MacKinnon's opponents point out that to defend this claim one must deny the sincerity (or self-knowledge) of women who work in pornography, but say that they do so willingly, and that they have not been abused.[17] Dismissing the testimony of women who defend pornography is a problematic move for those who oppose the silencing of women. Without this move, however, stories like Marchiano's only give reason to condemn certain pieces of pornography—those whose making involves coercion, assault, or rape. And since those offences also occur outside pornography, this means that cases like Marchiano's do not point to a wrong specific to pornography.

Some also argue that anti-pornography legislation would lead to more abuses in the pornography industry. Gayle Rubin suggests that restrictions on pornography only serve to make it more difficult to improve working conditions in the industry:

> the degree to which sex workers are exposed to more exploitation and hazardous working conditions is a function of the stigma, illegality, or marginal legality of sex work. People in stigmatized or illegal occupations find it difficult to obtain the protections, privileges and opportunities

[16] It is worth noting, though, that she explicitly denies this in MacKinnon (1993: 20–1).

[17] For example, Candida Royalle, a feminist and former pornography star who now produces and directs pornography, writes, 'It is often taken for granted that women get into porn because they are victims or prostitutes or self-destructive. It's very hard for this culture to accept that women could choose to do this as a job, which was certainly the case with me and many other women' (Royalle 2000: 541). She also writes, 'The only time a director wanted me to do something that I didn't want to do, I refused' (p. 542). Obviously, not all pornography actresses have experiences like Royalle's, but her experience shows the difficulty of generalizing from a single case.

available for other jobs. Prostitutes, porn models and exotic dancers have less recourse to police, courts, medical treatment, legal redress or sympathy when they are subjected to criminal, violent or unscrupulous behaviour. It is more difficult for them to unionize or mobilize for protection as workers.

(Rubin 1993: 33)

If this is correct, then interest in the real lives of those involved in making pornography should motivate feminists *not* to oppose pornography, but instead to support the efforts of those involved in pornography who are trying to improve their working conditions.[18]

Rapists' and murderers' use of pornography

The fact that some rapists and murderers have been users of pornography shows very little on its own—MacKinnon and her followers hold that many, if not most, men are users of pornography. Even the rapists' and murderers' use of *violent* pornography shows little. It seems reasonable to suppose that one who is attracted to sexual violence in real life might also enjoy depictions of sexual violence—so whatever it is that makes someone want to commit rape might also make them want to use violent pornography. However, rapists and murderers have also apparently acted out scenarios that they learned of from pornography: surely this, one might think, is an indication of pornography's power in causing crime. Defenders of pornography, however, have suggested that without pornography such rapists and murderers would merely have carried out different acts of violence. In short, these facts alone do not show that pornography *causes* sexual violence (Williams 1993). Moreover, studies have shown that sex offenders tend to have had *less exposure to pornography* than other men, not more (Segal 1990: 33). It is more difficult than it might seem, then, to link pornography and sexual violence.[19]

Rapists and murderers have, however, actually claimed that pornography led to their crimes. This testimony, it might seem, surely gives reason to believe that pornography has caused sexual violence. However, one might question whether rapists' own testimony as to

---

[18] For more on this see Rubin (1993), and also Cornell (2000).
[19] On this issue, see also Cameron and Frazer (2000: 240–53).

the causes of their crimes should be believed. Most people have rather poor knowledge of the causes of their own behaviour; even if rapists and murderers are trying to be as honest as possible, they may simply be wrong. Moreover, everyone likes to find a way of avoiding blame for wrongdoing. As Henry Louis Gates notes,

> Criminals, like the rest of us, are happy to attribute their bad behaviour to an external agency (mother, Hostess Twinkies, demon rum, *Playboy*), thus diminishing, in some measure, their own culpability.

(Gates 1992: 902)

The testimony of rapists and murderers, then, cannot be taken to show conclusively that pornography causes rape or murder. However, it can be taken as a piece of evidence to be weighed with the rest of the information available on pornography's relationship to violence.

Experimental evidence[20]

Links to actual violence

Some have argued that the experimental evidence cited earlier is insufficient to prove harm to women, because it does not show that viewing pornography actually makes men more likely to commit rape or other acts of violence in the real world (Strossen 1995; Segal 1990). At best, it only shows changes in viewers' *attitudes*. While this is correct, it is difficult to see how the experiments could be improved upon. It is simply impossible to carry out proper laboratory experiments in an ethical manner which test pornography's tendency to contribute to actual violence. Moreover, changes in attitudes are at the heart of feminists' claims about pornography. If pornography makes men view rape as more acceptable, and makes men view women as sex objects,[21] then MacKinnon has shown much of what she wants to show. These attitude changes in themselves, for MacKinnon, constitute significant evidence that pornography contributes to the subordination of women.

---

20 For further concerns about the experimental evidence regarding pornography's effects, see Segal (1990).

21 Some studies can be interpreted as showing this, though there is room for debate over exactly what counts as *viewing women as sex objects*.

Non-sexually explicit material

A more important objection to the use that MacKinnon and her followers make of psychological evidence comes from the fact that non-sexually explicit material pairing violence and sex also seems to produce worrying changes in attitudes toward women and rape (see e.g. Segal 1990; Linz et al. 1987).[22] This means, critics argue, that the psychological evidence cannot support a law that specifically targets sexually explicit material. If the idea is to target material which leads to the sexual objectification of women and greater acceptance of rape, then all such material should be encompassed, not only sexually explicit material.

There are several responses available to this argument. One is to maintain that this shows a need for alteration of MacKinnon's understanding of pornography: according to this line, pornography, properly understood, also includes material that is not sexually explicit. Diana Russell advocates just such a view of pornography (Russell 1993: 1–22). However, it would be politically difficult to make a successful case against all such materials, and this difficulty could well motivate a focus just on sexually explicit materials. If we know that a certain class of materials produces harms that we take seriously, this gives us the reason to act against as much of this material as possible. It is better, this line goes, to target some of it than none of it.

Linkage with inequality in general

Many have questioned the centrality that MacKinnon assigns to pornography. Feminists have spent many decades documenting ways in which a wide variety of media—fiction, textbooks, non-pornographic movies, television, commercials, and the like—contribute to the damaging of views of women. Moreover, they have argued that many social forces other than the media contribute to keeping women in a subordinate position. (The other chapters of this book discuss some of these forces.) Why, then, single out

---

[22] Many of these studies involve 'slasher' movies. But one can easily imagine views of sexuality being negatively affected by positive depictions of rape in even classic movies like *Gone with the Wind*. Indeed, one might expect the effect to be stronger, since these movies are considered respectable—what they depict may seem more socially acceptable.

pornography in the way that its opponents do? It is very difficult to justify claims that pornography is *the* key to the current inequalities between men and women, and that eliminating pornography is *the* key to ending these inequalities. Further, inequalities between the sexes seem to have been present since long before pornography was widely available, and some societies with very strict restrictions on pornography are very oppressive of women (Strossen 1995: 255). This does not conclusively show that MacKinnon is wrong—it could be that there are many causes of inequality in different societies, but that in our current society pornography *is* the key—but it certainly casts doubt on her claims.

Moreover, some have suggested that the campaign against pornography is a damaging distraction from the need to directly address these other problems women face.

> ... responsibility for discrimination is shifted to porn rather than the individuals and institutions that actually commit such acts, and women's anger and fear of violence are directed away from rapists and batterers and shifted to dirty magazines. But discrimination and violence are caused by many things; they will not stop just because sexist, sexually explicit material becomes unavailable. [An anti-pornography law] is no more than a comforting placebo.
>
> (Califia 1994: 123)

The idea that a single-minded focus on pornography is a mistake does not necessarily mean that all worries about pornography are a mistake. One may still think that pornography is often (or even always) problematic without thinking that it assumes the kind of importance that MacKinnon and many anti-pornography campaigners assign it. Carole Vance, for example, criticizes the anti-pornography focus as an excessively simple-minded attempt to make sense of an extremely complicated reality:

> Initially, most feminists could agree with the contention that pornography was often sexist. Before long, however, it became clear that the claims and characterizations of anti-pornography leaders and groups were grandiose and overstated. No longer an organic part of commercial media and images which often presented women in a demeaning, trivializing, and sexist manner, in their monolithic account pornography

became monstrous in ways that mainstream TV, *Good Housekeeping* magazine, or the Bible could never be.

(Vance 1992: xviii)

Vance calls for a careful, nuanced investigation of the ways in which many different forces may combine to perpetuate inequality. When it comes to pornography, she holds that what is needed is an exploration of the many different facets and varieties of both women's and men's responses. MacKinnon's view of pornography, according to Vance, is not only implausible but also a barrier to the sort of research and discussion that would be needed for genuine understanding. But objecting to MacKinnon on these grounds (as Vance would admit) by no means sets aside all feminist concerns about pornography. Accordingly, there are still important questions regarding some of the more specific claims made by opponents of pornography—such as the claim that it silences women.

Pornography as silencing

Silencing and rape

The experimental evidence seems to support Langton's and MacKinnon's claims that pornography silences women by making rape seem more acceptable, and making rape more difficult to perceive as rape. These are terrible effects, and it is terrible for women to be silenced in this way. However, nothing follows from this alone regarding what should be done about pornography. If, as some have argued, legislation directed against pornography would not effectively combat its effects, then proposals like MacKinnon's may be misguided. In particular, if the best way to fight pornography's effects is by speaking out against rape myths, legislating against pornography is not the answer.

Silencing and protest

One way of fighting pornography and its effects, we have seen, would be to speak out against it. But MacKinnon and Langton have also argued that pornography renders it impossible for women to protest, which would mean this technique would not meet with much success. The key example used in support of this claim is Linda Marchiano's failed attempt to protest pornography with her book *Ordeal*.

It is not clear, however, that this example can do the work that MacKinnon and Langton need it to do. It is appalling that Marchiano's protest has been sold as pornography, but generalizing from one case to all (or even many) women is too big a leap. Langton recognizes this, and argues more generally that pornography's tendency to make men see women as unworthy (perhaps combined with its ability to define what sex is) means that women's criticisms of pornography will not be taken as genuine protests. This argument, however, needs substantially more support. In particular, there is good reason to suppose that its conclusion is false. The world at large has had no trouble understanding that MacKinnon is opposing pornography. Her protests have been heard, and she has built a large and influential movement. Her views have influenced laws, court rulings, and the findings of government commissions on pornography.[23] It seems just false to say that women have been silenced so thoroughly by pornography that they cannot be recognized as protesting against it; or even that their protests are doomed to be ineffectual.

Fighting pornography's effects

Some studies seem to show that pornography's harmful effects can be successfully countered. After subjects have participated in experiments involving the viewing of pornography, it is standard to give them debriefings that explain that rape myths are false, that women suffer a great deal when they are raped, and that films like those they have seen serve to perpetuate false and damaging ideas about women. Studies have shown that those who view pornography and receive debriefings are less likely to accept rape myths, even many months later, than those who have experienced neither the pornography nor the debriefing during their experimental sessions. If this is correct, then educational messages have the potential to do a great deal

---

[23] In addition to the Canadian Supreme Court decision discussed earlier, MacKinnon played a central role in shaping laws passed in Minneapolis (though vetoed by the mayor) and Indianapolis (though struck down by the court), and influenced the findings of the Meese Commission on pornography (Dwyer 1995: 243–5).

toward eliminating the negative effects of pornography (Linz and Donnerstein 1989).

Even if these studies are right, however, it is unclear whether or not effective educational policies could be devised which might counter-act the harmful effects of pornography. Although the experimenters responsible for these studies advocate educational policies rather than restriction of pornography, they themselves raise concerns regarding the difficulty of devising effective policies. In particular, debriefings are most effective when tailored to the specific works of pornography that viewers have seen. Generalized, brief warnings like those found on cigarette cartons seem not to have much effect. This means that devising and carrying out an effective mass education programme to counteract pornography's effects might be a difficult feat (Linz and Donnerstein 1989).

Interpretation, fantasy, and role play

One key point made in defence of pornography is that pornographic images and narratives, like any others, are open to interpretation. To some, a woman asking repeatedly and enthusiastically for sex is a degrading image. To others, this may be an empowering image of female sexual assertiveness. Some pornography, however, may seem not to be open to such varied interpretations. In particular, scenes of domination seem rather unambiguous. (Feminist opponents of porn-ography do not in fact focus on just pornography of this sort, but this would be a possible approach.) However, use of pornography tends to involve a complicated interplay between the pornography and the user's fantasies. Jean Grimshaw has noted that fantasy is particularly murky—it may even be difficult to say just what role one is identify-ing with in a sexual fantasy (Grimshaw 1997).[24] This can surely hap-pen with the viewing of pornography as well. In a similar vein, Sue George notes, 'just because women appear submissive in much porn does not mean that a woman watching it has to be submissive in her

---

[24] Susan Dwyer, however, notes that we only feel tempted to claim that fan-tasies are indeterminate when we are uncomfortable about these fantasies: 'When someone fantasizes about puppies and fresh apple pie, or about living a successful and happy life, the urge to interpret diminishes to zero' (Dwyer 2003).

fantasies. Women can manipulate porn to fit their existing fantasies, as men do' (George 1988: 111).

Some feminists defend even violent images, without any reference to reinterpretations or ambiguous fantasies. Pat Califia argues that there is nothing wrong with images of domination and subordination (Califia 1994). She takes there to be nothing wrong with being aroused by sadomasochism: sexual desire is a complicated matter, and power often plays a crucial role in it. Not only is there nothing wrong with being aroused by thoughts of dominating women, according to Califia, but there is nothing wrong with acting on such desires.

The key for Califia is that all sexual activity—including sado-masochistic sexual activity—must be fully consensual. She argues that sadomasochism, far from involving lack of consent, instead involves exceptionally careful consent. Sadomasochists make use of 'safe-words' which, when uttered, will immediately put a stop to whatever activity is taking place. Further, sadomasochists engage in careful negotiation regarding what activities they would like to engage in. This, she claims, makes it just about the most consensual sexual community around. And this claim has considerable force: how many people outside this community have explicit pre-sex discussions with their partners regarding what sex acts they like, or agree to a safeword that will be an unambiguous 'no'? Given feminist concerns about fail-ure to recognize women's refusals, the latter is especially important.

Sadomasochists who fail to respect these rules soon find themselves ostracized by the community, so the rules are adhered to. With this sort of consensuality, Califia argues, there is no reason to object to sadomasochistic sex. Sadomasochistic sex also helps to reveal some problems with inferences from sexual practices to other spheres of life: Califia notes that many men who are submissive sexually are extremely powerful outside the bedroom. It is wrong, then, to assume (as MacKinnon does) that sexualized inequality must carry over into other areas of life.

Those who view images from sadomasochistic pornography with-out properly understanding the sadomasochistic community and its emphasis on consent will fail to appreciate the use that is made of this pornography. It is designed for a community who—far from being likely to rape—have an unusually explicit commitment to consensuality. One might worry, however, that sadomasochistic pornography will be widely viewed by those outside the community that Califia describes. Against this, however, several authors claim that violence is rare in mainstream pornography (Segal 1990; Donnerstein et al. 1987).[25] Further, studies have shown that most men are not aroused by violent pornography; instead, they are disgusted (Segal 1990).

Summary

Feminists who want to restrict pornography do so because they take it to subordinate and silence women, in part through helping to cause sexual violence and shaping negative attitudes toward women. Feminists who oppose restriction of pornography do so for a variety of reasons. Some question the evidence that pornography is especially crucial to shaping attitudes toward women and causing sexual violence. Others argue that restricting pornography is not the best way of undermining these effects of pornography. Still others defend pornography, even as it currently is, as important to women's sexual freedom. Who is right? We have seen that much turns on (a) the extent to which women actually are silenced by pornography; (b) how important pornography is in shaping attitudes toward women; and (c) what the best way of fighting pornography's negative effects is. The answers to these questions remains unclear, and so therefore does the right approach to pornography.

SUGGESTIONS FOR FURTHER READING

General

Chester, G., and Dickey, J. (eds.), *Feminism and Censorship: The Current Debate*. Bridport, Dorset: Prism, 1988. (*Especially useful for British readings.*)
Cornell, D., *Feminism and Pornography*. New York: Oxford University Press, 2000.

[25] The Internet, however, may well have made it far easier to gain access to less mainstream pornography (see Dwyer 2003).

Dwyer, S. (ed.), *The Problem of Pornography*. Belmont, Calif.: Wadsworth, 1995.

Itzin, C. (ed.), *Pornography: Women, Violence, and Civil Liberties*. New York: Oxford University Press, 1992. *(Especially useful for British readings.)*

Pornography as silencing or subordination

Hornsby, J., 'Disempowered Speech', in S. Haslanger (ed.), *Feminist Perspectives on Language, Knowledge, and Reality*, special issue of *Philosophical Topics* 23(2) (1995): 221–59.

—— 'Feminism in Philosophy of Language: Communicative Speech Acts', in M. Fricker and J. Hornsby (eds.), *The Cambridge Companion to Feminism in Philosophy*. Cambridge: Cambridge University Press, 2000, 87–106.

Jacobsen, D., 'Freedom of Speech Acts? A Response to Langton', *Philosophy and Public Affairs* 24 (1995): 64–79.

Langton, R., 'Speech Acts and Unspeakable Acts', *Philosophy and Public Affairs* 22 (1993): 293–330.

MacKinnon, C., 'Francis Biddle's Sister', in *Feminism Unmodified*. Cambridge, Mass.: Harvard University Press, 163–97.

—— 'On Collaboration', in *Feminism Unmodified*. Cambridge, Mass.: Harvard University Press, 198–205.

—— 'Pornography, Civil Rights, and Speech', in C. Itzin (ed.), *Pornography: Women, Violence, and Civil Liberties*. New York: Oxford University Press, 1992, 456–511.

—— *Only Words*. Cambridge, Mass.: Harvard University Press, 1993.

Other arguments against pornography

Dworkin, A., *Pornography: Men Possessing Women*. London: Women's Press, 1981.

Dyzenhaus, D., 'John Stuart Mill and the Harm of Pornography', *Ethics* 102 (1992): 534–51.

Forna, A., 'Pornography and Racism: Sexualizing Oppression and Inciting Hatred', in C. Itzin (ed.), *Pornography: Women, Violence, and Civil Liberties*. New York: Oxford University Press, 1992, 102–12.

Itzin, C. 'Legislating Against Pornography without Censorship', in C. Itzin (ed.), *Pornography: Women, Violence, and Civil Liberties*. New York: Oxford University Press, 1992, 401–34.

Longino, H. 'Pornography, Oppression, and Freedom: A Closer Look', in S. Dwyer (ed.), *The Problem of Pornography*. Belmont, Calif.: Wadsworth, 1995, 34–47.

MacKinnon, C., 'Francis Biddle's Sister', in *Feminism Unmodified*. Cambridge, Mass.: Harvard University Press, 1987, 163–97.

—— 'On Collaboration', in *Feminism Unmodified*. Cambridge, Mass.: Harvard University Press, 1987, 198–205.

—— 'Pornography, Civil Rights, and Speech', in C. Itzin (ed.), *Pornography: Women, Violence, and Civil Liberties*. New York: Oxford University Press, 1992, 456–511.

—— *Only Words*. Cambridge, Mass.: Harvard University Press, 1993.

Russell, D., 'Introduction', in D. Russell (ed.), *Making Violence Sexy: Feminist Views on Pornography*. Buckingham: Open University Press, 1993, 1–20.

Concerns regarding attacks on pornography

Califia, P., *Public Sex*. Pittsburgh, Penn.: Cleis, 1994.

Cornell, D., 'Pornography's Temptation', in *Feminism and Pornography*. New York: Oxford University Press, 2000, 551–68.

Feminists Against Censorship, *Pornography and Feminism*. London: Lawrence and Wishart, 1991.

George, S., 'Censorship and Hypocrisy: Some Issues Surrounding Pornography that Feminism has Ignored', in G. Chester and J. Dickey (eds.), *Feminism and Censorship: The Current Debate*. Bridport, Dorset: Prism, 1988, 110–18.

Palac, L., 'How Dirty Pictures Changed My Life', in A. Stan (ed.), *Debating Sexual Correctness*. New York: Delta, 1995, 236–52.

Rubin, G., 'Misguided, Dangerous and Wrong: an Analysis of Anti-pornography Politics', in A. Assiter (ed.), *Bad Girls and Dirty Pictures*. London: Pluto Press, 1993, 18–40.

Strossen, N., *Defending Pornography*. New York: Anchor, 1995.

Vance, C., 'More Pleasure, More Danger: A Decade After the Barnard Sexuality Conference', in *Pleasure and Danger*. London: Pandora 1992, xvi–xliii.

Experimental evidence

Donnerstein, E., Linz, D., and Penrod, S., *The Question of Pornography: Research Findings and Policy Implications*. New York: Free Press, 1987.

Einsedel, E., 'The Experimental Research Evidence: Effects of Pornography on the "Average Individual"', in C. Itzin (ed.), *Pornography: Women, Violence, and Civil Liberties*. New York: Oxford University Press, 1992, 248–83.

Linz, D., and Donnerstein, E., 'The Effects of Counter-information on the Acceptance of Rape Myths', in D. Zillman and J. Bryant (eds),

Pornography: Research Advances and Policy Considerations. Hillsdale, NJ: Erlbaum, 1989.

Segal, L., 'Pornography and Violence: What the "Experts" Really Say', *Feminist Review* 36 (1990): 29–41.

Zillman, D., and Bryant, J., *Pornography: Research Advances and Policy Considerations.* Hillsdale, NJ: Erlbaum, 1989.

4

Abortion

Most of the issues discussed in this book are ones that were introduced by feminists, or ones whose discussion is dominated by feminists. Abortion, however, is not like this. In fact, a key feminist insight on abortion has been to notice the many ways in which standard discussions overlook issues that are of vital concern to feminists. In particular, such discussions have a remarkable tendency to overlook the fact that abortion involves not just a foetus but also a pregnant woman. The tendency to overlook this is well symbolized by the standard image of a foetus used by opponents of abortion, described by Barbara Rothman as follows.

> Picture to yourself the photos you have seen of fetuses in utero, wriggling, sucking their tiny fingers. Where did they lie in their mothers? Where was that fetus in relation to her body, to her navel, to her heart, her pelvis? It existed as if in space. Indeed, the fetus in utero has become a metaphor for the 'man' in space, floating free, attached only by the umbilical cord of the spaceship. But where is the mother in that metaphor? She has become empty space.
>
> (Rothman 1986: 114, quoted in Cannold 2000: 37)

The literature on abortion is enormous, so our focus in this chapter will be selective. The discussion will centre on three issues regarding which feminists have made particularly distinctive and important contributions to the debate. I will begin by looking at ways that feminists have broadened the discussion of abortion, widening the focus to include pregnancy and motherhood, and the social conditions surrounding mothers and children. Next I will look at some ways that feminists have criticized the standard formulation of the abortion debate in terms of rights. Finally, I will turn to worries about taking the rights of foetuses more seriously than the rights of born human beings, including especially the rights of pregnant women.[1] Although many of the arguments I discuss support a pro-choice position according to which women should be able (legally and practically) to choose abortion, the point of the chapter is not to settle the issue of abortion, but rather to examine ways that feminists are changing and developing the abortion debate.

Laws in the US and the UK

Before we begin our main discussion, it is worth noting the legal status of abortion in the US and UK, at the time of this writing. US law on abortion is currently governed by the 1973 *Roe* v. *Wade* decision, in which the Supreme Court recognized a right to abortion, based on women's right to privacy. According to the ruling, women have a legal right to abortion until the end of the second trimester, the point at which the foetus becomes viable—that is, the point at which it could survive outside the womb.[2]

In England, Scotland, and Wales, women have the right to abortion (for the first twenty-four weeks) only when it is needed for the sake of a woman's health—but the law construes women's health very broadly, to include social considerations as well as more strictly medical ones (Fredman 1997: 130). A woman can only obtain an abortion if she can find two doctors willing to say that her health requires it[3]

---

[1] This chapter's focus on abortion should not be taken to suggest that abortion is the only issue of reproductive freedom of concern to feminists. Other important issues include forced or coerced sterilization, availability and affordability of contraception, sex education, and the provision of resources adequate to raise children.

[2] The idea that viability is a morally significant juncture in a foetus's existence is a problematic one. For an excellent discussion of it, see Shrage (2002).

[3] *Roe* v. *Wade* also requires physician approval for abortion. But this decision has nonetheless been interpreted as leaving the decision of whether or not to abort in the woman's hands. Physicians need to 'sign off' on abortion decisions, but the decision is taken to be the woman's. In the UK, the decision is considered the

(Cannold 2000: 24). In Northern Ireland, however, the law construes threats to a woman's health much more narrowly. Thus, many women travel from Northern Ireland to other parts of the UK to obtain abortions (BBC 2001).

Broadening the discussion

Since this chapter aims to show ways that feminists are altering standard debates on abortion, it is worth beginning with a little background on the nature of standard discussions. I will be arguing that these standard discussions overlook much that is of importance.[4]

The status of the foetus and the right to life

Humanity, personhood, and the foetus's right to life

Most debate over abortion in the philosophical literature concerns the status of the foetus, and whether or not this status is such that the foetus should be taken to have a right to life. A standard anti-abortion argument has it that it is wrong to kill anything that is human and alive. A foetus is human and alive. Therefore, the argument concludes, abortion is wrong.

This standard argument, however, is problematic. As Mary Anne Warren has pointed out, it can be seen as running together two distinct senses of 'human' (Warren 1973). One meaning of 'human' applies simply to all entities that are, biologically, *Homo sapiens*. Another refers to all of those that we consider to be members of the human moral community: those that have a right to life that we are morally obligated to respect. This distinction is an important and

---

physician's, and one that he or she may be required to defend in court (see Cannold 2000: 23).

[4] Despite this, many of the issues raised in standard discussions are well worth serious consideration. For example, one potentially important issue that I do not discuss here is whether, if one supports the right to abortion, there should be any restrictions on e.g. very late abortions.

widely (even if not explicitly) recognized one, both for abortion and for other issues. A brain-dead individual is still biologically human, but many of us think that it is acceptable to turn off their life-support machine. Moreover, a zygote (fusion of egg and sperm prior to implantation in the uterine wall) is biologically human. One of the ways in which birth control pills work is by preventing the implantation of a zygote in the uterine wall. Nonetheless, moral qualms about the pill are much rarer than moral qualms about abortion,[5] again suggesting that most of us do not consider all entities that are biologically human to be members of the human moral community.[6] Even more problematic for those who wish to understand biological humanity as sufficient for membership in the human community, human cancer cells are biologically human (Marquis 1989). We certainly do not consider such cells to be members of the human community, and we certainly do not consider it wrong to kill them.

The moral sense of the term 'human'—in which it designates a member of the moral community—is often referred to by a different term, 'person', in order to emphasize the distinction drawn above. Thus, the question of whether the foetus is a member of the moral community becomes the question of whether it is a person. Many traits have been proposed as criteria for personhood. One of the best-known standards is Michael Tooley's. Tooley argues that, very roughly, personhood requires self-consciousness. Less roughly, he takes a self-conscious creature to be one that 'possesses a concept of itself as a continuing subject of experiences and other mental states, and believes that it itself is such an entity' (Tooley 1981: 220). Foetuses clearly are not like this. Importantly, however, neither are newborn infants. If Tooley's criterion is accepted, then, foetuses do not have a right to life; but neither do newborn infants. Tooley accepts this consequence. He argues that self-consciousness is required for personhood, and that because neither foetuses nor infants are persons,

---

[5] Of course, many do object to the pill precisely because they take it to involve destruction of a member of the human moral community.

[6] Indeed, the pill is generally considered a *birth control method* rather than an abortion method, suggesting that the zygote does not even have the morally questionable status of a foetus.

neither has a right to life.[7] Thus, abortion is acceptable, but so is infanticide—at least very early on. This conclusion is a shocking one, and unwelcome to virtually all proponents of women's right to choose abortion. 'Just as acceptable as infanticide' is not much of a recommendation!

A future like ours and the foetus's right to life

Don Marquis argues against abortion without taking a stand on foetal personhood. He claims that the foetus's right to life derives neither from biological humanity nor from personhood (Marquis 1989). Instead, he claims, it is wrong to kill anything that has a future significantly like ours. We value our lives, and we should therefore think it wrong to deprive others of lives like ours. A foetus, if it is not aborted and all goes well, has a future like ours, and it is therefore wrong to kill it. Cancer cells and brain-dead humans do not have this possibility, so killing them is morally acceptable. This is clearly an improvement on the view that anything human has a right to life. But it still has the consequence that using the birth control pill might be a violation of a zygote's right to life. While this will be acceptable to many opponents of abortion, there are many others who worry about abortion but feel quite comfortable with this contraceptive method.

Pregnant women

Thomson, pregnancy, and the attached violinist

The above arguments assume that the key to the permissibility of abortion lies (at least largely) in the status of the foetus. In general, they proceed as though foetuses are things that we happen to come across, sitting all by themselves, and that we then try to decide

---

[7] Although it *seems* to have this consequence, it actually need not. Mary Anne Warren, for example, holds that newborns are not persons and, therefore, lack a full-blown right to life, but that it is nonetheless wrong to kill them. Indeed, she argues that it may often be appropriate to treat newborns *as if* they were persons. For Warren, the key difference between foetuses and newborns is that 'it is impossible to treat fetuses *in utero* as if they were persons without treating women as if they were something less than persons' (Warren 1989: 59).

whether it is acceptable to kill them. If the foetus has a right to life, we cannot kill it. If it lacks one, we can. This is typical of much of the literature on abortion.

It should not need to be pointed out that something is missing from this picture—the woman who is carrying the foetus. One of the first papers to pay attention to the pregnant woman's perspective was Judith Jarvis Thomson's 'A Defense of Abortion' (1971). This paper—one of the most famous in philosophy—has been much criticized even by feminists, for reasons that we shall see shortly. However, it makes a very important and still surprisingly infrequently made point: a discussion of abortion must take into account not only the foetus but also the pregnant woman. More specifically, Thomson argues that even if a foetus *is* a person, it may still be acceptable to abort it. Thomson argues in this way not because she actually believes that a foetus is a person, but rather to make the strongest possible case for abortion by granting its opponents the claim that is often considered sufficient to establish abortion's wrongness.

Thomson's argument makes crucial use of an analogy. Imagine, she suggests, that you wake up one morning to find that you have been kidnapped and a famous violinist has been attached to your body. He is using your kidneys, and he will need to do so for the next nine months. He has been attached your body by a society of music lovers who sought to preserve his life and found that your body was the only one which could fulfil his needs. If you now detach him, he will die. Most of us, Thomson suggests, would agree that you have no obligation to remain attached to the famous violinist for nine months. And we would agree to this even though we know that detaching yourself will kill him, and even though we believe that violinists have a right to life. It would be very good of you, according to Thomson, to save the violinist's life by allowing him to remain attached to you, but it would not be wrong to detach yourself, and therefore to kill him. This shows, Thomson argues, that the right to life is not absolute. Sometimes killing is acceptable, as it would be in order to avoid nine months attached to the violinist.

Thomson's argument captures something important about pregnancy. This is that it takes place in a woman's body. A foetus is not something which is simply found, but rather something growing inside the body of a woman, and dependent on her supporting it, generally for nine months. The pregnant woman thus has a special relationship to the foetus, which may give her special rights with respect to it. This is ignored in discussions that focus only on the foetus and its status.

Nonetheless, it has often been noted that Thomson's violinist argument also overlooks some important things about abortion. One key fact about abortion is that, except in cases of rape, the woman carrying the foetus has voluntarily acted in a way that has helped to bring it about that she is pregnant. This is very different from simply waking up in bed attached to a violinist. Thomson offers other analogies that are designed to be closer to cases of pregnancy resulting from voluntary sex. We will not discuss these here, as the main point I am interested in is the idea that considering the pregnant woman, and in particular the foetus's relationship to the pregnant woman, can convince us that a foetus's right to life is not absolute.[8] Once we recall that pregnancy involves not only a foetus but also a woman, it no longer seems that considering only a foetus's right to life can show us whether abortion is morally acceptable.

Thomson's discussion also draws attention to the fact that preserving a foetus's life requires much more than just not killing it: it requires the use of another human's body for nine months. Legally forbidding abortion, then, amounts to legally obligating someone to keep another being alive. Even if we grant that the being who is kept alive is a person, this is strongly at odds with most countries' legal systems, and especially at odds with American law. Although many European countries have 'good Samaritan' laws, which require one to do things such as summon help to the scene of an accident, none have laws requiring citizens to preserve each other's lives for months at a time. Most American states do not even require the minimal

---

[8] Even leaving aside Thomson's argument, there is something very odd about simply assuming the right to life to be absolute. Most of us do not believe in an absolute right to life—anyone who thinks it is acceptable to kill in self-defence or who accepts the possibility of a just war has already abandoned the idea that persons have an absolute right to life. Anti-abortion arguments that take a right to life to be absolute, then, actually rest on a rather unpopular view of the right to life. Thomson's argument, if successful, shows that the right to life is even weaker than these considerations would suggest.

assistance that European law does. American law students are generally taught about this lack of obligation via the example of an Olympic swimmer who sees an adorable child drowning in a shallow pool. The swimmer pulls up a chair and watches the child drown. Students are taught that (in most states) this swimmer has done absolutely nothing illegal (Glendon 1991: 78). If the swimmer is not even legally obligated to effortlessly save the drowning child, how could a woman be required to preserve another's life at considerable physical cost, and over many months? A right to life that includes the right to such support from a particular person is far stronger than a right to life is generally taken to be.[9]

Pregnancy and intimacy

Thomson's article draws attention to the moral relevance of the pregnant woman in discussions of abortion. In particular, she focuses on the fact that the foetus's continued life is dependent on quite large investments, and potentially significant sacrifices, from the pregnant woman. Margaret Little, however, has recently argued that this discussion, like nearly all others, still neglects a key feature of pregnancy: it pays insufficient attention to the fact that it takes place *within* a woman's body (Little 1999). She points out that gestation involves a profound degree of intimacy. (Little's argument, like Thomson's, grants the assumption that the foetus is a person.) The degree of intimacy involved in gestation is one that, she argues, standard political philosophy is ill equipped to deal with. She notes that 'under mainstream political theory . . . the very notion of a person is someone physically separate from others' (Little 1999: 296). Pregnancy is not like this.

> For a foetus, to be alive is to be occupying someone's body, to be using it, to be living in a particularly intimate physical relationship with another. Even assuming fetal personhood, that is, we have here a person in extraordinary physical enmeshment with another—a person whose blood is oxygenated by another's, a person whose hormonal activity in turn

---

[9] A country that takes citizens' right to healthcare seriously may well take citizens to have a right to very substantial support. However, the obligation to provide this support would not be taken to fall on particular private citizens, but rather on the state as a whole.

affects that other's brain and metabolism, a person whose growing physical size enlarges another's physical boundaries.

(Little 1999: 296)

Pregnancy, then, involves a unique degree of attachment and intimacy. Intimacy is a wonderful thing when it is entered into and continued voluntarily. Involuntary intimacy, however, is generally taken to be a great violation. To see this point one need only consider the difference between consensual sex and rape. Little notes that gestation which one consents to and embraces can be, and often is, an emotionally wonderful experience—even sometimes when it is physically very difficult indeed. Pregnancy that one does not want, however, is an experience of involuntary intimacy. To force someone into continuing this sort of intimacy is, she argues, wrong.

> Whatever the state's beneficent motives for protecting the interests of the foetus, it matters that the method used for that protection involves forcing others to have another entity live inside them.

(p. 301)

One might suppose that viewing involuntary pregnancy in this way undermines the joy and meaningfulness of pregnancy. Little, however, disagrees:

> To think that the above concern insults the meaningfulness of pregnancy is simply to misunderstand the point. We don't impugn how meaningful it is to have willing sex when we protest against rape; the fact that sexual intercourse can be wonderful doesn't mean we would think it appropriate for the state to conscript people into serving as prostitutes.

(p. 302)

Once we see gestation as the intimacy that it surely is, Little argues, we can see a new reason that women must have the right to abortion: nobody should be forced into unwilling intimacy.[10] Philosophers

---

[10] One might object to Little's understanding of pregnancy as intimacy by noting that one can be unaware of being pregnant, and intimacy of which one is unaware seems an odd notion. Yet other forms of intimacy can take place without one's awareness as well—women are sometimes raped while drugged into unconsciousness, and it seems reasonable to take these cases to be ones of involuntary intimacy.

have failed to see this justification, because they have failed to think seriously about the nature of pregnancy. Indeed, Little notes that discussions of abortion often take as their starting point discussions of rights and obligations toward others who are separate. In order to try to make sense of abortion, philosophers are forced to build in improbable details, like Thomson's violinist who has been attached to one's kidneys. But Little argues that philosophers should begin instead from the nature of pregnancy. We can see this as an instance of a phenomenon that we will explore further in Chapter 8: the way that women's experiences and perspectives can give us new ways of seeing and understanding old issues.

Appreciation of motherhood as reason for abortion

Little criticizes Thomson for not taking the experience of pregnancy seriously enough. Others have argued that—in a sense—Thomson takes it too seriously. In the violinist example, the reason you wish to detach yourself from the violinist is simply that otherwise you will be forced to spend nine months attached to him. Obviously, the analogy here is meant to be one with pregnancy. But women do not, in general, have abortions simply in order to avoid the experience of pregnancy. In most cases, the decision has much more to do with *whether or not a woman wants to become a mother.* Many feminists have argued that it is vital for those writing on abortion to consider the actual thoughts and reasoning processes of women deciding whether to have abortions. Invented examples with little connection to these reasons, they argue, have little bearing on the rightness of women's actual decisions. As Rosalind Hursthouse writes,

[I]n the violinist case . . . the only question is, can I stand remaining in this condition for the next nine months for his sake? I do not have any worries at all about the future beyond these nine months. But very few abortions are sought because the pregnant woman is concerned solely about her present physical condition in itself, with no worries about the future beyond the next nine (or rather, eight or seven) months. If I do not unhook myself from the violinist then the upshot after nine months is that some adult human being, with whom I can shake hands and bid goodbye, survives. If I do not have an abortion, after nine months the upshot is that there will be a *child*, a new person in the world, and more-over, that child will be mine—I shall have become a mother, and in one sense will remain one for the rest of my life.

(Hursthouse 1987: 206)

Considering this makes it clear that there is more at stake in abortion than whether or not one wishes to spend nine months pregnant. Becoming a mother means bringing a human life into the world, and many women take this to entail an inalienable responsibility for this new human life. Thus, women who do not feel that they would be capable of providing a good life for a child of theirs seek abortion for precisely this reason. Indeed, this seems to be one of the most common reasons that motivate women to seek abortions. Sometimes this is because the woman is a single teenager, unable to support even herself; sometimes it is because the woman already has several children and feels she cannot support more; sometimes it is because the woman simply feels emotionally unable to take on the burden of child-rearing. Dr Elizabeth Karlin, Director of the Women's Medical Center in Madison, Wisconsin, writes,

> There is only one reason I've ever heard for having an abortion: the desire to be a good mother. Women have abortions because they are aware of the overwhelming responsibility of motherhood.

(quoted in Cannold 2000: 98)

At first, Karlin's claim seems paradoxical: how could an abortion be motivated by the desire to be a good mother? Yet one who values being a good mother but does not feel able to be one might well opt for abortion.

Thomson's case suggests that the conflict at the core of abortion decisions is between the foetus's right to life and the woman's right not to be pregnant. Instead, however, many women are concerned not so much with a *right* not to be pregnant as with a *responsibility* not to bring life into the world for which they cannot adequately care. For this reason, Hursthouse suggests that Thomson's analogy is inadequate to real abortion decisions.

It might be argued, however, that focusing on the right not to be pregnant is absolutely essential to defending the right to abortion. This is because one who gives birth is legally and morally able to give her child up for adoption, and indeed there are many infertile couples eager to adopt. How, then, could a woman's knowledge that she cannot adequately care for a child provide adequate reason for choosing abortion? This line of thought accepts that a right not to be pregnant, such as that which Thomson defends, could confer the right to abortion. But it rejects the idea that the responsibility not to bring life into the world that one cannot adequately care for could do so.

The key flaw in this line of argument is that it still does not take adequate account of women's experiences of being pregnant. Many women know that if they carry a pregnancy to term and give birth, they will be psychologically incapable of putting the child up for adoption. If they know this, then they know that the decision is really not one between abortion, adoption, and keeping the child, but rather one between abortion and keeping the child. If they also know that they would be incapable of adequately caring for a child, then they will take the only responsible decision to be abortion. Margaret Little describes this well:

> One of the most common reasons women seek abortions is that they do not have room in their life just then to be a mother, but they know if they continue the pregnancy they will not be able to give up the child. What has seemed paradoxical (and indeed ethically confused) to many strikes me as a perfectly sensible, and often wise, appreciation of the different moral contours involved with entering, existing in, and exiting relationships. One may decline to enter a relationship that, once extant, changes the contours of your psyche such that you couldn't leave it . . .
>
> (Little 1999: 312)

Little takes pregnant women who abort to be declining to enter into the relationship of being mother to a baby (by carrying a pregnancy to term and giving birth) because they know that they could not leave that relationship once they had entered it.

The relevance of societal support for mothers

Most of the debate over abortion in the philosophical literature focuses, as we have seen, on the foetus. Much less attention is paid to the woman carrying the foetus. We have already seen that considering the woman's perspective introduces new and important considerations to the discussion. But the debate can be broadened still further, to include discussion of the society in which women find themselves. In particular, feminists have urged that it is important to pay attention to the ways in which the nature of a woman's culture affects the meaning and effects of motherhood and child-rearing.

As we have already seen in Chapter 1, it is still the case that mothers perform the vast majority of childcare tasks. Fathers generally contribute little, and what childcare is available outside the home is often of poor quality or prohibitively expensive. After having children, many women will be unable to work at the jobs that they previously held or hoped to hold and many will find it impossible to pursue the sort of education that they might otherwise wish to pursue. For single mothers, the situation is even more difficult. Many single mothers find that struggling to raise children while working in insecure and poorly paid jobs plunges them into poverty. For teenagers especially, having a child may mean the end of educational plans that would have allowed secure economic prospects for themselves and their future families.

> We live in a society that defines childrearing as the mother's job; a society in which most women are denied access to work that pays enough to support a family, childcare facilities they can afford, or any relief from the constant, daily burdens of motherhood; a society that forces women into dependence on marriage or welfare and often into permanent poverty . . . Under these conditions the unwillingly pregnant woman faces a terrifying loss of control over her fate.
>
> (Willis 1992: 84)

Abortion as self-defence

Jane English uses the effect of motherhood on women's lives to argue that abortion can legitimately be considered a form of self-defence— even if one accepts the assumption that the foetus is a person (English 1998). English notes that most people suppose that a self-defence justification would only allow abortion in order to save the mother's life. However, she argues that in fact our conception of self-defence extends beyond this. She asks when we consider it acceptable to kill another person in self-defence, and suggests that we allow this even in cases where something less than our life is at stake.

You may not shoot someone merely to avoid having your clothes torn. This might lead one to the mistaken conclusion that the defense may only equal the threatened injury in severity; that to avoid death you may kill but to avoid a black eye you may only inflict a black eye or the equivalent. Rather, our laws and customs seem to say that you may create an injury somewhat, but not enormously, greater than the injury to be avoided. To fend off an attack whose outcome would be as serious as rape, a severe beating or the loss of a finger, you may shoot; to avoid having your clothes torn, you may blacken an eye.

(English 1998: 318)

English then suggests that, given the potential effects of motherhood on women's lives, abortion may be justified in self-defence—even if the foetus is a person. She does this by way of an analogy. In English's example, you are to imagine that you are a surgeon, attacked by an innocent person who has been hypnotized into kidnapping you. The attacker's plan is to take you to a mad scientist who will induce 'a permanent mental block against all your knowledge of medicine' (1998: 319). This would automatically destroy your career and have an enormous impact on your family and personal life. So, English argues, if the only way you can escape it is to kill the attacker, killing him is justified—and this is so even though the attacker is an innocent person. Further, she argues that this is the case even if you have done something which can be seen as contributing to your kidnapping: perhaps you have gone out at night, even though you know that the kidnappers only operate at night. English thinks you would still be justified in killing your kidnapper, and that this shows abortion may be justifiable even if the foetus is a person. She adds, 'I think it is no exaggeration to claim that unwanted pregnancies (most obviously among teenagers) often have such adverse lifelong consequences as the surgeon's loss of livelihood' (pp. 319–20). This, English argues, means that at least some abortions are justified on grounds of self-defence.[11]

[11] There are some difficulties for this argument. The general principle that a person may kill anyone whose actions would destroy their career and have a large impact on their personal life is surely too strong. It might legitimate killing rivals for jobs, or killing those who discover that one has been embezzling company funds, and English surely would not want this. However, it is possible that her justificatory principle could be refined to avoid these consequences.

The role of societal factors in English's argument is not at first obvious. But the effects of motherhood are crucial to her discussion. The reason motherhood has these effects is, as we saw in Chapter 1, that child-rearing is consigned largely to women and that workplaces are structured in such a way as to make many jobs incompatible with childcare duties. As we also saw in Chapter 1, society does not have to be structured in this way: thus, the structure of society is crucial to English's argument.

Jaggar and the centrality of societal arrangements

Allison Jaggar focuses more sharply on the significance of society's role in bringing it about that the responsibility to raise children falls so heavily on women. She argues that the strength of a woman's right to choose abortion depends at least in part on the nature of the society in which she finds herself.

Jaggar makes two arguments, both of which are important to her case. The first focuses on women's entitlement to make abortion decisions. She suggests that decisions should be made by those who are most affected by them.

> Biology, law, and social conditioning work together to ensure that most women's lives are totally changed as the result of the birth of a child while men can choose how much they wish to be involved.
>
> (Jaggar 1973: 353)

This means that the decision of whether or not to have an abortion should be made by the pregnant woman. This argument depends on the fact that women are those whose lives are so dramatically affected. If men's lives came to be changed as much as women's by the birth of a child, they might well deserve a say in abortion decisions, according to this line of argument.[12] Nonetheless, she insists that pregnancy does give women a special sort of status in any abortion

---

[12] There are relationships even now in which men's lives would be affected as much as women's by the birth of a child. In these relationships, if Jaggar is right, it seems to me that men should be seen as having a moral right to a say in the abortion decision. However, it is so overwhelmingly the case that child-rearing is left to women that abortion decisions must—as things currently stand—be legally those of women alone. In a more equitable society, things might be different.

decision—and that therefore the pregnant woman will always be entitled to a stronger say than any others in such decisions. She writes that a pregnant woman must have

> a strong voice in the decision: she is not just an ordinary member of the community in this matter, for it is still she who must carry and bear the child. Her wishes must therefore be accorded special weight.
>
> (Jaggar 1973: 359)

Jaggar's second argument concerns the state's right to have a say in abortion decisions. According to her, many governments are on extremely shaky ground when they claim to be protectors of a foetus's right to life. This is because, she claims, a genuine right to life includes not only a bare right to continued existence but 'the right to a full human life and to whatever means are necessary to achieve this' (Ibid.: 351). Governments (like the US government) that do not even *attempt* to provide for the medical and nutritional needs of all cannot claim to truly be protectors of a right to life. They cannot, then, outlaw abortion on the grounds of protecting a foetus's right to life.

Jaggar, then, takes a two-pronged approach to the issue of abortion, and both of her arguments make crucial reference to surrounding social circumstances. First, she argues that women—as those most affected by the birth of a child—are the only ones who can legitimately decide whether or not to have an abortion. If women were not the only ones so strongly affected, things might be different. Second, she denies the legitimacy of current governments' claims to be protectors of a foetus's right to life. A government that took on a great deal of responsibility for giving all citizens a full human life might have a legitimate claim to be protecting a foetus's life. Jaggar does not hold that this could ever justify outlawing abortion, although she thinks it is conceivable that such a government might legitimately 'shape public policies in ways designed to influence [women's] abortion decisions' (Jaggar 1997: 132).

Jaggar argues, then, that it is only due to our current social structures that women should have an exclusive right to decide whether or not to have abortions. As things stand now, however, women very clearly do have the right to abortion. As we have seen in Chapter 1, many feminists take it to be vital to bring about a world in which the full burden of child-rearing does not fall on women. If feminists succeed in bringing it about that men share equally in the work of child-rearing, then if Jaggar is right an important plank in the argument for a woman's *exclusive* right to choose abortion disappears. If the burden of raising a child does not fall exclusively on the woman, it becomes much more difficult to argue that the decision of whether or not to have a child should be hers and hers alone.

Societal arrangements and arguments against abortion

Abortion as a barrier to meeting women's needs

Interestingly, some feminists have used the very features of society that Jaggar describes to argue for an opposite conclusion. These arguments begin from the now familiar idea that we live in a society which does not sufficiently support those who do the vital work of bringing up children. Those raising children need social support mechanisms like childcare, flexible time, healthcare, and the assurance that they will not fall into poverty simply because they are devoting substantial time and energy to childcare. Some anti-abortion feminists argue that the availability of abortion makes it possible for this lack of support to continue.

Sidney Callahan argues that some of women's most pressing needs are for effective contraception and adequate support for mothers and children (Callahan 1984). As long as abortion is available, she suggests, these needs will not be met. The reason is that abortion allows women something which provides a *substitute* for some of what they really need: it gives women some control over their fertility, even if they lack effective contraception, and it offers a way of avoiding motherhood for those who cannot afford it. Since abortion is far cheaper and easier than reforming society to be more responsive to the needs of women and children, its availability makes it easier to neglect the broader range of women's needs. Callahan, then, sees abortion as an obstacle to giving women full and genuine control over their lives:

> As far as society goes, it is far, far easier to give individual women permissive access to abortion than it is to collectively support child-care, health care, or even preventive programs of sex education.

> (Callahan 1984: 328)

There are several problems with this argument. The first problem is that it seems to make the unrealistic assumption that we are living in a society in which the government is committed to meeting women's needs in one way or another. Thus, if abortion is outlawed, women will be more likely to obtain what they need by the other methods Callahan discusses. But this is very far from being the case—especially in Callahan's own country, the United States. As I write this chapter in 2002, George W. Bush's anti-abortion administration looks especially unlikely to provide for the needs discussed above. Bush is committed to scaling back social programmes, rather than increasing support for mothers and children; he favours abstinence-only sex education programmes, which provide no information about contraception; and he has tried to eliminate contraceptive coverage from the Federal Employee Health Benefits Plan. At the time that Callahan wrote her article, under the Reagan administration, the situation differed in some particulars, but was no more favourable to the programmes Callahan supports. An argument like hers only makes sense (if at all) in the context of a government that seems likely to meet women's needs by one method or another. Sadly, this is not the situation in which most of us find ourselves. In the world that we live in, Callahan's argument seems hopelessly idealistic.[13]

We can also ask whether Callahan is right to suggest that all women's needs could be met without abortion. Even if women had access to effective contraception and sex education, and even if the needs of mothers and children were adequately provided for by the state, the right to abortion would arguably remain necessary. No method of contraception is perfect, and it is unlikely that a perfect method could be developed. Further, no matter what support is provided for mothers and children, being a mother will in all likelihood never be a responsibility that every woman would be willing to assume under all circumstances. If deciding the course of their reproductive lives is a vital need for women, then abortion would remain necessary even if society were reformed in the way that Callahan suggests.

---

[13] Callahan might respond that if abortion were illegal there would be a surge of pressure on governments to change their policies in such a way as to attend properly to women's needs. This seems to me quite a gamble to take.

Despite my objection to the way that Callahan connects abortion and the provision of support that women need, there is nonetheless an important connection. The more that women are given the support that they need, the fewer women will need to have abortions. Many women do have abortions because they lack access to adequate contraception; and many women do have abortions because they lack the supports that would allow them to bear and raise a child as they would otherwise like to do. Further, Callahan is right that true reproductive freedom for women demands the provision of all these services. The right response, it seems to me, is to accept all this without accepting her claim that abortion availability makes states less likely to provide these services. There is no reason to suppose that a United States without legal abortion would provide the services that Callahan suggests, and no reason to suppose that one cannot fight both for legal abortion and for services that would bring it about that fewer women would want or need abortions.

Abortion as devaluation of caregiving

Many women who oppose abortion see support for abortion as contributing to the devaluation of the caregiving work generally done by women. The availability of abortion helps to make motherhood optional. This, they hold, makes it seem like just one option among many, rather than the especially essential work that it is— humanity would not survive if there were no childbearers and childrearers. Moreover, arguments that abortion is needed often focus on negative aspects of motherhood, casting it as an undesirable fate. Faye Ginsburg writes of her interviews with anti-abortion women:

> [I]n their view, social changes that could be interpreted as casting reproduction and child rearing as a liability are anti-woman. Abortion is thus a condensed symbol for the devaluation of motherhood and the central attribute assigned to it in this culture—the self-sacrifice and nurturance of dependents.

> (Ginsburg 1989: 7)

Because abortion makes it possible for women to choose not to be mothers, and because defenders of abortion often focus their arguments on the costs of motherhood, opponents see abortion as an attack on the importance of motherhood.

There are several problems with this objection. First, it should be noted that this argument—if it works—would also work against contraception. Contraception does much to make motherhood optional. If allowing women to choose not to be mothers devalues motherhood, then contraception would seem to devalue motherhood just as surely as abortion does. (Similarly, those arguing for the importance of contraception emphasize the negative aspects of unplanned parenting.)

It seems to me, though, that the argument does not succeed—either against abortion or against contraception. It is difficult to see how understanding motherhood as a genuine choice rather than an inevitable fate devalues it. Many genuine choices—like the choice to jump into a burning building to save a life—are highly valued precisely because they are choices; and many inevitable fates—like death due to inoperable cancer—are considered extremely undesirable. Carrying through a pregnancy and devoting one's life to raising a child is difficult and vitally important work (like saving a person in a burning building). As things are, our society does indeed significantly undervalue this work. But it is hard to see why this work would be any more valued if it were unchosen. (Indeed, millennia of experience have shown us that lack of control over childbearing does not lead to proper valuing of the caregiving work that women do.) Moreover, discussing the negative aspects of motherhood need not be a devaluing of it: a key reason that we are so impressed by those who jump into burning buildings to save lives is that jumping into burning buildings is *dangerous*. Discussing the costs and difficulties of motherhood should make us value all the more those who choose it.

Finally, the reasons many women give (as noted earlier) for their choices to have abortions make it clear that they do value and appreciate the work of raising a child, and that this is precisely why they are choosing not to do it: they realize that this work requires an enormous investment and they do not feel able to make this investment. Ginsburg interviewed a pro-choice activist, who had an abortion because she and her husband did not feel able to raise a fifth child. This activist explained:

> The perspective that abortion is 'destroying the family' is a very, very narrow one. In my experience, people who've made the choice to have an abortion made it because they want a strong family.
>
> (Ginsburg 1989: 154)

The choice to have an abortion, then, may often stem from an awareness of the difficulty of child-rearing, and the importance of doing it well. The availability of abortion makes it possible for women to see becoming a mother as something that they should only do when (and if) they are ready and able to do so—which seems a sensible attitude toward work whose value they take seriously.

Worries about rights

The weakness of the right to choose

Recently, many feminists have argued that formulating the pro-choice position in terms of a woman's *right* to choose abortion is a mistake. A mere *right* to choose, they argue, will not suffice to give women real reproductive freedom.

A right to do something is often understood as simply a right not to be interfered with in one's efforts to do that thing. This doesn't guarantee that one will be able to do that which one has a right to do. Thus, the fact that I have a right to buy a BMW does not mean that anyone will act in order to bring it about that I can afford to buy a BMW. Since I cannot afford to buy a BMW, my right to buy one does not give me very much. The right to choose abortion is often understood on this model. Most importantly, it has been understood on this model by the US Supreme Court. The court ruled in 1981 that women can still be said to have freedom of choice even when public funding for abortion is unavailable—that is, even women who cannot afford abortions are still taken to have the freedom to choose them (Petchesky 1986: ix). These women would be able to obtain abortions if they could afford them, just as I would be able to buy a BMW if I had more money.

Access to abortion in the United States is severely limited.[14] Since 1977, Medicaid (the US federal programme that provides health insurance for the poor) has been forbidden to fund abortions, except in a very restricted range of circumstances.[15] Currently, funding is permitted only when the mother's life is threatened, or in cases of rape or incest. Many women are therefore unable to afford abortions, or forced to undergo risky second-trimester abortions because of delay due to lack of money (Cannold 2000: 62). In the 1980s further restrictions on federal funding for abortion were passed: federal funding is also unavailable for (among others) Native Americans, federal employees and their dependants, Peace Corps volunteers, and military personnel and their dependants (Boonstra and Sonfield 2000). Since military personnel and Peace Corps volunteers are often stationed in countries without legal abortion, the denial of government-supplied abortion services is especially likely to mean complete unavailability of abortion to these women. Even when women are able to afford abortions, they may still have difficulty obtaining them. Eighty-six per cent of US counties have no abortion providers, and the percentage of doctors offering abortion services has been sharply declining—in part due to a concerted campaign of violence (including murder) directed against abortion providers by anti-abortion activists.[16] As Eileen McDonagh writes,

14 In addition to the barriers described in the text, the Supreme Court has also allowed states to impose waiting periods and to require parental notification for teenagers. Waiting periods can be a very severe barrier for poor women who live hundreds of miles from their nearest abortion provider—they would need to either make two trips or pay for accommodation near the abortion provider. Parental notification requirements makes it much more difficult for teenage women to obtain abortions.

15 Initially, funding was only available when the mother's life was threatened. In 1978, rape, incest, and 'severe and long-lasting physical health damage' became grounds for Medicaid funding of abortion. The health damage exception only lasted until 1979; the rape and incest exceptions were removed in 1981, and only restored in 1992. (Boonstra and Sonfield 2000; 'Public Funding for Abortion Fact Sheet', ACLU, www.aclu.org/library/funding.html, 1. Consulted 12 Aug. 2002.

16 'Fact Sheet: The Shortage of Abortion Providers', www.abortionaccess.org/ AAP/publica_resources/fact_sheets/shortage_provider.htm. Consulted 12 Aug. 2002. According to the NARAL foundation's fact sheet, 'Clinic Violence and Intimidation' (28 June 2002), seven people involved in abortion provision in the US

In the years since *Roe* . . . abortion rights have become little more than a meaningless abstraction for millions of women who lack the means to pay for an abortion, are incapable of traveling great distances to obtain one, or are unable to wait a long period before having one.

(McDonagh 1996: 3)

Because these availability problems are so severe, some feminists have argued that demanding a right to choose is insufficient. Women need not just the choice of abortion, but the real possibility of it. Abortion needs to be affordable and available to all women, not just offered as an empty and unattainable possibility.

The narrow understanding of rights described above, however, is not the only one available. There are also understandings of rights that would place a much greater obligation on the state to make abortion available and affordable. Industrialized countries other than the United States, for example, recognize their citizens as having a right to healthcare. This right is understood as conferring upon the state the obligation to make free healthcare available to all of its citizens. If the right to abortion were understood on the model of this sort of right to healthcare, it would be seen as carrying with it the obligation for abortion to be genuinely made available—that is, accessible and affordable—to all women. Defending this broader notion of rights, Rosalind Pollack Petchesky argues,

rights, to be meaningful, must carry the necessary enabling conditions that will make them concretely realizable and universally available. This is just another way of saying that certain social conditions—decent health care, education, housing, nutrition, etc.—are so fundamental to individual moral agency and citizenship that the society must provide them to everyone. Extended to abortion, such a concept of social rights implies, first, embedding abortion itself in a full range of social services—health care, prenatal care, child care, safe and reliable contraception, sex education, protection from sexual and sterilization abuse[17]—that make

have been murdered since 1993 and many more murder attempts have been made; between 1977 and 2001, there were at least 41 clinic bombings, 165 arsons, 82 attempted bombings, and 554 bomb threats.

[17] The US (along with other countries) has a history of sterilizing women without their consent or under coercion. The women singled out for this have generally been non-white, poor, or disabled. Although mainstream feminism neglected

up authentic reproductive choice; and, second, standing in solidarity with all women, however young or poor, to make sure they have access to those services.

(Petchesky 1986: xv)

On an understanding of rights like Petchesky's, the right to choose abortion requires much more than the US Supreme Court has taken it to require. The right to choose, then, *need not* be understood so narrowly that it does not require giving women genuine access to abortion services. Nonetheless, it is problematic that it has often been understood so narrowly. Unless it is understood more richly, it is a rather empty promise to the many women who cannot afford abortions or must drive hundreds of miles to find abortion providers.

European countries tend to understand rights in a way closer to Petchesky's suggestion, but this does not mean that women have the sort of access to abortion that Petchesky would like. Because citizens are viewed as having the right to healthcare, for example, European governments take themselves to be obligated to provide healthcare at taxpayers' expense. So a right to abortion is far more likely to be understood as requiring genuine availability of abortion. However, things are actually more complicated than this. As we have seen, British women can only obtain abortions if they can find two doctors willing to say that it is required for the sake of their health. If it is deemed necessary to a woman's health, however, the National Health Service will provide an abortion free of charge, just as it would provide other medical treatments.

The situation in Great Britain, then, is very different from that in the United States. For example, the cost of abortion is not a barrier to the same extent as it is in the United States.[18] However, a woman's access to abortion is greatly affected by whether or not her physician is willing to give her a referral. Not all physicians are willing to do this, and there are some regions where it is difficult to find a physician to

these issues for some time, focusing almost exclusively on abortion and birth control, reproductive rights are now generally understood as including freedom from coerced or involuntary sterilization. For more discussion of these issues, see e.g. Petchesky (1986).

[18] It can still be a barrier. If a woman is unable to obtain an abortion through the National Health Service, she will need to pay for it herself.

approve an abortion. Moreover, the National Health Service is under-staffed, especially in the area of abortion provision, and this means that women are often placed on waiting lists for long periods of time. These waiting lists can make the difference between a relatively easy first-trimester abortion and a much more difficult second-trimester abortion. If the woman is unable to obtain approval for an abortion, she has to turn to the private sector, where there are clinics dedicated to providing abortion services for women, staffed by doctors commit-ted to supporting women's abortion decisions. A woman forced to resort to such clinics will have to pay for abortion just as an American woman would, and she may not be able to afford it.[19]

The strength of the right to choose

Feminists have also criticized 'the right to choose' as too strong a formulation, in a very particular way. The problem is that it is often supposed that a right to do something means one's decision to do or not do that thing is beyond the bounds of moral criticism. If a woman has a right to abortion, then, there is no room for making moral judgements about particular abortion decisions. Although some have argued that abortion decisions have absolutely no moral significance, increasing numbers of feminists have recently argued that it is important to acknowledge the moral dimension of abortion decisions. In part, this comes from taking seriously the way that pregnant women themselves view abortion. Some women do not attribute any moral significance to their abortion decisions. However, many women consider the decision of whether or not to have an abortion to be a deeply moral one. Indeed, we have seen that many women feel they are doing something morally right or even obligatory in having abor-tions—because they do not feel that they would be able to care adequately for a child or to give it up for adoption. Insisting that abortion decisions have no moral significance means not taking ser-iously what these women say about their decisions. It also makes it difficult to criticize particular abortion decisions coherently.

[19] For information on availability of abortion in the UK, see Cannold (2000: 21, 62).

... recognizing abortion as a woman's basic right makes it difficult for us to articulate our concerns about the abortions chosen by women because the fetuses they are carrying are female, or the abortions risked by women because they don't want to postpone or diminish their partner's sexual pleasure. For if it is a woman's fundamental moral right to choose abortion, then it will seem inappropriate to question her reasons.

(Shrage 1994: 56)

Certainly some take the assertion of a right to seal off the possibility of any further discussion of morality. However, it does not follow that talk of rights need have this effect. Most of us think, for example, that we should have the right to vote for the political party of our choice. Nonetheless, we might still make moral judgements about the voting decisions that people make—judging, for example, that it is morally wrong to vote for a racist party while insisting that those who do have every *right* to do so. The right to choose abortion, then, does not automatically rule out any moral dimension to individual abortion decisions. However, it is perhaps important to go out of one's way to make this clear: rights are often misunderstood as sealing off moral discussion.

Women's rights and foetal rights

Feminists have recently drawn attention to the fact that foetuses are increasingly taken to have rights well beyond those accorded to children or adults; and pregnant women far fewer rights than other citizens. We have already seen, in our discussion of Thomson's article, that those who oppose abortion take foetuses to have a right to quite an extraordinary level of support from another human. But foetuses are increasingly taken to have rights even beyond this.[20] Women have been forced to have Caesarean sections against their will, even over religious objections and at the cost of their lives; and women have been jailed for consuming alcohol while pregnant (ACLU 1997). The justification for these actions is concern for the foetus. An

---

[20] Privileging a foetus's rights over a woman's is especially common when the woman is poor or non-white (see Bordo 1993: 71–98; ACLU 1997).

especially clear statement of this justification can be found in the New Jersey Supreme Court's ruling that 'a child has a legal right to begin life with a sound mind and body' (Bordo 1993: 87). This right, if upheld as absolute, could justify state intervention into all the minutiae of a pregnant woman's life. It would certainly justify the interventions mentioned above.

However, there are two problems with this justification for the interventions. The first is that it is very difficult to see how the right described could be upheld as absolute: it conflicts with the mother's right to control her own body. A person's right to control of their own body, *especially* when it comes to medical interventions, has traditionally been taken very seriously. Susan Bordo discusses a case in which the father of a dying child refused to give a bone marrow donation that might save the child's life. Although the child's mother sued, the father's right to refuse this procedure was upheld. Judges discussing the possibility of forced marrow transplants have argued with great passion against any bodily invasion. Consider the following comment from the judge in a related case, *McCall* v. *Shimp* 1978:

> For a society which respects the rights of *one* individual, to sink its teeth into the jugular or neck of one of its members and suck from it sustenance for *another* member, is revolting to our hard-wrought concepts of jurisprudence. Forcible extraction of living body tissue causes revulsion to the judicial mind. Such would raise the specter of the swastika and the Inquisition, reminiscent of the horrors this portends.
>
> (quoted in Bordo 1993: 74)

If a man cannot legitimately be compelled to donate marrow to save the life of his already born son, it is difficult to see how a woman could, in the interests of her foetus, be compelled to undergo such invasive surgery as a Caesarean, or jailed for ingesting legal substances. And, indeed, this is what courts have found: ignoring the pregnant woman's will in the interest of protecting her foetus has been found, over and over, to be unacceptable—on appeal. Although courts have consistently upheld women's rights over their own bodies, these eventual rulings have often come too late—after a pregnant woman was jailed (in at least one instance, for drinking alcohol) or compelled to have non-consensual surgery, and—in one case—after the woman died as a result of a forced Caesarean (ACLU 1997).

The second problem with the idea that a child has a 'legal right to begin life with a sound mind and body' is that, at least in the US, this would grant foetuses rights that children and adults lack. This right, if taken seriously, would (at least) give a foetus a right to adequate nutrition and medical care, and an environment free of toxins. These are not rights that the US recognizes for born human beings. As Susan Bordo puts it, this leave us with 'a strange set of affairs ... that a two-year-old child has far fewer rights than a six-month old foetus.' (Bordo 1993: 88)

It is difficult indeed to see how this disparity could be justified: even the strongest opponents of abortion have failed to offer criteria that would entitle foetuses to *more* extensive rights than children. Of course, there is more than one direction in which one could now take the discussion. One might argue that foetuses should not have the legal rights described above, as this would deprive mothers of their right to bodily integrity. But one might also argue that not only foetuses, but children and adults, have a right to all that is needed for a sound mind and body. This latter argument would still face the problem of denying pregnant women control over their bodies, but it would not give foetuses more rights than children.

The privileging of foetuses' rights and the disparaging of pregnant women's rights make a disturbing pair. This contrast is made especially vivid by the words of a pro-choice Catholic theologian describing his visit to an abortion clinic, during which he asked to see the products of abortions.

I asked to see the contents of one of the bags of a typical abortion—a six- to nine-week pregnancy—and it was opened and placed in a small metal cup for examination. I held the cup in my hands and saw a small amount of unidentifiable fleshy matter in the bottom of the cup. The quantity was so little that I could have hidden it if I had taken it into my hand and made a fist.

It was impressive to realize that I was holding in my hand what many people think to be the legal and moral peer of a woman, if not, indeed, her superior. I have held babies in my hands and now I held this embryo. I know the difference.

(Maguire 1993: 146)

The arguments of this chapter show that incorporating feminist thought can change the shape of an important debate. This debate has had an unfortunate tendency to focus on foetuses to the neglect of the women carrying them. Once we take women's perspectives seriously, however, we see that much more than the foetus needs to be considered. I have not attempted here to settle the issue of abortion—there are elements of standard debates that are worthy of more discussion than they have received here. Nonetheless, it seems clear that these debates go badly wrong by paying insufficient attention to women, and that debates over abortion would be substantially enhanced by bringing these concerns to the fore.

SUGGESTIONS FOR FURTHER READING

General

Baird, R. M. and Rosenbaum, S. E., *The Ethics of Abortion, rev. edn.* Amherst, NY: Prometheus, 1993.

Cannold, L., *The Abortion Myth: Feminism, Morality and the Hard Choices Women Make.* Hanover, NH: Wesleyan University Press, 2000. (*Includes good brief statements of current status of abortion in the US, the UK, and Australia.*)

Petchesky, R. P., *Abortion and Woman's Choice.* London: Verso, 1986.

Pojman, L. P., and Beckwith, F. J. (eds.), *The Abortion Controversy: 25 Years After Roe v. Wade.* Belmont, Calif.: Wadsworth, 1998.

Shrage, L., *Abortion and Social Responsibility: Depolarizing the Debate.* Oxford: Oxford University Press, 2003.

Against a focus on the status of the foetus

English, J., 'Abortion: Beyond the Personhood Argument', in L. P. Pojman, and F. J. Beckwith (eds.), *The Abortion Controversy: 25 Years After Roe v. Wade.* Belmont, Calif.: Wadsworth, 315–24.

Jaggar, A., 'Abortion and a Woman's Right to Decide', *Philosophical Forum* 5 (1973): 347–60.

Little, M. O., 'Abortion, Intimacy, and the Duty to Gestate', *Ethical Theory and Moral Practice* 2 (1999): 295–312.

Markowitz, S., 'A Feminist Defense of Abortion', in L. P. Pojman and F. J. Beckwith (eds.), *The Abortion Controversy: 25 Years After Roe v. Wade*. Belmont, Calif.: Wadsworth, 1998, 389–399.

McDonagh, E., *Breaking the Abortion Deadlock: From Choice to Consent*. Oxford: Oxford University Press, 1996.

Thomson, J., 'A Defense of Abortion', *Philosophy and Public Affairs* 1 (1971): 47–66

Abortion access and affordability

Cannold, L., *The Abortion Myth: Feminism, Morality and the Hard Choices Women Make*. Hanover, NH: Wesleyan University Press, 2000, ch. 2.

McDonagh, E., *Breaking the Abortion Deadlock: From Choice to Consent*. Oxford: Oxford University Press, 1996, ch. 6.

Petchesky, R. P., *Abortion and Woman's Choice*. London: Verso, 1986.

Shrage, L., *Abortion and Social Responsibility: Depolarizing the Debate*. Oxford: Oxford University Press, 2003.

Foetal rights vs. women's rights

Bordo, S., *Unbearable Weight: Feminism, Western Culture, and the Body*. Berkeley: University of California Press, 1993, 71–98.

Cannold, L., *The Abortion Myth: Feminism, Morality and the Hard Choices Women Make*. Hanover, NH: Wesleyan University Press, 2000, ch. 3.

Petchesky, R. P., *Abortion and Woman's Choice*. London: Verso, 1986, ch. 9.

Young, I. M., 'Punishment, Treatment, Empowerment: Three Approaches to Policy for Pregnant Addicts', in *Intersecting Voices: Dilemmas of Gender, Political Philosophy, and Policy*. Princeton, NJ: Princeton University Press, 1997, 75–94.

Anti-abortion feminism

Callahan, S., and Callahan, D. (eds.), *Abortion: Understanding Differences*. New York: Plenum, 1984. (*Several articles are by anti-abortion feminists; others are pro-choice.*)

Callahan, S., 'Abortion and the Sexual Agenda', *Commonweal* (25 Apr. 1986): 232–8.

Wolf-Devine, C., 'Abortion and the "Feminine Voice"', *Public Affairs Quarterly* 3(3) (1989): 81–97.

5

Feminine Appearance

Feminists are famous (perhaps notorious) for their concerns about standards of feminine attractiveness. Rejection of the pressure to live up to such standards has been important enough to feminism—or at least to popular conceptions of feminism—that it plays a key role in the stereotype of a feminist as a woman who wears men's clothes, eschews makeup, burns her bras, and rejects adornment and attractiveness of any sort. This may even contribute to the reluctance of many women to call themselves 'feminists'.

The stereotype of feminists (like many stereotypes) is far from the truth. Bra-burning was always a myth (Rhode 1997), and most feminists (today, at least) would strongly reject any attempt to impose a new, feminist ideal of how women should look. But even many of those who realize that this stereotype is false may be reluctant to accept feminist criticism of current standards of attractiveness. There are many reasons for this. One is surely that clothing, makeup, and dieting seem like personal matters—individual choices—that couldn't possibly have political significance. A key insight of feminism, however, has been that what seem to be purely personal and individual matters (like how one's family is structured—see Chapter 1) do indeed have political significance. It is very difficult, if not impossible, to cordon off some areas of life as immune to political analysis.

Even if one accepts, however, that there isn't a sharp line to be drawn between the personal and political, it may still seem that feminist criticism of women's appearance-related ideals and efforts is a mistake. One reason for this is that many women enjoy spending time on their appearance—they enjoy shopping for clothes, wearing makeup, and successfully losing weight. Feminist criticism seems to be insisting either that women *do* not enjoy these activities or that they *should* not. Moreover, the enjoyment that women get from these activities seems as though it could form the basis for an appealing argument against any feminist criticism: if feminists aim to improve the lives of women, criticizing activities that women enjoy does not seem a promising strategy.

This chapter will begin by laying out in a bit more detail why it is that feminist concern over matters of appearance may seem misguided. In particular, we shall see that any adequate discussion of these issues must be able to take account of the enjoyment women get from time spent on their appearance, and of the fact that women do in general feel that they are choosing to do this, rather than being pressured into it. I will argue, however, that such feminist discussions are available: feminist worries about women's appearance-related pursuits are not criticisms of women who engage in and enjoy such pursuits, and they are perfectly compatible with such enjoyment.

Women's enjoyment and feminist discussions

Enjoyment and choice

The effort that women spend on their appearance is not generally experienced as a horrible trial to be endured for the sake of living up to externally imposed standards. Many women *feel* a strong desire to be thinner, or to wear the clothes and makeup they see in magazines and stores, and they get a lot of pleasure from doing so. Indeed, as Natasha Walter notes, women spend some of their happiest hours shopping for clothes and makeup together:

> Feminists frequently write as if women's relation to their bodies is invariably tortured and full of self loathing. But this is not the only, or even the main truth about that relation. If you watch women in shops, holding dresses up to their bodies and dreaming in the mirrors; if you watch them reading fashion magazines, flicking idly through the pages until, with an indrawn breath, they laugh out, 'look at that! Look at that blue, that's the blue I want . . .' . . . you know that there is a real, fresh, happy

sensuality about women's feeling for self-decoration that can never be expunged.

(Walter 1998: 86–7)

Women's efforts on their appearance often feel playful and harmlessly entertaining. One who looks for political content in such efforts can therefore seem simply confused—to be missing the point, and trying to find serious aspects to a mere diverting entertainment. A black woman describes her decision to wear coloured contact lenses in the following way: 'What's the fuss? When I put on my blue lenses, it makes me feel good. It makes me feel sexy, different, the other woman, so to speak, which is like fun' (Bordo 1993: 251). Listening to what women actually think and feel is vital to feminism. And many women insist that they enjoy their appearance-related efforts—that they choose them freely, and pursue them happily, for their own satisfaction. Where, then, is there room for feminist criticism?

In fact, we can quickly see that enjoyment and choice of an activity do not rule out political criticism of it if we consider an imaginary example. Suppose that there came to be a fashion in twenty-first-century America for adult female foot-binding, and 90 per cent of women had their feet bound, rendering it difficult to walk and causing permanent damage. Imagine also that these women reported that they genuinely wanted this, and found it enjoyable. The fact that women reported their experience in this way would not keep us from worrying about the fashion and its effects, or from criticizing it. And that seems the right reaction.

Bordo on cultural patterns

Feminist worries about women's beauty-related pursuits are not criticisms of women who engage in these pursuits. Instead, they result from the examination of cultural patterns. This is a common feminist strategy. We have seen, for example, that individual women's choices about their careers and families are revealed in a new light once we examine the culture in which these choices take place. We saw, in Chapter 1, the way that social structures (including both workplace and family expectations) work to limit women's choices. Feminist discussion of this chapter's issues takes a similar form. Women's efforts to beautify themselves seem at first to be a non-starter as a political issue: if women are happy doing this, why should feminists care? However, a closer examination of cultural patterns reveals that all is not what it at first seems to be.

Examining cultural patterns allows us to notice a homogeneity to the choices that women often describe as purely playful and pleasurable self-expression. Susan Bordo, for example, notes that black women often describe hair-straightening as simply a matter of individual preference, to which no political significance should be attributed. They each just like 'hair that swings from side to side', as Oprah Winfrey put it (Bordo 1993: 255). But in 1989, 68 per cent of Essence magazine readers polled straightened their hair (p. 254). This uniformity casts doubt on the idea that individual preferences can tell the whole story.

Bordo notes that women are strongly encouraged by advertisements to think of their choices as free and playful—even while the advertisements are pushing particular ideals as the only acceptable ones. An Evian ad asks, 'If you could choose your own body, which would you choose?' A Nike ad maintains 'The body you have is the body you inherited, but you must decide what to do with it'.[1] These ads, which speak of choice, are accompanied by pictures only of a certain sort of body—in great shape, with perfect faces and 'hair that swings'. When they suggest choosing the sort of body you want, Bordo argues, they mean choosing that body from a *very* narrow range of choices.

If Bordo is right, then we can acknowledge a sense in which women's choices about their appearance are free and enjoyable (in the vast majority of cases, women are not being *forced* to do what they do) while still finding reason to worry. In particular, it is possible to criticize the narrow range of choices that are deemed acceptable, and that give enjoyment. Moreover, one can examine the political content of the ideals women are striving to attain. Bordo asks, for example, 'Does anyone in this culture have his or her nose reshaped to look more "African" or "Jewish"?' (Bordo 1993: 25). Marcia Ann Gillespie

---

[1] Increasingly, ads like this are directed at men as well as women. We will return to this point later in the chapter.

writes that when black women are considered beautiful by the media, they are nearly always blacks with features close to white ideals:

> When they do decree a Black woman beautiful, nine times out of ten she conforms to the white aesthetic. Take a close look at the women who are selected as models. Black but not really black: café au lait, not black coffee; pouty rather than full-lipped; a bit of butt but not too much.
>
> (Gillespie 1998: 185)

Gillespie recounts her conversations with Korean women about whom they consider beautiful: exclusively 'tall, all with blond or brunette hair, none of them who looked even vaguely like an Asian woman'.

Bordo argues, plausibly, that the uniformity of the looks which women choose to pursue suggests that more than individual preference is at work. In particular, it is worthwhile to examine the ways in which the range of acceptable bodies is carved out, and the political significance of the ideals that women are pursuing. With that in mind, I'll turn now to an examination of what I will call 'norms of feminine appearance'. In this examination, I will focus on negative aspects and effects of these norms. Later, I will return to the seeming paradox of how these negative aspects could coexist with the enjoyment we have already discussed.

Norms of feminine appearance

I will be using the phrase 'norms of feminine appearance' to refer to the standards of appearance that women are expected to live up to. By 'norms of feminine appearance' I do not mean the way that it is normal for women to appear. Rather, I mean the standards that women *feel* they should be living up to. Bordo is right, it seems to me, to maintain that these standards do exist, and that they are worthy of examination. The exact content of these norms changes rapidly and drastically over time. By the time you read this, the norms that I describe may well be outdated in certain respects.[2] Nonetheless, I will attempt to give a few examples of norms of feminine appearance.

---

[2] Indeed, this is one of the things that guarantees the norms will be a challenge to live up to: few (if any) women can naturally manage short hair one season followed by long hair the next.

Bodies

At the moment I write this, the prevailing body ideal in the US and UK includes large breasts and slim legs.[3] As Carol Tavris (Tavris 1992: 32–3) has pointed out, this sort of ideal is particularly difficult for most women to live up to: in general, if you diet enough to have the slim legs, your breasts will not be large. Living up to it fully will often require surgery—either liposuction for the legs or breast enlargement. This has not always been the desired body—norms have ranged from famously generous 'Rubenesque' proportions to the 'heroin chic' of the 1990s. Ideals of other times, though, are just as unnatural for many women. The simple reason is that women naturally come in a wide variety of sizes. Any one ideal will guarantee that large numbers of women will look 'wrong'.

The pressure to attain the culturally desirable body plays a very important role in the lives of most women today. It is a cultural commonplace that women are obsessed with dieting, and such concerns have increasingly been noticed even in young girls. According to some estimates, up to 80 per cent of women in the UK are 'concerned about their weight or dieting at any one time' (Farrell 1995: xi), and 80 per cent of US girls between grades three and six[4] 'feel bad about their bodies', while 70 per cent are on diets at any one time (McNaught 1998). We see this even in new products, like Samsung's A400 mobile phone for women. What makes it suited for women is that (aside from its makeup-mirror look), it includes a calorie counter and 'fatness calculator' (Quin 2002). Constant dieting is not a healthy way of life.

Susan Bordo has, in addition, argued that there are important connections between the rather standard phenomenon of dieting and the non-standard but disturbingly common[5] diseases of anorexia and

---

[3] The extent to which body ideals vary by cultural sub-groups is unclear. While some studies indicate, for example, that black women's and girls' ideals are less thin than white women's and girls', other studies show no difference, or even the reverse (Dittrich 2002).

[4] Approximately 8–10 years old.

[5] It is estimated that 0.5–3.7% of American women suffer from anorexia and that 1.1–4.2% of American women suffer from bulimia, over the course of their lives (National Institute of Mental Health 2002).

bulimia (Bordo 1993). While anorexia is far from fully understood and is almost certainly caused by more than just cultural pressure, Bordo suggests that it would be very surprising if constant pressure to be thin did not play a major role in this condition. It would be a remarkable coincidence, she suggests, if anorexia and bulimia just happened to be much more common in women than men (men make up only 5–15 per cent of US sufferers according to the National Institute of Mental Health 2002); and women just happened to face much more pressure than men to be thin. Bordo suggests that the connection is stronger than this. In particular, she focuses on the fact that many thought patterns initially thought to be crucial to understanding the motivations of anorexics and bulimics have turned out to be widespread among women. For example, anorexics and bulimics tend to perceive their bodies as larger than they are. This initially led researchers to suppose that perceptual anomalies might be responsible for these eating disorders. They later learned, however, that such distorted perceptions are extremely common among women—according to one study, 95 per cent of women without eating disorder symptoms overestimated the size of their bodies (Bordo 1993: 54–7). Bordo argues, on the basis of comparisons like these, that eating disorders among women should be seen as connected to norms of feminine appearance. Women with anorexia and bulimia are, according to her, taking cultural standards of female beauty (or even acceptability) to their natural—if extreme—conclusion.[6]

Many women also engage in plastic surgery in order to obtain the currently desirable body. Liposuction to remove fat and breast enlargement are the most popular operations. In the US in 2001, over 300,000 women had liposuction and over 200,000 had breast augmentation. In each case, the number of women embarking on the surgical procedure more than doubled over the five-year period 1997–2001 (American Society for Aesthetic Plastic Surgery 2002). The desire for surgery of this sort is strong enough to overcome the high cost (averaging, in 1999, $1,700 for liposuction and $3,800 for tummy tucks, according to Kiplinger's Personal Finance

---

[6] The emaciated body of the anorexic or bulimic, of course, does not live up to prevailing standards of feminine beauty, and Bordo does not deny this.

Magazine)—which is not paid by health insurance—and the risk of complications.[7]

Faces

A recent article in *Cosmopolitan* notes that:

> At our age, most of us are more concerned with mastering the art of walking in stiletto heels, than fending off wrinkles. But just because we can't see them, doesn't mean they're not lurking in our lifestyles, waiting to make an appearance.

> (Steinherr 2001a: 291)

Women are expected to keep themselves wrinkle-free for as long as possible, and to conceal any wrinkles that they may acquire. Images of women in magazines are carefully airbrushed to remove wrinkles in order to conceal all signs of ageing. One editor of two women's magazines writes, 'By now readers have no idea what a real woman's 60-year-old face looks like in print because it's made to look 45. Worse, 60-year-old readers look in the mirror and think they look too old, because they're comparing themselves to some retouched face smiling back at them from a magazine' (cited in Wolf 1991: 82–3). The demand to avoid wrinkles is especially problematic when combined with the common demand for tanning—sunbathing and tanning booths in one's youth lead to increased wrinkles later.[8]

Wrinkle-free skin is of course impossible in reality, beyond a certain age. But the pressure to postpone or conceal wrinkles is great. Women will go to great lengths to achieve these goals. Relatively harmlessly, Arlene Dahl's 1965 *Always Ask a Man* suggests a range of wrinkle-preventing exercises, including the following.

> To strengthen cheek muscles and maintain youthful facial contours: keeping upper and lower teeth slightly apart, make a large, round O with your mouth. Hold position for a count of 5. Then force mouth back into a wide grin (teeth still parted) and say 'aagh'. Hold for count of 5. Repeat five times.

> (Dahl 1965: 56)

---

7 $1,700 is approximately £1,133, and $3,800 is approximately £2,533.
8 Their carcinogenic tendencies should of course also be noted.

Wrinkle prevention is still a popular concern: a friend of mine was recently given (un-ironically) a twenty-fifth-birthday present of Oil of Olay, and the shelves of wrinkle-prevention creams in any drugstore will attest to the fact that this was not a bizarre aberration (except possibly in terms of social skills). Still, trying to prevent wrinkles via exercises and creams seems a pretty harmless waste of time (though, perhaps, a less harmless waste of money). Substantially more harmfully, plastic surgery to maintain a youthful appearance has become increasingly popular. One popular surgery to remove wrinkles is a face peel, described by one who underwent the procedure in the following words.

> Essentially, it is no different from a second-degree burn . . . [It] makes you go brown and crispy, then a scab forms and drops off . . . [it] takes several hours because it is so poisonous and you can't risk getting it into the bloodstream.
>
> (quoted by Wolf 1991: 256)

Most recently, botox injections—which involve injections of botulinum toxin (a toxin produced by the organism that causes botulism)—have become extremely popular. These injections hide wrinkles because they paralyse facial muscles. There were 1.6 million botox injection procedures performed in the United States in 2001, a 2,356 per cent increase in the five years since 1997 (American Society for Aesthetic Plastic Surgery 2002). Movie directors have begun to complain that the popularity of botox makes it difficult to find stars who are able to show facial expression (LeMieux 2002).

Wrinkles in men are often considered a mark of character, and are even taken to be attractive. In women, however, wrinkles are to be avoided at all costs. Aside from the very real price (financial, psychological, and physical) of efforts to conceal wrinkles, there is an important message carried by this double standard. Bartky notes that 'the face of the ideally feminine woman must never display the marks of character, wisdom, and experience that we so admire in men' (Bartky 1990a: 73). Instead, women must try to look as youthful as possible.

Freedom from wrinkles is not the only demand made on women's faces. Women also spend enormous amounts of time, energy, and money trying to achieve the right appearance for their faces—even if the current look is 'natural'. *Cosmopolitan* also weighs in on this topic: ' "Natural" doesn't equal no makeup. The season's low-key look still requires some effort and a few perfect products' (Steinherr 2001b: 269). Exactly what hairstyles and what sorts of makeup are desired changes dramatically across times and places. But not 'making an effort' is almost always unacceptable—particularly in the workplace. In 1982 Ann Hopkins, a successful accountant, was turned down for a partnership on the grounds that she needed to learn to 'walk more femininely, talk more femininely, dress more femininely', and 'wear makeup'.[9] One might think that such demands are a thing of the past, but a recent study claims that women who wear makeup earn 20–30 per cent more than those who do not (Reed 2002).

We have already noted the fact that plastic surgery is used to conceal signs of ageing. It is also used simply to obtain 'beautiful' faces, as these are culturally defined. Importantly, understandings of what is beautiful are not racially neutral. All too often, the feminine ideals that are applied to all women are based on the 'ideal' features for Anglo-Saxons, leading to a very disturbing racist element in views regarding what appearance is desirable.

> Jewish women demand reductions of their noses so as to be able to 'pass' as one of their Aryan sisters who form the dominant ethnic group . . . Adolescent Asian girls who bring in pictures of Elizabeth Taylor and of Japanese movie actresses (whose faces have already been reconstructed) demand the 'Westernizing' of their own eyes and the creation of higher noses in hopes of a better job and marital prospects.
>
> (Morgan 1998: 155)

Eugenia Kaw notes that the Asian women who have eyelid surgery that makes their eyes look more Western are reluctant to describe what they are doing in these terms. Instead, they will describe their

---

[9] Hopkins sued for sex discrimination and won. The court found that her employer had judged her behaviour by reference to a sex stereotype. (See *Hopkins v. Price-Waterhouse*, 741 F. 2d 1163; S. Ct. 1775; *Price Waterhouse v. Hopkins*, 490 U.S. 288.) The sex stereotype understanding of sex discrimination is discussed in more detail in Chapter 2.

eyes as looking unpleasantly 'slanted' or 'sleepy', and say that they want their eyes to look 'more open'. Often, they will report that they had difficulty properly applying eye makeup. (This last comment, notably, assumes that the way Westerners apply makeup must be the proper way.) Kaw argues that the descriptions these women give of their reasons for surgery show them to have internalized negative stereotypes of Asians, and that the result of this is a desire to rid themselves of Asian features. She further notes that Asian-Americans are more likely than any other ethnic group (including whites) to have cosmetic surgery (Kaw 1997: 55–73).

Those considering plastic surgery are encouraged to do so by plastic surgeons who present perfectly normal facial features as inadequate. As Kaw notes, there are worryingly racist overtones in writings like the following, from a 1990 textbook.

> . . . given an appreciation of the physical diversity of the Asian population, certain features do form a distinct basis for surgical intervention . . . These facial features typically include the upper eyelid, characterized by an absent or poorly defined superior palpebral fold . . . and a flattened nose with poor lobular definition.
>
> (McCurdy 1990: 1, cited in Kaw 1997: 176)

Eyelid surgery, which is the most popular cosmetic surgery among Asian-American women, is the third most popular form of plastic surgery overall in America. In 2001, over 200,000 women underwent eyelid surgery, an increase of 51 per cent since 1997 (American Society for Aesthetic Plastic Surgery 2002). Eyelid surgery costs from $1,000 to $3,000,[10] and carries risks of 'bleeding and hematoma', 'hemorrhage' and 'formation of a gaping wound' (Sayoc 1974: 162–6, cited in Kaw 1997: 177).

Lisa Jervis, a Jewish woman who was pressured by her mother to have a nose job, writes,

> [G]iven the society in which we live, the proximity of white features to the ideal of beauty is no coincidence. I think anyone who opts for a nose job today (or who pressured her daughter to do so) would say that the reason is to look 'better' or 'prettier'. But when we scratch the surface of

---

[10] $1,000–3,000 is £666–2,000.

what 'prettier' means, we find that we might as well be saying 'whiter' or 'more gentile'.

(Jervis 2000: 64)

Clothing

Women's clothing, of course, differs a great deal from one time and place to another. At some times and places they have been seriously damaging to women's bodies: an obvious past example is that of corsets, in which women had great difficulty moving and frequently fainted (Bordo 1993: 162). Of course, modern fashion is not this extreme.[11] But it can still pose problems. Women's clothes are far more likely than men's to restrict movement. And women still suffer foot problems from decades of forcing their feet into high-heeled and/ or excessively small shoes (American Academy of Orthopaedic Surgeons 2002), or—as in the north of England—shiver in February while wearing skimpy dresses at night.

The financial cost of the clothing women are expected to wear may also be considerable. Women's clothes tend to be more expensive and less durable than men's. Moreover, women are expected to own a far greater variety of outfits. This means that women will have to spend significantly more of their income on clothing than men do, and will thus have less money to spend on other items, or to save for the future.

Movement

Women are expected to keep close track of the way that they move their bodies. In general, women's movements are tightly constrained. Where men take large steps relative to their bodies, women take smaller ones, and women hold their arms closer to their bodies and sit so as to make themselves as small as possible. The postures women adopt in conversation—keeping their legs close together and not

---

11 Some have doubted, however, whether the manner in which we have moved away from corsets can be seen as much of an improvement: where corsets imposed a particular shape on bodies from the outside, the demand is now for bodies themselves to be shaped via dieting, exercise, or surgery (Davis 1995: 41).

taking up space, nodding deferentially and smiling a great deal—are exactly those which subordinates adopt when talking to those in power. The feminine way of carrying oneself and moving one's body, then, is the same as that which signals subordination.

> Women's typical body language, a language of relative tension and con-striction, is understood to be a language of subordination when it is enacted by men in male status hierarchies. In groups of men, those with higher status typically assume looser and more relaxed posture: the boss lounges comfortably behind a desk while the applicant sits tense and rigid on the edge of his seat . . . What is announced in the comportment of superiors is confidence and ease . . . women tend to set to and stand with legs, feet, and knees close or touching . . . One thing is clear: woman's body language speaks eloquently, though silently, of her subordinate status in a hierarchy of gender.
>
> (Bartky 1990a: 74)[12]

Inadequacy

A key message of many of these norms individually, and of the norms collectively, is that women are, by and large, *simply not good enough.* Arlene Dahl's advice manual suggests that all readers should 'Make this Beauty Resolution now: *"I hereby resolve to be more attractive!"'* (Dahl 1965: 23). This means she assumes that absolutely every woman who reads her book (it is very clearly directed at women)— no matter how attractive she already is—needs to be more attractive. This explicit statement seems laughable today, and my students gen-erally find it very funny. However, nearly every women's magazine at the newsagent's features on its cover articles on how 'you'—the reader—can improve your appearance. The assumption that all women's looks are in need of improvement is still alive and well. Moreover, this should not be surprising—few women manage natur-ally to live up to all of the rather demanding norms of feminine appearance. Women are told that they should 'at least make an effort'; many feel that they should not leave the house without makeup (or,

---

[12] On female movement, see also Young (1990a). For a critical discussion sug-gesting that Bartky (1990a; 1990b) and Young (1990a) idealize male movement, see Grimshaw (1999).

as some say, 'putting their face on'); and women who no longer adhere to standard beauty regimes are accused of 'letting themselves go'. The message of all this is that there is something inherently inadequate about women's natural appearance.

Adherence to norms

In the text above, I have occasionally juxtaposed discussions of norms of appearance with quotations from women's magazines. But it is far too simple-minded to suppose that women follow these norms simply because they read women's magazines and do everything that they are told to do. The elements of the culture that contribute to women's adherence to these norms deserve further analysis—and even women's magazines are not as simple as they seem.

The complex message of women's magazines

Women's magazines do not actually give only one message to their readers. *Cosmopolitan's* May 2002 issue provides a good example of this. This issue has a cover story entitled 'Banish Your Body Hang-Ups', surely a good sign for those who want to fight women's negative body images. The article consists of interviews with women and their partners, in which women explain what they hate about their bodies and their partners explain why they actually love those very of traits. Again, this sounds good—and it is. But, unfortunately, the page about a woman who thinks her hair is too 'wild' and 'thick' is faced by an advertisement featuring a model with perfectly smooth hair; and the page about women who find their noses too large is faced by an ad featuring a model with a small nose, half hidden by her hair. The body-positive message of the article is repeatedly undermined by the messages of the advertisements appearing throughout it.

Part of the explanation for women's magazines' mixed messages may come from a conflict between editors' desires and advertisers' demands. Although women's magazines are known mainly for their fashion and beauty articles, this is not all that they contain. Julia Hanigsberg writes:

Women's magazines have covered most of the critical feminist issues of recent years. All have emphasized that women who are battered are never at fault, that the glass ceiling should be fought, that women should earn equal pay for equal work, that 'no means no,' that women have a right to fight unwelcome sexual advances, that men should be equal participants in housework and childcare responsibilities, and that the criminal and judicial systems are prejudiced against rape victims.

(Hanigsberg 1997: 74–5)

Indeed, *Glamour*'s editor-in-chief, Ruth Whitney, describes her publication as 'a mainstream feminist magazine' (Hanigsberg 1997: 73). Editors, then, *may* want to promote a feminist agenda, and even specifically to improve women's body images (as in the *Cosmopolitan* issue mentioned above).[13] Nonetheless, these magazines remain filled with insecurity-inducing advertisements, and articles on how to get just the 'right' look.

Magazines cannot survive without advertising. A key method advertisers use is that of generating new wants or needs in people. One of the most powerful ways to do this is to generate or build on insecurities in such a way as to make people believe products can help them to overcome what they see as their inadequacies (Kilbourne 2000). There is a great deal of money to be made from women's appearance-related insecurities. Advertisers, then, do not want women to be secure about themselves. They also exercise enormous control over the magazines in which they advertise. Advertisers not only place advertisements designed to make women insecure enough to buy their products, but they also make content-related demands of magazines. They often insist that certain sorts of stories must run next to their advertisements: they want articles on makeup to accompany their makeup ads, articles on hair care to accompany their hair product ads, and so on.

Food advertisers have always demanded that women's magazines publish recipes and articles on entertaining (preferably ones that name their products) in return for their ads; clothing advertisers expect to be

---

[13] I do not mean to suggest that all editors' of women's magazines are like this— merely that some are, and that the content of women's magazines is more complicated than it is generally taken to be.

surrounded by fashion spreads (especially ones that credit their designers); and shampoo, fragrance, and beauty products in general insist on positive editorial coverage of beauty subjects . . . That's why women's magazines look the way they do.

(Steinem 2002: 60)

Whatever the women running the magazines may want, then, if they wish their magazines to survive they must do what advertisers want them to do—and advertisers want insecure women who will spend a fortune on their products. Even *Ms.* magazine, founded as an explicitly feminist magazine, was forced to accept advertisements which undermined its message to such an extent that—when *Ms.* finally gave up on advertising revenue altogether—it featured some of these ads as examples of destructive images of women.[14]

Women's magazines do sometimes have editors who want to publish articles that combat common female insecurities. And they even sometimes publish such articles. But even when such articles are published, they are swamped by other articles and advertisements whose message is quite the opposite. The thought that women are influenced by the media, then, remains plausible despite the mixed messages of women's magazines.

Some think it insulting to suggest that women are influenced by the media in this way—that it portrays women as easily manipulated dupes of advertisers. But the fact is that women, like men, *are* influenced by advertising. That is why companies spend so much time, money, and effort on it. There is nothing insulting about saying that women are affected by advertising. Nonetheless, we would miss a great deal if we focused only on what norms are touted by advertisers as desirable. We need to examine other elements of the culture, and also to look closely at the complicated ways that women (and men) relate to them.

---

[14] There have very recently been some interesting changes in advertisers' demands, due to the discovery that women are especially interested in reading certain sorts of news stories in women's magazines. 'Now, the ad pages that accompany domestic and international rights abuse stories are getting top dollar in *Marie Claire*, largely because readers polled say these are among the pages they read the most' (Sandler 2002).

Culture at large

Advertising does not take place in a vacuum. It taps into elements that are already present in a culture, and presumably would not be so successful if it didn't do so. So, for example, advertisements and beauty articles will focus on goals such as 'taking control of your life' or 'becoming who you've always wanted to be'.[15] Women (like men) want to feel that they are in charge of their lives, and want to improve themselves. Moreover, these goals seem worthy ones. It may seem, however, that nobody should be so easily taken in as to suppose that weight loss and beauty products are the right ways to achieve these goals. However, it is not only advertisements spreading the message that beauty and weight loss should have this importance. To name a few other sources of this idea: most girls grow up with mothers who worry about their weight; we all see many thin women, perhaps thinner than we are, complaining that they are too fat; we read critical commentary on the slightest 'flaws' in celebrities' appearances. Moreover, all this is too often presented as of great importance. Boys, too, grow up in this culture—and they also learn how women 'should' look.[16] Susan Bordo notes that women in her classes write in their journals about their boyfriends' pressure to lose weight, or to look like particular celebrities; and that men write about their girlfriends' 'flaws' in a perfectly parallel manner (Bordo 1993.). We are all taught, from a large variety of sources, that women's appearance is vitally important. It is not surprising, then, that women respond to messages suggesting that they improve themselves by improving their appearance.

---

[15] Susan Bordo gives many examples of this in *Unbearable Weight*.

[16] Actually, the relationship between men's desires and women's attitudes is complex. Several studies have presented women with drawings of women's bodies, and asked them what size men find attractive. The size women pick is smaller than the size men actually pick, when they are presented with the drawings. Still, the size men pick is smaller than (women's self-reports of) women's actual size. See e.g. Forbes et al. (2001) and Rozin and Fallon (1988).

Internalization of norms

Many of my students maintain that discussions like those in the previous two sections just don't ring true for them: they don't feel that they are following the dictates of fashion magazines, or even of broader cultural pressures, when they spend time on their appearance. Instead, they feel quite strongly that they are doing this *for themselves*. Sometimes this is described as something they do simply for the fun of it, but more often as the effort to live up *to their own* standards: they just won't be happy with themselves if they don't look the way they want to look.

Sandra Bartky discusses this sort of conviction that the pressure is self-imposed. She suggests that it reflects the way that society's norms have been internalized. This sort of internalized pressure is, according to Bartky, potentially even more debilitating than merely trying to live up to the standards of others—it cannot be escaped in the way that pressure from outside can be. Women are 'self-policing subjects', who place upon themselves a constant and relentless pressure (Bartky 1990a). Her analysis is based on Michel Foucault's discussion of the Panopticon (Foucault 1979), a model prison proposed by the philosopher Jeremy Bentham (1748–1832). This prison would consist of a central watchtower surrounded on all sides by cells with windows that were lit from behind. The inmates in these cells would know that they might be watched at any time by the guards in the watchtower, but they would never know at any particular time whether they were in fact being watched. If they were being watched, anything they did would be seen, and the prisoners would be aware of this fact—whether or not they *were* actually being watched. Bentham considered this to be an ideal prison arrangement because, he thought, the prisoners would have to constantly behave *as though* they were being watched—for fear that they *might* be. They would, then, become self-policing, because the knowledge that they might be watched would cause them to engage only in actions that are acceptable to their watchers. Thus, external constraints are transformed into constraints that one places on oneself.

Bartky argues that women, like the inmates in the Panopticon, are self-policing. Women, according to Bartky, think of themselves as always potentially being observed and judged. So, she argues, they constantly watch themselves for any deviation from acceptable standards of appearance. This causes women to exist somewhat at a distance from themselves, always watching, judging, and criticizing. Self-policing, Bartky argues, renders women—in a very important respect—unfree. Every waking moment of every day, women must make sure that their appearance conforms to acceptable standards:

> The woman who checks her makeup half a dozen times a day to see if her foundation has caked or her mascara run, who worries that the wind or rain may spoil her hairdo, who looks frequently to see if her stockings have bagged at the ankle, or who, feeling fat, monitors everything she eats, has become, just as surely as the inmate of the Panopticon, a self-policing subject, a self committed to a relentless self-surveillance.
>
> (Bartky 1990a: 80)

Or, as Arlene Dahl approvingly put it in her 1965 advice manual for women,

> Each woman has an audience (hopefully, male!), and must live up to the image she wants to project. She should present her best self at all times. (You never know who's looking.)
>
> (Dahl 1965: 7)

Dahl actually takes this requirement to go beyond the waking hours of the day, discussing what colour lipstick women should wear to bed, and worrying that the curlers women must wear to bed are aesthetically displeasing. (She helpfully designed and marketed a boudoir cap to conceal curlers and thus deal with the problem (Dahl 1965: 112, 171).)

Dahl's advice, of course, probably seems dated—surely no such advice would be given today, you may think. But, flipping through the pages of *Cosmopolitan*, one might wonder how much times really have changed. The following comes from an article from February 2001 entitled, 'You, but sexier—18 showoff positions to flatter your figure in bed'. A sample suggestion:

> While in the missionary position, the flesh on your stomach falls back and to the sides, making your stomach look flatter. But be warned: one

false move—like rolling over onto your side or bending double—and any
little rolls of fat will be magnified.

(Kelly 2001: 101)

If women do think in the way suggested by this article, then it is surely
right that women are self-policing—that they constantly scrutinize
their bodies disapprovingly, striving at all times to live up to the norms
of appearance that they have internalized. And most women will
acknowledge that (whether or not they have the particular insecurities
suggested by the *Cosmopolitan* article) there is something to the idea
that they police their bodies for deviations from the desired norms.

Self-policing may easily go unnoticed, and it can be hard to see it as
a problem. The idea that one places restrictions on oneself and that
this constitutes a lack of freedom is a strange and un-obvious one.
Moreover, following one's own constraints and restrictions can be a
vital part of living as one wants to live. Forcing oneself to get up every
morning and work toward a long-term goal can be very important to
living well. We do not see people who do this as unfree because they
are placing constraints on themselves. Even monitoring one's appearance does not necessarily seem problematic: it is hard to imagine
worrying much about the lack of freedom exhibited by making sure
one's fly is fastened, or remembering to brush one's teeth.[17] But
Bartky is not committed to the idea that all self-monitoring is a problem. For Bartky, women's self-policing is a problem because the
norms women impose on themselves are often unattainable ones, and
the effort to live up to them leads to psychological or physical damage.

This claim of psychological damage may not seem to sit well with
the enjoyment women get from their appearance-related efforts. But
policing oneself in damaging ways is perfectly compatible with
enjoyment. Bordo writes, for example:

> Putting on makeup, styling hair, and so forth are conceived of only as free
> *play*, fun, a matter of creative expression. This they surely are. But they
> are also experienced by many women as necessary before they will show
> themselves to the world, even on a quick trip to the corner mailbox.

(Bordo 1993: 253)

---

[17] Exercise routines, even the much-criticized aerobics classes, may also be
empowering (Grimshaw 1999).

Women enjoy putting on makeup, according to Bordo, but they also *demand* it of themselves. The fact that enjoyment can co-exist with this sort of feeling of obligation allows Bartky to argue that women's enjoyment does not count against the idea that they are self-policing.

We have noted already that women enjoy buying makeup, reading about fashion, and losing weight. Bartky argues that these pleasures are not what they seem. The satisfaction that women experience from conforming to feminine norms is what she calls a 'repressive satisfaction': repressive satisfactions serve to keep women attached to and invested in a system that is ultimately damaging to them. In particular, the satisfaction stems from a state of mind that she describes as one of 'infatuation with an inferiorized body'(Bartky 1990b: 40). Rather than making women feel good about themselves, all the attention devoted to appearance only serves to reinforce each woman's idea of her own inadequacy. Susan Bordo describes the combination of enjoyment and inadequacy nicely:

> I love shopping for makeup with my friends . . . Women bond over shared makeup, shared beauty tips. It's fun. Too often, though, our bond is over shared pain—over 'bad' skin, 'bad' hair, 'bad' legs. There's always that constant judgment and evaluation—not only by actual, living men but by an ever-present, watchful cultural gaze which always has its eye on our thighs—no matter how much else we accomplish.
>
> (Bordo 1999: 217)

This situation is made worse by the fact that women, as well as men, view excessive concern with one's appearance as self-indulgent: 'women are ridiculed and dismissed for the triviality of their interest in such "trivial" things as clothes and makeup' (Bartky 1990a: 73). So, at the same time that women feel they must work hard to conform to feminine ideals, they think that the time and effort they devote to doing this is wasted on a trivial and unworthy activity. The pleasure women get from time, effort, and money spent on their appearances is reduced not only by physical and psychological damage they may do themselves, but also by their own view that such efforts are unworthy. If Bartky is right, then the mixed messages of women's magazines may actually be seriously problematic: on the one hand, they contain articles telling women that they *shouldn't* obsess about their bodies; on the other hand, they contain advertisements (and other articles) that help to perpetuate these obsessions. As a result—whatever good intentions there may be—these mixed messages contribute to the very problematic state of mind of feeling on one hand that one must worry about one's appearance and on the other that it's wrong to do so.

Reasonableness of women's responses

Feminists are often thought to believe that any woman who follows norms of feminine appearance has been brainwashed into a completely irrational behaviour. But if feminist criticisms are right, then women who follow prevailing norms of appearance may be behaving in perfectly reasonable ways. According to feminist criticisms, there are constraints in the world that can make it difficult for women to function without living up to these norms of appearance. This means that one way for women to do the things they want to do may well be to follow these norms. In addition, successfully following norms of appearance may be crucial to women's self-esteem. Living up to these norms, then, can be seen as reasonable.

As we have seen, the need to live up to feminine norms is reinforced in a multitude of ways—in the media, but also in the attitudes of employers, family, and peers. A woman who thinks that adhering to these norms is important cannot be understood simply as brainwashed and irrational. Susan Bordo suggests instead that she is someone who sees, accurately, that living up to these norms is important for her goals in life. She writes, discussing women who had dangerous silicone breast implants,

> These women take the risk, not because they have been passively taken in by media norms of the beautiful breast (almost always silicone-enhanced), but because they have correctly discerned that these norms shape the perceptions and desires of potential lovers and employers . . .
>
> (Bordo 1993: 20)

Kathy Davis argues, on the basis of interviews with women who have undergone dangerous plastic surgery, that women's desires for such operations should not be understood as irrational. Women who undergo such surgery live in societies that place a high premium on attaining the proper feminine appearance, and women who cannot do this may be gripped by powerful feelings of inadequacy. Such feelings not only get in the way of women's pursuit of non-appearance-related goals, but also block women from achieving a comfortable relationship with their own bodies. Davis argues that having surgery, for such women, *may* be a way to change their lives for the better. It may also be combined with a serious and well-considered critique of the norms that make them view their bodies as inadequate.

> Contrary to the popular stereotypes of the scalpel slave and the female with a predilection for the surgical fix, these women seemed highly critical of the beauty norms which compelled them to take such a drastic step. They were invariably skeptical about cosmetic surgery as a general remedy for women's dissatisfaction with their appearance. Instead it was presented as the lesser of two evils rather than as an answer to all their problems.
>
> (Davis 1995: 162)

Having plastic surgery, for some women at least, can be a way of dealing with the social pressures—external or internal—that cause them to be consumed by feelings of inadequacy. Surgery may, in some cases, be a way to set aside appearance-related anxieties so that they can live the lives they want to live. Susan Bordo discusses TV star Sara Gilbert's rationale for her decision to have a nose job, which seems to come from just such thoughts:

> I think it's important to be attractive to yourself. Your body just kind of gets in the way of what you want to do. So if you're concentrating that much energy on your body, then just change it so you can move on and deal with the intellectual.
>
> (Bordo 1993: 296)

Gilbert's decision to have plastic surgery seems a carefully thought-out response to her own concerns about her appearance. She did not want to continue to spend time and energy being worried and unhappy about her appearance, so she changed it.

How effective is plastic surgery as a response to cultural pressures? It is unclear. Davis insists that most of the women she interviewed were happier post-surgically than they were prior to surgery, even though many of them had suffered repeated and debilitating side-effects of surgery, and even though in some cases the surgery worsened the woman's perceived original problem (as with breast implants gone wrong). These women, Davis insists, felt stronger, happier, and more in control of their lives because they had attempted changes that meant a great deal to them, whether or not their attempts were successful. On the other hand, Bordo writes of women who are never satisfied with a single operation, and instead constantly strive to get closer to their desired perfection—a striving which consumes huge amounts of time, money, and psychological energy, and which may lead to serious health problems.

It is uncertain whether or not surgery—or, more generally, an effort to adhere to norms of appearance—is an individually effective response to the pressures women face. Nonetheless, it is important to recognize that these may be rational and well-thought-out responses. As writers like Bartky insist, these pressures *are* strong ones, and they may for some be pressures that cannot be overcome through strength of will. Or, even if they can be overcome in this way, doing so may not be the best use of a woman's time and energy. One who takes seriously the strength and extent of appearance-related pressures on women should recognize the possible rationality of women's efforts to live up to norms of appearance. To do otherwise is, according to Davis, a failure of respect. She describes her response to a paper that describes women who undergo plastic surgery as Stepford Wives, 'diabolically transformed into robots by husbands in search of perfect wives' (Davis 1995: 176):

> . . . I remembered the women who [I interviewed] . . . I found myself jumping to their defense: their faces had not been empty or vacuous; *they* had not been placid robots, merely complying with their husbands' desires for a servant with big breasts. In short, *they* were nothing like Stepford Wives. I became increasingly irritated at this image, which erased their suffering, their struggles, their protest against circumstances which made cosmetic surgery their only viable course of action.

Recognizing the possibility that women like those interviewed by Davis were responding thoughtfully and rationally to the pressures placed on them by no means robs us of the ability to criticize these pressures. Indeed, the very fact that engaging in dangerous plastic surgery could be considered a rational action is a powerful indictment of the pressures placed on women.

Self-policing and reflection on oneself

We have seen that women often enjoy spending time and effort on their appearance, and take themselves to be exercising their own individual preferences. Yet, I have argued, this is perfectly compatible with feminist critiques of norms of feminine appearance. Nonetheless, the positive aspects of women's experience with feminine norms of appearance make it more difficult to discern the problems. Some problems are obvious: silicone breast implants are dangerous and tanning booths cause cancer. But most women do not have silicone breast implants, and do not go to tanning booths. Without obvious problems like this, it can be harder to see grounds for worry.

If all women felt (as some of course do) that norms of appearance are damaging to them, the problem would be hard to miss. But, as we have seen, the grounds for feminist critique emerge most clearly when we step back from individual experiences to look at the system of norms and its patterns of effects. These patterns include both societal patterns (such as seeking out only particular sorts of noses) and patterns in individuals' lives (such as self-policing). The self-observation involved in self-policing is a worrying one. But, as Pamela Anderson has pointed out, not all self-observation is so worrying. In particular, the sort of self-observation involved in coming to see one's relationship to norms of feminine appearance, and in realizing that one is self-policing, can be an immensely valuable one.

Some of my students resist the criticisms that Bartky makes of women's beauty-related pursuits, insisting that there is something insulting in her portrayal of women. What they find insulting is the idea that women are victims of external forces that push them into self-destructive pursuits. But Bartky's view does not require that women be especially sensitive to external forces: although the content of the norms she discusses is specific to women, the internalization of external norms is not. Moreover, the capacity for self-observation, so crucial to self-policing, can be turned to useful ends.

For Susan Bordo, this capacity is vital to feminism. She calls for reflection upon oneself and one's relationship to cultural forces. For Bordo, this reflection is the primary course of action that feminism can recommend. Reflection on oneself and on cultural patterns can allow one to distinguish what is genuinely valuable and pleasurable from what is in fact destructive, and to weigh up the pleasurable and destructive elements of particular norms or ways of pursuing them. As a result of such reflection, one *may* still decide to follow the norms, but one will do so with a greater awareness of their full cultural context and effects.

> [F]eminist cultural criticism is not a blueprint for the conduct of personal life (or political action, for that matter) and does not empower (or require) individuals to 'rise above' their culture or to become martyrs to feminist ideals. It does not tell us what to *do* . . . whether to lose weight or not, wear makeup or not, lift weights or not. Its goal is edification and understanding, enhanced *consciousness* of the power, complexity, and *systemic* nature of culture, the interconnected webs of its functioning. It is up to the reader to decide how, when, and where (or whether) to put that understanding to further use in the particular, complicated, and ever-changing context that is his or her life and no one else's.
>
> (Bordo 1993: 30)

Men, too?

Men, like women, are expected to dress, look, and move in particular ways. Indeed, Marilyn Frye has argued that both men and women are required to engage in what she calls sex-marking behaviour (Frye 1983a). According to Frye, we begin to see the emphasis that our society places on sex when we realize the extent to which each person is expected to make clear what sex they are. Even when clothing styles are relatively androgynous, as they sometimes are, there will be differences in the ways that males and females dress. Men may wear earrings, but there are certain kinds of earring that only women wear. Women's hairstyles will generally be somewhat different from men's, even during periods when relatively similar male and female hair lengths are in style. Even at their most androgynous, then, women and men can generally be distinguished from one another at a glance. And most of the time, men and women are not at their most androgynous. Workplace clothing, in particular, remains sharply distinct for men and women. A student of mine in 1999 was told that if she must wear a black trouser suit to a job interview, she should be sure to wear a pink shirt, in order to look sufficiently feminine. Also important are the less obvious markers of maleness and femaleness—as we have already noted, there are distinctive postures and forms of movement associated with maleness and femaleness.

> There are different styles of gait, gesture, posture, speech, humour, taste and even of perception, interest and attention that we learn as we grow up to be women or to be men and that label and announce us as women or as men.

> (Frye 1983a: 24)

In order to engage in normal social interaction, then, we are required to know the sex of others and to constantly announce our own sex in countless ways. As Frye notes,

> We are a gregarious species. Our lives depend on our abilities to interact with others in relations of work, of exchange and of sympathy. What one cannot do without seeming excessively odd or unintelligible, one cannot do without severe disturbance to patterns of interaction upon which one's life depends. Sex-marking behaviour is not optional; it is as obligatory as it is pervasive.

> (Frye 1983a: 21)

This pressure to dress, look, and move in appropriate ways for one's sex falls no less heavily on men than on women. It would be wrong, then, to suppose that only women are subject to norms of appearance.

Moreover, men are increasingly subject to appearance-related pressures similar to those faced by women. They have, of course, always been expected to wear particular styles of clothing, or to have particular hairstyles. But in recent years, the expectations have grown. Men's magazines have proliferated—a few of them nearly as filled as women's magazines with stories on how to get the perfect body, and what clothes to wear. Men's makeup has in recent years become a booming cosmetic industry. Male appearance-related insecurity is growing. According to a 1994 survey, three of men's top six desires for themselves were to be 'attractive to women', 'sexy', and 'good-looking' (Bordo 1999: 219). From 1994 to 1999, the number of men having liposuction tripled (Fraser 1999). All of this leads some of my students to insist that feminist criticism of norms of appearance is now misplaced—these norms and their effects, at least now, have nothing in particular to do with women. Everyone faces such pressures, and we should all simply accept this.

One way to respond to this argument is to point out that there are differences in the sorts of expectation placed on men and women: women are expected to wear more uncomfortable clothing, to have more outfits, to spend more time on their appearance, and certainly to wear more makeup. Frye's 1983 comments still largely ring true:

> As feminists have been saying for two hundred years or so, ladies' clothing is generally restrictive, binding, burdening and frail; it threatens to fall apart and/or to uncover something that is supposed to be covered if you bend, reach, kick, punch or run. It typically does not protect effectively against hazards in the environment . . . Men's clothing is generally the opposite of all this—sturdy, suitably protective, permitting movement and locomotion. The details of feminine posture serve to bind and restrict. To be feminine is to take up little space, to defer to others, to be silent or affirming of others, etc . . . the behavior which announces femaleness is in itself both physically and socially binding and limiting as the behavior which announces maleness is not.
>
> (Frye 1983a: 32)

Appearance-related pressures are still far stronger on women than men. Women still spend far more money on cosmetic surgery (Fraser 1999), and far more time and effort on their appearance. In addition, women seem to feel far greater dissatisfaction with their bodies. The pressures on women seem (at least so far) to have a much more damaging effect than the pressures on men.[18] All these are good reasons for feminists to take a particular interest in norms of feminine appearance and in the effects of these norms.

---

[18] Grimshaw (1999) argues, however, that there is to some extent a problematic idealization of male modes of movement in claims like these.

But it is important also to acknowledge that the appearance-related demands on men are indeed well worth discussing. Acknowledging this does nothing to undermine feminist criticisms. The fact that men, too, are increasingly subject to the sorts of pressure that women have traditionally faced should not be cheering to anyone. If men are now becoming self-policing subjects, this signals not a desirable gender equity but a very sad state of affairs. If anything, the fact that norms of appearance place serious pressure on both women and men only demonstrates the urgency and importance of criticizing them. Susan Bordo has now turned her attention to masculine appearance, as well as feminine appearance. In *The Male Body*, she writes:

> If someone had told me in 1977 that in 1997 *men* would comprise over a quarter of cosmetic-surgery patients, I would have been astounded. I never dreamed that 'equality' would move in the direction of men worrying *more* about their looks rather than women worrying *less*. I first suspected that something major was going on when the guys in my gender classes stopped yawning and passing snide notes when we discussed body issues, and instead began to protest when the women talked as though they were the only ones 'oppressed' by standards of beauty.
>
> (Bordo 1999: 217–18)

The increasing pressure on men to conform to unattainable standards of beauty is far from a sign of progress: it is, instead, a sign that the problem has grown.

SUGGESTIONS FOR FURTHER READING

Worries regarding feminine norms

Bartky, S., 'Foucault, Femininity, and the Modernization of Patriarchal Power', in *Femininity and Domination*. New York: Routledge, 1990, 63–82.

—— 'Narcissism, Femininity, and Alienation', in *Femininity and Domination*. New York: Routledge, 1990, 33–44.

—— *Unbearable Weight: Feminism, Western Culture, and the Body*. Berkeley: University of California Press, 1993.

Frye, M., 'Sexism', in *The Politics of Reality: Essays in Feminist Theory*. Freedom, Calif.: Crossing Press, 1983, 17–40.

Gillespie, M. A., 'Mirror Mirror', in R. Weitz (ed.), *The Politics of Women's*

Bodies: Sexuality, Appearance, and Behaviour. Oxford: Oxford University Press, 1998, 184–8.

Jervis, L., 'My Jewish Nose', in O. Edut (ed.), *Body Outlaws: Young Women Write about Body Image and Identity*. Seattle: Seal Press, 2000, 62–7.

Kaw, E., 'Medicalization of Racial Features: Asian-American Women and Cosmetic Surgery', in R. Weitz (ed.), *The Politics of Women's Bodies: Sexuality, Appearance, and Behaviour*. Oxford: Oxford University Press, 1998, 55–73.

Morgan, K. P., 'Women and the Knife: Cosmetic Surgery and the Colonization of Women's Bodies', in R. Weitz (ed.), *The Politics of Women's Bodies: Sexuality, Appearance, and Behaviour*. Oxford: Oxford University Press, 1998.

Young, I. M., 'Throwing Like a Girl: A Phenomenology of Feminine Body Comportment, Mobility, and Spatiality', in *Throwing Like a Girl and Other Essays in Feminist Philosophy and Social Theory*. Bloomington: Indiana University Press, 1990, 141–59.

Emphasizing enjoyment of femininity

Richards, J. R., 'The Unadorned Feminist', in *The Sceptical Feminist*. London: Routledge, 1980, 181–206.

Walter, N., *The New Feminism*. London: Little, Brown, 1998.

Young, I. M., 'Women Recovering Our Clothes', in *Throwing Like a Girl and Other Essays in Feminist Philosophy and Social Theory*. Bloomington: Indiana University Press, 1990, 177–88.

Defending the rationality of women's plastic surgery decisions

Davis, K., *Reshaping the Female Body: The Dilemma of Cosmetic Surgery*. New York: Routledge, 1995.

Website offering body image facts

About-Face: www.about-face.orgshr/facts/ses.html

6

Feminism and Language Change

Some of the most familiar demands of feminism are demands for language reform. Nearly everyone is acquainted with the idea that feminists object to certain traditional uses of language—such as using 'man' to refer to the entire human species. In some quarters, such as academia, proposals for change have been fairly successful. In others, they have met with great resistance, and been viewed as pointless and objectionable instances of political correctness gone mad. The public prominence of reform proposals, and the diversity of views over their legitimacy, is one good reason to look closely at this topic. Another reason is the sheer interest of what comes from a close look at it. While feminists generally agree that some reform is a good idea (though there are differences of opinion over which proposals are good ones, their prospects for success, and their importance), there is much less agreement on the reasons for reform. Although I find fault with some of the arguments that have been given for feminist reforms of language, I argue below that many of the reforms are justified, and that their prospects for success are sufficiently promising to make them worthwhile. Nonetheless, there are compelling arguments showing that one should not take reform of specific terms to be enough to bring about an end to sexist language use, and that reform of language alone cannot succeed.

I will begin by discussing some of the best-known examples of feminist calls for reform of language. I've chosen just a few examples to discuss simply because it is impossible to cover the full range of proposals in one chapter. (For more comprehensive discussions, see Miller and Swift 1976; Cameron 1985; 1998; Penelope 1990; Spender 1985.) I will begin with complaints about supposedly gender-neutral uses of the terms 'he' and 'man'. Interestingly, worries have also been raised about the gender-specificity of terms such as 'manageress'[1] or 'waitress'. I will discuss these worries individually, but I shall also tackle the question of how well concerns over gender-specificity fit with concerns over gender-neutrality. After this, I will turn to problems with these calls for reform. The first set of objections comes from those who think that all feminist reforms of language are either undesirable or impossible. I will argue that none of these objections succeeds. However, another set of criticisms accepts the desirability of reform, but raises the worry that the most common feminist reforms either do not or cannot go far enough. I will conclude that while some of these suggestions are misguided, others are quite compelling.

Gender-neutrality

The problem

There are some terms in English that are said to have both gender-neutral and gender-specific meanings. 'Man' is used gender-specifically in a sentence like 'A man does not have ovaries': clearly women are not meant to be the subject of the sentence. 'Man' *might* be meant gender-neutrally in 'Man is a rational animal': the speaker might well mean to include women among those she is discussing. 'He' is used gender-specifically in a sentence like 'My brother went to the store and he bought a lot of garlic'. 'He' might be used gender-neutrally in a sentence like 'When an American arrives in Britain he will be surprised by the number of words that he does not understand'. (Similar considerations apply to the closely related terms 'men' and 'his'.)

Many feminists have objected to the gender-neutral use of 'he' and 'man', arguing either that these terms are not truly gender-neutral or that there are good reasons to avoid the gender-neutral use of words that also refer exclusively to males. It is important to note that these

---

[1] 'Manageress' is a relatively common term in the UK, though not in the US.

arguments do not depend on the idea that one who uses the terms 'he' and 'man' intending them gender-neutrally is somehow blameworthy, or that such a person must intend to give offence, or to exclude women. Such an argument would be implausible, as the gender-neutral usage of these terms has been taught to many speakers as correct, and need not be an indication of any particular mindset. Instead, feminist objections turn on the idea that, whatever speakers intend, there is still something wrong with (supposedly) gender-neutral usage of these terms.

Potential for confusion

A first reason for opposing apparently gender-neutral uses of terms like 'man' and 'he' is the potential for confusion that they bring with them. Because these terms have both gender-specific and gender-neutral meanings, one might have difficulty discerning which meaning is intended in a particular use. Imagine that an exam is given, after students have been taught the stereotypical version of early humanity's existence, with women as gatherers and men as hunters. The exam contains the question,

> Was early man a gatherer?

Students might quite legitimately be confused by this question: If 'man' is meant gender-neutrally, the expected answer is 'yes', while if 'man' is meant gender-specifically the expected answer is 'no'.[2] Perhaps more worryingly, one might be confused by a job advertisement that read,

> The successful applicant will have the following traits: he will be friendly, energetic, hard-working, and punctual.

A woman reading this advertisement might be uncertain about whether it was appropriate for her to apply. In order to avoid the potential for this sort of confusion, then, terms that function as both gender-specific and gender-neutral should be avoided.

---

[2] This sort of example is inspired by Mercier (1995). I am, however, not using the example she uses to make this point, which involves the question 'Who was the first man to fly westerly across the Atlantic?' My reason is that I am not certain that the 'gender-neutral' meaning of 'man' even seems to be available in it.

This argument does not depend on the idea that one should in general avoid ambiguous words (words that have more than one meaning). This idea would be ludicrous, as most languages are filled with ambiguous words like 'bank' and 'rose'. Attempting to avoid all ambiguous words would be an enormous and unnecessary effort. Most of the time, it is very clear what is meant by an ambiguous term. When someone says, 'I am going to the bank to deposit some money', nobody supposes (at least in ordinary circumstances) that the speaker is heading to the river. The situation is different, however, with terms like 'he' and 'man'. Because the gender-neutral use is meant to include all of those people who are excluded by the gender-specific use, the potential for confusion is much greater and has the potential to do more harm: there are many more cases in which one might be unsure which meaning is intended.

Nonetheless, an argument for linguistic reform based only on the potential for confusion would not get very far. As Deborah Cameron has pointed out, in the vast majority of cases we *are* able to tell which uses are meant to be gender-neutral and which gender-specific.

> If I see a banner saying 'All men are equal' I know I can join the demonstration; if I see the word MEN on the entrance to a public lavatory, I know I am not supposed to enter.
>
> (Cameron 1998: 10)

Cameron's first example is a little unfortunate: 'All men are equal' is precisely the sort of phrase that has (at least historically) involved a very limited meaning of 'men'—limited not just to males, but to white, property-owning males. Still, she is right to note that even if the potential for confusion is greater with terms like 'men' and 'he' than with terms like 'bank', it is far from ubiquitous. In most real-life contexts, confusion is not likely to arise. The desire to avoid confusion might well motivate us to avoid gender-neutral terms where there is potential for confusion, but would give us no motivation to do so when context makes the meaning clear.

Effects on thought

A more compelling problem for the use of gender-neutral terms is that even when they do not confuse us, they do affect the way that we think. In particular, studies have shown that readers of terms like 'man' and 'he' tend to think more readily of males than of females (Erlich and King 1998: 168). Many experiments have compared the effects of such terms and more neutral ones, such as 'people', 'he or she', or 'they'. These studies show that subjects are more likely to generate male mental images to accompany 'man' and 'he', and when asked to select appropriate illustrations they are more likely to select images of men.[3] Female subjects were more interested in jobs described using 'he or she' or 'they' than those described using 'he' (Stericker 1981).

The use of 'he' and 'man', then, does have effects on our thoughts. And these effects can be important ones. If women are less likely to apply for a job because of the pronoun used in its description, this is clearly important. But the other effects matter too. Historically, there has been a tendency to focus on men and their actions as the important ones.[4] There are also strong tendencies to view certain activities as male. This is well illustrated by the continued success[5] of the riddle below:

> A boy and his father were driving when suddenly a truck careened around a corner and hit their car head-on. The car was crushed, and when their bodies were removed from the wreck the father was already dead. The son, badly injured but still alive, was rushed to the hospital, where hasty preparations were made for immediate surgery. As the boy was brought in for the operation, the surgeon saw him and said, 'I can't operate, that's my son.' How is that possible?

> (Moulton 1981: 100–1)

Although the riddle is by now fairly old, people still have trouble realizing that the surgeon is the boy's mother. Female doctors still have difficulty convincing patients—especially older patients—that

---

[3] See e.g. Erlich and King (1998: 168), Gastil (1990), Martyna (1978), Moulton et al. (1978), Wilson and Ng (1988). There have been some criticisms of this research in Cole et al. (1983). But see also the response to these criticisms in Gastil (1990).

[4] As in e.g. the way that political theorists have neglected issues of justice within the family, to which women are traditionally consigned. (I discuss this issue in Chapter 1.)

[5] This may well not succeed when read in a chapter on feminism and language. But try it on friends and acquaintances, and it probably will.

they are doctors. When a critically ill patient refused to take his medicine because he wanted 'the doctor' to give it to him, one female doctor was forced to ask a male cleaner to dress up as a doctor and give the man his pills.[6] The riddle and this story suggest not only that people strongly assume doctors will be male, but that this assumption is exceptionally difficult to shake.

It is very difficult to overcome presumptions that males are under discussion. These assumptions are by no means always due to language—indeed, there is nothing in the riddle or example above to indicate that language plays a role in generating the presumption that doctors are male. However, using 'he' and 'man' only reinforces already strong tendencies to assume maleness in certain contexts. If we want our general claims about, for example, people or doctors to be genuinely seen as claims about *people* or *doctors*, rather than just men or male doctors, we should not use terms that make readers even more likely to assume maleness.

Not really neutral

Janice Moulton argues that terms like 'he' and 'man' are not really gender-neutral (Moulton 1981). She argues for this point by offering cases in which a gender-neutral meaning is clearly intended, but fails to come across. Here are some examples of intended but unsuccessful gender-neutral use of 'man' and 'men'.[7] (I am following a convention of linguists by indicating unacceptable or problematic examples by *.)

> *Man has two sexes. Some men are female.
> *Early man breastfed his young.

Similar examples can be constructed with 'he' and 'his':

> *Ask the job candidate about his husband or wife.
> *When a person is first breastfeeding, he may find it useful to seek the advice of a midwife.

If 'he' and 'man' had genuinely gender-neutral uses, the sentences above would be unproblematic. It is clear that the speaker intends the terms to be understood gender-neutrally, so they should be. Our

---

6 I thank Komarine Romdenh-Romluc for this anecdote.
7 The first example is from Moulton (1981: 111); the second is mine.

failure to understand these terms as fully gender-neutral, even when it is clear that they are so intended, indicates that they are not really gender-neutral terms.

Adele Mercier argues that the meanings of terms like 'he' and 'man' are more complicated than has commonly been supposed (Mercier 1995). Each term can be used either when the person (or people) at issue are known to be male or when their sex is unknown. But if sex is known to be female, they become unacceptable. To see this vividly, consider the dialogue below:

A: Whoever left his hat behind has very strange taste.
*B: That was Gloria, and yes, he does have strange taste.

Unless Gloria is male, B's answer is unacceptable, despite the fact that it is clearly picking up on the 'gender-neutral' use of 'he' in B's utterance. True gender-neutral terms do not work like this. To see this, consider the following closely related dialogue, with 'person'.

C: Whoever left this hat behind has strange taste.
D: That was Gloria, and yes, she is a person with odd taste.

D's utterance is a bit stilted, but it is by no means unacceptable in the way that B's is. 'Person', unlike 'he', remains acceptable even when we know that its referent is female.

These arguments are compelling. However, showing that 'he' and 'man' are not truly gender-neutral terms is insufficient to show that these terms should not be used in the way that they are. Instead, what Moulton has demonstrated is, arguably, simply that it is incorrect to describe these terms as truly gender-neutral. They are not gender-neutral terms, but rather terms with a more restricted usage. To argue that there is something wrong with *the use made of these terms*, one needs to argue that there is something wrong with the more restricted usage that they're given. Otherwise, all that can be established is that it is wrong *to describe them as gender-neutral*. This, on its own, is just a classificatory error, like calling something an adjective when it is really an adverb. It doesn't show that there is anything wrong with the words or the use that is actually made of them.

Message: men as norm

Moulton notes that the phenomenon of specific terms being used as if they were non-specific ('man' and 'he' being used as if they were more general than they are, for example) is a familiar one, well-known to advertisers. Moreover, it is one generally accepted to have significance. Some product brand names, like 'Hoover' (in the UK) and 'Xerox' (in the US), have come to function as terms for products as well as brands. Advertisers know that it is a significant achievement when a brand name becomes a generic term. When a brand obtains this sort of prominence, it indicates that the brand is taken as the norm or model of that product type.[8] Similarly, terms like 'man' and 'he' are thought of as generic terms despite their specificity. This, Moulton argues, is what is *wrong* with the supposed gender-neutral use of 'man' and 'he':

> A gender-specific term, one that refers to a high-status subset of the whole class, is used *in place of* a neutral generic term. Many of us who deplore the efforts of drug companies to get us to use the brand name rather than the generic name of a product have failed to recognize that the use of 'he', 'man', etc. in place of 'they', 'one', 'person', or 'human' is a similar phenomenon with similar effects.

> (Moulton 1981: 113)

Purveyors of other brands of vacuums become rightly resentful when 'Hoover' becomes the name for vacuums: the message of this is that Hoover is the best, or at least the normal, brand. The use of 'he' and 'man' as if they were gender-neutral treats men as the norm for humanity. It can therefore be considered a sort of insult to women.

Laurence Horn and Steven Kleinedler have recently argued that Moulton's account cannot be quite right about 'man' (Horn and Kleinedler 2000). A key reason for this is that 'man' began its life as a truly gender-neutral term ('mann'), with no gender-specific use. The gender-specific use *followed* the gender-neutral use. Nonetheless, they suggest that 'man' is currently only acceptable in its so-called

---

[8] Moulton suggests that purveyors of the brand happily embrace this. Laurence R. Horn and Steven R. Kleinedler (2000) argue otherwise, noting that makers of the brand in fact generally take such developments as a risk to copyright and therefore resist them.

gender-neutral use when males would seem appropriate referents. We can see this by comparing the acceptability of the first sentence below with the unacceptability of the second.

Man is the only animal that is embarrassed by his nakedness.
*Man is the only animal that is embarrassed by his pregnancy.

For Horn and Kleinedler, this occurs because we take males to be the prototypical referents for 'man' and 'he'. Where males do not make sense as referents, these terms seem inappropriate. Their analysis, then, allows for much the same objection to 'gender-neutral' use as Moulton's: it seems to take males as the exemplars of humanity.

It can sometimes be difficult to recognize factors like this regarding one's own language, and regarding usage that is as familiar as the 'gender-neutral' use of 'he' and 'man'. With this in mind, Douglas Hofstadter wrote a parody piece imagining that English had race-linked terms that functioned in the way that sex-linked terms function. In the passage below, he discusses (and 'defends') an imagined 'race-neutral' use of 'white'. His point here is not one of comparing racism and sexism, but instead one of making vivid the strangeness of an often taken-for-granted use of 'man'.

> Most of the clamor, as you certainly know by now, revolves around the age-old usage of the noun 'white' and words built from it . . . The Negrists claim that using the word 'white', either on its own or as a component, to talk about all the members of the human species is somehow degrading to blacks and reinforces racism. Therefore the libbers propose that we substitute 'person' everywhere where 'white' now occurs. Sensitive speakers of our secretary tongue of course find this preposterous. There is great beauty to a phrase such as 'all whites are created equal' . . . Think how ugly it would be to say 'all persons are created equal' or 'all whites and blacks are created equal'. Besides . . . such phrases are redundant. In most contexts, it is self-evident when 'white' is being used in an inclusive sense, in which case it subsumes members of the darker races just as much as fairskins.

(Hofstadter 1998: 141)[9]

---

[9] The Hofstadter example may suggest another, slightly different, view on why using gender-specific terms as if they were gender-neutral is insulting. One reason that the Hofstadter example is so offensive is the existence of a history in which

Solutions

The main solution proposed for the problems raised by the supposedly gender-neutral use of 'man' is a simple one: substitute an appropriate yet genuinely neutral term, such as 'humanity', 'humankind', or 'people'. The proposals made for such substitutions are generally pretty conservative. Most advocates of reform do not suggest rewriting Shakespeare. Instead, the proposals are generally concerned only with making suggestions for the future.[10]

The proposals made for dealing with the problems posed by the supposedly gender-neutral use of 'he' are more varied. Some suggest attempting to rewrite so as to avoid the need for a third person indefinite pronoun. This can be done, for example, by recasting the sentence 'Each student should make sure that he picks up a handout' as 'Students should make sure that they pick up handouts'. Other solutions commonly used are to alternate of the use of 'he' and 'she' so far as this is possible, to use exclusively 'she', to use 'he or she', or to use 's/he'. Some have argued that English needs to have a new third person singular pronoun created which can be genuinely gender-neutral. This last solution has not met with widespread acceptance. (For discussion of a range of proposed solutions, see Cameron 1998: pt 2.)

In many ways the most interesting proposal is to use 'they' as a third person singular gender-neutral pronoun. Discussing this proposal properly requires us to draw a distinction between descriptive and prescriptive grammar rules. Descriptive grammarians take as their goal describing languages as they actually are—as they are spoken and

---

blacks have been treated as not fully human. A clear illustration of this is the fact that 'All men are created equal' was not originally meant to include blacks. Similarly, there is a history of treating women as not fully human and not including them either under slogans like 'All men are created equal'. Due to this sort of history, one might argue, terms that suggest either whites or men to be the paradigm cases of humanity are offensive.

10 Some, however, do suggest some retranslating or rewriting, both for specifically feminist reasons and in order to clarify the original meanings of texts which were written when different usages were common (see e.g. Mercier 1995).

written by their native speakers. Prescriptive grammarians are interested in languages *as they should be*. This may have little or nothing to do with how languages are actually used. For example, speakers of English often use 'that' and 'which' relatively interchangeably. However, there are prescriptive grammar rules for American English that draw subtle distinctions between contexts in which one term is appropriate and contexts in which the other term is appropriate. These rules are unknown to, and unfollowed by, most speakers.[11] Nonetheless, prescriptive grammarians insist that these rules are right. Professional linguists are interested in the descriptive rather than prescriptive side of language, and prescriptivism is often rather hard to justify. It is especially difficult to justify a prescriptive rule that fails to accord with the practice of speakers. Appealing to tradition would not accomplish much, since languages change over time. (If prescriptivists never allowed that change was acceptable, they would be forced to advocate some long-dead precursor to modern English.) Prescriptive grammarians will often invoke considerations of elegance, but it is not at all clear that such considerations—especially if opinions regarding the elegance of a particular phrase vary—should be decisive. Some prescriptive rules, however, can be justified on grounds such as clarity. (For a thorough discussion of prescriptivism and its justifications see Cameron 1995.)

Use of 'they' and its variants ('their' and 'them') as singular pronouns is generally forbidden by prescriptive grammarians—it is considered ungrammatical. However, 'they' and its variants come very naturally to speakers of English in sentences like the following, which prescriptive grammarians would take to be incorrect:[12]

Anyone can do it if they try hard enough.
Who dropped their ticket?
Either Mary or John should bring a schedule with them.

The gender-neutral use of 'they' is obviously a part of English, descriptively speaking. In particular, it is extremely common in speech. (In writing, people tend to be more careful to adhere to prescriptive

---

[11] The particular rules concerning 'which' and 'that' are viewed as recommendations rather than requirements of correct usage in Britain (Cameron 1995: 50–1).

[12] These examples are from Bodine (1998: 125)

grammar rules.) Prescriptive grammarians argue that this use is illogical—it is wrong to use a plural pronoun as a singular one. However, those who object to 'they' on these grounds are generally perfectly willing to accept the use of 'he' to refer to women. These positions are in tension with each other. 'They' is no more illogical than 'he': one fails to agree in number, the other in gender. (For more on this, see Bodine 1998: 126.) So the appeal to logic fails. Descriptively, the singular use of 'they' is a part of our language. One who advocates it on feminist grounds, then, is only urging that we alter a prescriptive rule by bringing it into line with actual use. It is worth noting, however, that 'they' does not offer a universal solution. Imagine that we don't know what sex Pat is, and we want to say that Pat will pick up his or her shoes. We cannot do this with the sentence below:

*Pat will pick up their shoes.

Gender-specificity

'Manageress', 'waitress'

Feminists criticize supposedly gender-neutral uses of terms like 'he' and 'man' because those who encounter these uses will tend to think of men rather than women, and because using a male-specific term as if it were generic carries the message that men are the norm. Interestingly, feminists also criticize certain gender-specific terms like 'manageress', a term still fairly common in the UK. Obviously, their criticisms of this term cannot take exactly the same form. Use of the term 'manageress' to describe one in a particular position of authority cannot be accused of obscuring the fact that women hold positions of authority. Rather, it calls attention to it. If people tend to assume, as they might, that managers are male, using the term 'manageress' clearly cancels this assumption by making it explicit that the individual in question is female.

So what is the objection to terms like 'manageress'? The difficulty is that the general term for the job held by a manageress is 'manager'. Nonetheless, this general term is seen as not applying to a woman who holds this position. A woman is somehow not suited to be a manager, and must instead be known as a 'manageress'. So, the objection goes, we have yet another instance of taking men as the norm. Supposedly gender-neutral uses of 'he' and 'man' are one way of taking maleness as the norm, while insistence on the gender-specific 'manageress' is another way. Terms like 'manageress', according to this line of thought, serve to reinforce already powerful stereotypes about the sorts of work to which men and women are suited.

It seems to me that it is consistent for a feminist to argue both against the gender-neutral use of 'he' and 'man' and against the gender-specific term 'manageress'. But it is important to be careful about which arguments are made. If one's objection to the terms 'he' and 'man' is solely that they make the contributions of women invisible, leading readers to assume that males are under discussion, then surely one cannot consistently object to the term 'manageress'. After all, as I have noted, this term makes women very visible rather than invisible. If one's concern is with female invisibility, then, one should positively advocate the use of terms like 'manageress'. If one's concern, however, is with the tendency to take maleness as the norm, the situation is different. One can make a coherent case both against the gender-neutral uses of the terms 'he' and 'man' and against the term 'manageress'—but one needs to be careful how the case is made.

Gender-specific 'he', 'she'

We have already considered worries about the gender-neutral use of 'he'. One might think that the gender-specific use of 'he' would be free of concerns. This is not so, however. One can raise worries about the gender-specific use of 'he' and 'she' as well: these worries centre on the fact that we have so few other options.

The nature of English pronouns has the effect that one cannot use pronouns to refer to a particular individual unless one knows what sex they are. Normally, we take this very much for granted. However, sometimes we want to write or talk about someone whose first name we do not know, or whose first name does not indicate what sex they are. When this happens we find ourselves at a loss. Marilyn Frye nicely brings out the absurdity of this.

If I am writing a book review, the use of personal pronouns to refer to the author creates the need to know whether that person's reproductive cells are the sort which produce ova or the sort which produce sperm.

(Frye 1983a: 22)

It does seem absurd that, no matter what the context, it is so very important to know the sex of the person under discussion. The need to know this is only increased by the continued use of terms like 'manageress' and 'waitress'. Frye takes this to be a further instance of the 'sex-marking' behaviour we discussed in the previous chapter. In endless ways, including our language, we indicate that it is always vital to know what sex someone is. This, Frye suggests, helps to create the illusion that there are two very sharply defined sexes, differing enormously and importantly from each other in every context. She takes breaking down this illusion to be an important project for feminism.

'Miss', 'Mrs', 'Ms'

Note: The use of 'Ms' is more widespread in the US than in the UK. In the US, it is rare not to be offered the choice of 'Ms', and it is often used as a default by businesses and others who have no way of knowing a woman's marital status. In the UK, 'Ms' does not have the status of a default, and it is very common not to be offered 'Ms' as a choice when selecting a title. It is perhaps also worth noting that the use of titles is far more common in the UK than in the US: it is rare to be asked for one's name without being asked for a title in the UK, while in the US it is very common.

Feminists have advocated the use of the title 'Ms' as a female equivalent of the male 'Mr'—a title that gives no indication of marital status. The fact that feminists advocate this is well known. Feminists' reasons for advocating it are less well understood. In this section, I consider the reasons given in favour of substituting 'Ms' for 'Miss' and 'Mrs'.[13]

---

[13] Another solution, which I can only mention here, is to simply stop using titles.

Message

First, consider the message conveyed by the use of the terms 'Miss' and 'Mrs', combined with the lack of similar terms for men. There is no title in standard use that indicates a man's marital status. If one wishes to address or refer to a man formally, one simply prefixes his last name with the term 'Mr'. However, if 'Miss' and 'Mrs' are the only options available for referring to women (as is still often the case in the UK), the situation is very different. In order to refer to a woman or address her formally, one must know her marital status. This only makes sense if we assume that a woman's marital status is, at the very least, significantly more likely to be relevant—whatever the context— than a man's. Very few of us today (at least in the US and UK) would agree that a woman's marital status is more often relevant than a man's.[14]

Privacy

Because one must know a woman's marital status in order to refer to her as 'Miss' or 'Mrs', women are regularly expected to reveal their marital status unless a term like 'Ms' is available. As a result, women regularly reveal facts about their personal lives, and it is difficult or impolite to refuse to do so. There is no such expectation that men will regularly reveal facts about their personal lives.

---

[14] Michael Levin (1981) argues against the adoption of 'Ms' precisely because he *does* assume that a woman's marital status is more often relevant than a man's. He claims that the titles 'Miss' and 'Mrs' are needed because men are (he claims) the initiators of sex, and that they therefore need to know which women are sexually available. The titles 'Miss' and 'Mrs', according to Levin, offer this information (only unmarried women are sexually available). Since women do not, according to Levin, initiate sex, they have no need for corresponding information about men. This is why there is no need for titles declaring men's marital status. According to Levin, then, there are good evolutionary reasons for the use of 'Miss' and 'Mrs': they are vital to the survival of our species. There are, to put it mildly, many objections that could be raised to Levin's argument. For some of them, see Soble (1981) and Purdy (1981).

Convenience

A final problem for the titles 'Miss' and 'Mrs' is not an especially feminist one, but simply an issue of convenience. The use of these titles requires knowledge of a woman's marital status. One does not always have such knowledge, and asking can be awkward. For this reason, 'Ms' first began to gain popularity not amongst feminists but in the business world of 1950s America (Baron 1986: 167–72). Moreover, 'Ms' is useful for women who have married but retained their original names. 'Mrs' is traditionally not affixed to a woman's original name, while 'Miss' seems inappropriate for a married woman (Purdy 1981). Simply on grounds of convenience, then, 'Ms' is a very useful term.

Arguments against reform

History

Feminist proponents of linguistic change are often accused of ignoring linguistic facts and historical reality. For example, those opposed to linguistic change often insist that 'he' simply *is* the correct gender-neutral pronoun in English, and that it has always been so. One popular usage guide maintains:

> The use of 'he' as a pronoun for nouns embracing both genders is a simple, practical convention rooted in the beginnings of the English language. 'He' has lost all suggestion of maleness in these circumstances.
>
> (Strunk and White 1979: 60)[15]

We have already seen some reasons for disagreeing with this—both from Moulton's argument that 'he' is not gender-neutral, and from psychological studies which reveal that there does seem to be a suggestion of maleness. In addition, however, the usage guide's claim has the history wrong. 'They' was commonly used even in writing until

15 The 4th edn. (2000) has dropped the claim that there is no suggestion of maleness, but the first sentence quoted remains.

relatively recent times, as several studies of literature have shown (Bodine 1998: 126). In the mid-eighteenth century, some prescriptive grammarians began to argue that singular 'they' was incorrect, and that 'he' should always be used in its place, but other prescriptive grammarians failed to forbid use of singular 'they'. By the mid-nineteenth century, condemnation was universal, and it has continued to this day. Nonetheless, as Ann Bodine notes,

> despite almost two centuries of vigorous attempts to analyse and regulate it out of existence, singular 'they' is alive and well. Its survival is all the more remarkable considering that the weight of virtually the entire educational and publishing establishment has been behind the attempt to eradicate it.

> (p. 126)

The longevity of singular 'they', despite its condemnation, makes it seem that 'they' has a very good claim be English's real gender-neutral singular pronoun.

Impossibility of deliberate change

It would be hard to deny that language changes over time. However, there is at least some plausibility to claiming that we cannot deliberately decide to change language and then successfully bring this about. This is what Michael Levin argues:

> Granted, English idioms change with social patterns. WWII gave us 'Rosie the riveter.' But we cannot even predict these changes, let alone try to dictate them.

> (Levin 1981: 219)

Because we cannot dictate linguistic change, Levin suggests, feminist attempts to reform language are doomed. This argument is an interesting one, especially when considered in light of the history discussed above. That history shows just how difficult it can be to make deliberate linguistic changes: the singular use of 'they' has persisted despite the best efforts of prescriptive grammarians. However, it also shows that, in at least one case, feminist efforts would be on the side of accepting usage as it is—what feminists want to change with regard to 'they' is the (often ignored) rule against its singular use. Those who oppose this usage are the ones fighting the fruitless battle Levin describes.

It is also important to note that, however difficult it may be deliberately to change language, it is far from impossible. The Académie Française, for example, a French government body, dictates language use. Moreover, politically motivated change not dictated by a government can also succeed. To take just one example of such change, very few in America or Britain today would use the word 'Negro', which forty years ago was common. Moreover, while the rarity of 'Ms' in British English could be thought to count against the possibility of change, its frequency in American English surely shows that change is possible. It seems clear that it is wrong to suppose deliberate linguistic change to be impossible. Such change is difficult, and it is well worth looking at the factors that make it more likely to occur (see Erlich and King 1998), but it cannot be considered impossible.

Ease of thought

Michael Levin suggests that:

> language is the vehicle of thought and in an important sense we must be unconscious of our choice of words if we are to express our thoughts. When we become entangled with decisions about how to speak, we lose contact with the reality our speech is directed to.
>
> (Levin 1981: 218)

Feminist linguistic reforms, then, would impede our ability to think, and are therefore a mistake.

Levin maintains that we cannot properly express our thoughts if we are conscious of our choice of words. This is surely false. Even when *very* conscious of our choice of words, we successfully express our thoughts—in job interviews, delicate romantic situations, or negotiations, to name a few examples. It does seem, however, that it would be bad to be *always* so conscious of our words as we are in such situations. But this is not at all what feminists suggest. We regularly reflect upon and alter our speech without great cost to the flow of our thoughts: we may swear more or less in certain groups, or speak more formally in some settings than others. It is not debilitating to be somewhat aware of one's choice of words. Moreover, at least one suggested reform can be accomplished simply by *not* reflecting too carefully on one's usage: the third person singular 'they', we have seen, comes very naturally. One can easily avoid the use of 'he' as a gender-neutral term simply by speaking in the way that comes naturally.

One might even argue that the extra thought that may be involved in using or even encountering the sorts of use suggested by feminists would be a *beneficial* consequence of such usages. Not all thought is bad, after all—and a bit of extra thought about the problematic ways in which English takes maleness as a norm might well be a good thing. Deborah Cameron suggests just this in the quotation below.

> The strategy I believe is helpful is the one used in this book—every indefinite or generic referent is feminine. I and several other linguists use this practice all the time. When questioned by people who find it odd, we reply that we are practicing positive discrimination through positive language. If it comes naturally to men to say/write *he*, obviously it comes naturally to me to use *she* . . . I have no illusions that positive language will change the world . . . But what might be achieved is a raising of people's consciousness when they are confronted with their own and others' prejudices against saying *she*.
>
> (Cameron 1985: 88.)

The insufficiency of language reform

Language as male

Many feminist writers claim that existing languages reflect a male viewpoint, in ways far more sweeping than we have seen so far, and that the reforms needed go well beyond changes to the use of a few specific terms.

Male words

English can be seen—at least to some extent—as encoding male ways of conceptualizing the world. Words related to sex offer especially telling examples of this. Take, for example, the word 'foreplay'. Foreplay is the activity that comes before what is considered to really be sex. However, for many women the activities known as 'foreplay' are the ones that are the most sexually satisfying. If women were making up terms for sex, they arguably would not privilege the act of male penetration as 'sex' and relegate *their* most pleasurable activities to secondary status (Spender 1985: 178; Cameron 1985: 81). Some have even suggested that women would be less likely to use the term 'penetration', as from a female perspective the same act might better be described as 'enclosure' (Cameron 1985: 81). Legal examples are also revealing. Sally Haslanger discusses the term 'rape', which has often been taken legally to apply only to acts of penetration that involve more than 'the normal level of force' (Haslanger 1995: 109). This also seems to reflect a perspective that women are likely not to share.[16] As Haslanger suggests, sexual activities other than penetration might seem just as (or possibly more) violating to many women, and the presumption that it is acceptable for sex to involve some amount of force is certainly one that most women would reject.

Missing words

Another way languages are said to be male is that they may lack words for things that matter a great deal to women. We have already seen, in Chapter 2, that the term 'sexual harassment' is a recent feminist innovation. Lyn Farley's story of how this term came about provides a useful illustration of the way that gaps in language come to be recognized:

> there was an unmistakable pattern to our employment. Something absent in all the literature . . . was newly exposed. Each one of us had already quit or been fired from a job at least once because we had been made too uncomfortable by the behaviour of men.
>
> (Farley 1978: xi, quoted in Spender 1985:184–5)

As a result of the experience of talking to other women about this common unnamed problem that they faced, Farley coined the term

---

[16] Many men would also fail to share this perspective.

'sexual harassment'. This term has now been successfully introduced into English, and the concept has been recognized in law. Having a term to describe sexual harassment has made it more possible to recognize, analyse, and fight it. Undoubtedly we are not yet aware of all the ways in which our languages may prove inadequate to express important ideas.

All of language is man-made

Writers like Dale Spender (1985) and Julia Penelope (1990) have argued that language was created by men. As a result, the only words that we have are ones that describe the world as men experience it.

> Males, as the dominant group, have produced language, thought and reality. Historically it has been the structures, categories and the meanings which have been invented by males—though not of course by all males—and they have been validated by reference to other males. In this process women have played little or no part ... Women have been excluded from the production of language, thought, and reality.
>
> (Spender 1985: 143)

Men's power to make our language what it is allows them to control other areas as well, Spender argues:

> The group which has the power to ordain the structure of language, thought, and reality has the potential to create a world in which they are the central figures, while those who are not of their group are peripheral and therefore may be exploited.

Because men created and control language, a male worldview is imposed on all of us.[17] Women's experiences become unspeakable or at least difficult to articulate.

Mostly, these claims are overblown and obviously false. If men created reality, then they created oceans, amoebas, and chipmunks—which they clearly didn't do. Moreover, the idea that men have created reality does not even make sense, as men are themselves

---

[17] Spender does note that not all men have had language-making power. Although not much attention is devoted to this point, it would presumably follow that the worldview being imposed is that of white, economically and socially privileged males. If this is right, the language would seem likely to pose problems not only for women but also for men not of this group.

presumably a part of reality. Nor have men created thought. It is hard to understand even what is meant by the claim that men created thought. But it seems very clear that women have thoughts, and would have thoughts even if it were not for men. The idea that men created language fares little better. Although it is not obviously incoherent, there is no reason to suppose that it is true. Nor does it make sense to suppose that women have been totally excluded from the creation of language, thought, and reality. Indeed, even the most traditional thinkers would grant women an important role in creating reality, given their role in creating human beings.

These overblown claims, however, are motivated by some more plausible thoughts: while it makes little sense to suppose that men have *created* language, thought, and reality, it is not so clearly wrong to suppose that men have had a disproportionate influence on these things. It seems to me that the most plausible reading of these claims is that men's influence on language has meant that categories by which we divide up the world (such as, for example, what we call 'sex') reflect a male worldview. This fact could be taken to mean that our thoughts about reality reflect a male worldview. So, *in some extended sense*, language, thought, and reality reflect a male worldview, and this worldview is imposed on all of us. However, we would have to be careful in formulating this idea: the very fact that many women have managed to articulate feminist claims shows that their thoughts were not completely determined by this male worldview (Cameron 1985; Hornsby 1995). So the most plausible idea would be that men's disproportionate influence on language, thought, and reality makes it difficult to formulate and express ideas that do not reflect a male worldview.

Is it right, then, that men have had a disproportionate influence on language? It probably is, in certain respects. Over the years it has generally been men who wrote dictionaries and usage guides, and passed laws. Through these activities men have indeed had power over what is considered to be correct language. But most people do not learn language from dictionaries and usage guides, let alone legal documents, and real language usage often diverges quite sharply from what is considered correct. This sort of power over language, then, is not the sort of power that can be seen as shaping our thoughts and imposing a worldview. Nonetheless, there are indeed ways in which the meanings of certain words seem to reflect a male perspective. This limited claim, then, is right. (Note that this is not a claim about *all* words, but only about some words.) But we have also seen that women are able not only to think beyond these categories but to make changes to the language (like the introduction of the term 'sexual harassment') that help to diminish this male influence. Whatever constraints language places on thought, then, they are not insuperable. Nonetheless, Jennifer Hornsby notes:

> Without calling language 'man made,' we may agree that the language that any of us have at our disposal has been fitted historically to a social reality of which we are critical—that its use by speakers has carried assumptions . . . from which we should hope to be free.

> (Hornsby 1995: 129)

What to do about maleness of language

Some have argued that the biases inherent in English are so severe that women must create their own language in order to be able to express (or even to think) thoughts untainted by male assumptions.[18] But the idea of *a* 'women's language' is problematic: it seems to presuppose a similarity in the experiences of women. If English is too dominated by male assumptions to be usable by women, why should we suppose that women from different ethnic, socioeconomic, and cultural backgrounds will find a single language adequate?[19] Surely anyone concerned with finding words to capture all of women's experiences would need to argue for *many* women's languages.

A women's language also seems unnecessary. We have seen many ways that women have successfully criticized and even changed English. There seems no reason, then, to adopt the rather drastic solution of language creation. And this is a good thing. Creating one's own language makes it very difficult to communicate with others. Those who seek to change the world and to change the way that others see

---

[18] Suzette Haden Elgin (1985) has invented a women's language, Laadan, for just such reasons.

[19] For more on differences among women, see e.g. Lugones and Spelman (1983).

the world will not get very far if they cannot communicate. Whatever the problems of our common language, then, the virtues of having a language in common are considerable. It seems far more sensible to work within the language as we have it, attempting to make changes where they are warranted, than to create a new language.

Over-emphasis on specific terms

Deborah Cameron has argued that focusing on specific terms is a mistake (Cameron 1985: 84–6). She thinks it *is* right for feminists to call attention to problems with 'gender-neutral' usage of terms like 'he' and 'man', and right to try to do something about this. However, she thinks that focusing solely on such efforts cannot succeed in making language non-sexist, and that it may give a false impression of success: it is relatively easy to change one's usage of a few terms, but harder and more important to make bigger changes. Cameron points out that there are serious problems of sexist language use even when these problems do not involve specific terms that have been singled out for discussion by feminist critics. She offers the following example, from the British newspaper, *The Guardian*: '[A man] went berserk with a machete and killed his next-door neighbour's wife, Birmingham Crown Court heard yesterday' (Cameron 1985: 85). It is easy at first not to notice anything linguistically troubling about this quotation. To see what is wrong, ask yourself where the next-door neighbour's wife lives. The answer, unsurprisingly, is that she presumably also lives next door. So why is she not the 'next-door neighbour'? What is taking place, according to Cameron, is that a term that is not specific to one gender is used as if it is. Only the male neighbour is called 'neighbour'. To my knowledge, no feminists have called specifically for reform of the word 'neighbour', and none would be likely to do so. This word does not often pose problems, like 'he' and 'man' do. Nonetheless, it can be used in ways that, just as surely as uses of 'he' or 'man', encode the assumption that maleness is the norm. Supposing that changing a few terms can solve all the problems, then, is a mistake.

One might, however, argue that changing a few terms can have important effects on the way that we think. Suppose, for example, that sex-marking becomes less common in language. If people rarely encounter sex-marked words, it might well feel much less natural to impose sex-marking on terms like 'neighbour'. Thus, it might be that changing particular terms could have more sweeping effects than Cameron envisages. However, considerations in the next section cast some doubt on this hopeful thought.

Backfiring of reforms

In many cases, feminists have succeeded in getting new terms or new usages accepted. Unfortunately, however, things have not always gone according to plan. One good example of this is what has happened with the introduction of terms like 'chairperson' and 'spokesperson'. These terms were intended to be fully gender-neutral substitutes for 'chairman' and 'spokesman'. Instead, they have become terms that are used when women fill the positions in which men are called 'chairman' or 'spokesman' (Cameron 1985: 89; Erlich and King 1998: 168). Far from improving the situation, this leaves one with the impression that there is something improper about using the word 'woman', and that the euphemism 'person' must be adopted instead.

Another example is what has happened with the word 'Ms'. In the UK at least, when 'Ms' is offered as a choice, it is offered as an additional option along with 'Miss' and 'Mrs'. My British students tell me that selecting 'Ms' is seen as a declaration that they are 'difficult feminists'. When 'Ms' is offered as an additional option in this way, it cannot fulfil its original function of bringing it about that women are asked to provide no more information about themselves than are men. While women can avoid giving information about their marital status, they cannot do so without giving information about their political commitments.[20] In both the US and the UK, there is also widespread misunderstanding of the meaning of 'Ms': it seems to have a variety of interpretations, often ones somehow involving marital

---

[20] Moreover, the 'information' given may not even be accurate. One does not need to be a feminist in order to choose 'Ms' as a way of not indicating marital status; and one certainly does not need to be a *difficult* feminist.

status (some take it to indicate a divorced woman, for example) (Erlich and King 1998: 167–8).

Feminist proposals for change, then, have often not had the effects intended. Studies have even shown that use of 'he or she' or 'they' in place of 'he' does not completely counteract the tendency for most people to think of men rather than women (Erlich and King 1998: 169; Cameron 1995: 142). Some, like Susan Erlich and Ruth King, claim this shows that changing terminology will not have the desired effects unless the way that people think is also changed. As long as people consider males to be the norm, no amount of linguistic reform will prevent the assumption that males are the norm. Linguistic reform can only succeed if reform of the way people think takes place at the same time. This is undoubtedly right. However, it is important to recognize the significance of the progress that has already been made. It would be truly remarkable if using 'he or she' or 'they' completely eliminated people's tendency to think of males rather than females: there are many forces besides language which undoubtedly play a role in producing this tendency, so why should language change be sufficient to eliminate it? That language change has any effect on this at all is impressive support for the view that language change matters.

Insufficiency of *language* reform

Some have argued that attempting to reform language is a waste of time. It is not in itself wrong, but there are many more important issues for feminists to worry about. Barbara Ehrenreich writes,

> If you outlaw the term 'girl' instead of 'woman' you're not going to do a thing about the sexist attitudes underneath . . . there is a tendency to confuse verbal purification with real social change . . . Now I'm all for verbal uplift . . . [but] verbal uplift is not the revolution.
>
> (cited in Cameron 1995: 140)

There is something right in this objection and something wrong. What is right is the idea that language reform is neither the only nor the most important issue for feminists to worry about. However, it does not follow from this that language reform is completely ineffectual in changing sexist attitudes, and that feminists should spend no time attempting it. Although language does not affect thought in quite so strong a sense as some have supposed, it does still affect thought. We can see this from the experiments, discussed earlier, on the effects of using 'he' as a supposedly gender-neutral term. Moreover, making alterations to language is a way of highlighting the feminist projects of increasing the visibility of women, and of encouraging reflection on those assumptions about men and women that we take granted. 'Changing what counts as acceptable behaviour is one of the ways you go about changing prevailing attitudes—ask anyone who still smokes cigarettes' (Cameron 1995: 143).

An important goal of feminism is to change the way that people think about women, to bring it about that men no longer occupy such a privileged place in our thoughts. If changing language can make some small contribution to this, changing language seems a worthwhile thing. It by no means follows from this that language change *must* be pursued—it could be that changing language was so time-consuming that it would prevent feminists from pursuing other, more urgent goals. But this doesn't seem to be the case: a key aspect of changing language is changing the ways that individuals speak and write. Changing one's own language use is fairly easy. By doing this, one can relatively easily make a contribution to feminism. This is by no means so time-consuming a project that it prevents one from attending to other issues. It is wrong, then, to suppose that one is faced with a choice between, for example, pursuing the issue of language change and pursuing the issue of female poverty. Cameron also puts this point well:

> In 1970's when non-sexist language policies were a novelty, people who opposed them were fond of saying that modifying language would not get women equal pay. Some of us were equally fond of replying that we never thought it would; but no one was offering a binary choice, *either* equal pay *or* non-sexist language—nothing prevented us from campaigning for both. Nor did anyone that I know of dispute that if you *did* have to make the call, equal pay would win hands down. But the point is, that call was never necessary. Social change is not a finite process or a zero-sum game.
>
> (Cameron 1995: 141)

SUGGESTIONS FOR FURTHER READING

General

Cameron, D., *Feminism and Linguistic Theory*. Basingstoke: Macmillan, 1985.
—— (ed.), *The Feminist Critique of Language*, 2nd edn. London: Routledge, 1998.
—— 'Feminist Linguistic Theories', in S. Jackson and J. Jones (eds.), *Contemporary Feminist Theories*. Edinburgh: Edinburgh University Press, 1998, 147–61.
Miller, C., and Swift, K., *Words and Women: New Language in New Times*. New York: Anchor, 1976.
Vetterling-Braggin, M. (ed.), *Sexist Language*. Totowa, NJ: Littlefield & Adams, 1981.

'He' and 'man'

Bodine, A., 'Androcentrism in Prescriptive Grammar', in D. Cameron (ed.), *The Feminist Critique of Language*, 2nd edn. London: Routledge, 1998, 124–38.
Moulton, J., 'The Myth of the Neutral "Man"', in M. Vetterling-Braggin (ed.), *Sexist Language*. Totowa, NJ: Littlefield & Adams, 1981, 100–15.

'Ms'

Levin, M., 'Vs. "Ms"', in M. Vetterling-Braggin (ed.), *Sexist Language*. Totowa, NJ: Littlefield & Adams, 1981, 217–22.
Purdy, L., 'Against "Vs. Ms"', in M. Vetterling-Braggin (ed.), *Sexist Language*. Totowa, NJ: Littlefield & Adams 1981, 223–8.
Soble, A., 'Beyond the Miserable Vision of "Vs. 'Ms' "', in M. Vetterling-Braggin (ed.), *Sexist Language*. Totowa, NJ: Littlefield & Adams, 1981, 229–48.

Maleness of language

Cameron, D., *Feminism and Linguistic Theory*. Basingstoke: Macmillan, 1985, ch. 6.
Daly, M., and Caputi, J., *Websters' First New Intergalactic Wickedary of the English Language*. Boston: Beacon Press, 1987.
Hornsby, J., 'Disempowered Speech', *Philosophical Topics* 23(2) (1995): 127–47.
Penelope, J., *Speaking Freely: Unlearning the Lies of the Fathers' Tongues*. New York: Pergamon, 1990.

Difficulties for language reform

Cameron, D., *Feminism and Linguistic Theory*. Basingstoke: Macmillan, 1985.
—— 'Lost in Translation: Non-Sexist Language', in D. Cameron (ed.), *The Feminist Critique of Language*, 2nd edn. London: Routledge, 1998, 155–63.
Erlich, S., and King, R., 'Gender-based language reform and the social construction of meaning', in D. Cameron (ed.), *The Feminist Critique of Language*, 2nd edn. London: Routledge, 1998, 164–79.

7

Women's 'Different Voice'

The difference between men and women is like that between animals and plants. Men correspond to animals, while women correspond to plants ... When women hold the helm of government, the state is at once in jeopardy, because women regulate their actions not by the demands of universality but by arbitrary inclinations and opinions. Women are educated—who knows how?—as it were by breathing in ideas, by living rather than by acquiring knowledge.

(Hegel 1952 [1821]: addition to par. 166)

Men are different from women and women are on the whole psychologically and biologically better equipped to be the principal child nurturers.

(Lea 2000: 2)

The history of the 'different voice'

The idea that women are psychologically very different from men is one of enduring popularity. As the above quotations illustrate, this idea is closely linked to the thought that each sex has certain activities to which it is suited and others to which it is not—G. W. F. Hegel thought women should not enter politics, while Ruth Lea thinks they are better than men at childcare. Historically, the claim that women think differently from men has often been used to argue that it is right for women's role in life to be limited—that wives should be subordinate to husbands, that women should not be educated, that women should be confined as far as possible to the home, that women should not vote, and so on. Sometimes, it was clear that those making these arguments took women to be *inferior* to men: the nineteenth-century French thinker Pierre-Joseph Proudhon provided a convoluted set of calculations which he took to prove that 'the total value of man and woman, their relationship and consequently their share of influence will be as 3 by 3 by 3 is to 2 by 2 by 2, or 27 to 8' (Moses 1981: 155). The situation was far murkier, however, with other writers. By the time Proudhon was writing, it had become increasingly popular to see men and women as having different but *complementary* virtues, of equal importance. Women, unsurprisingly, were said to possess traits that rendered them perfectly suited for a life of domesticity while men's traits rendered them fit for life outside the home. Generally, women were taken to be emotionally sensitive and good at close personal relationships, traits needed for the family, while men were said to be rational, a trait thought to be much needed outside the home. Each sort of role was taken to be essential. This kind of claim, then, offered recognition and appreciation of the real and important work that women did in the home, and of the traits that women (were taken to) have. It also, however, served to provide a justification for restricting women to their traditional roles: if male and female roles were both essential, and sex determined which role one was suited for, a strict sexual division of labour was only rational (Okin 1981; 79 1992 [1979]).[1]

It is standard to contrast thinkers who claimed that women were inferior to men with those who claimed that women were merely different from men—as I have just done. But it is in fact harder than it might at first seem to maintain these categorizations. Immanuel Kant, for example, is often cited as a philosopher who took women to be complementary to men, possessors of unique virtues that should be cherished and preserved. But Kant held that only those who act from reason and a sense of duty (rather than emotion or compassion) could be truly moral. He also held that for women there is 'nothing of duty, nothing of compulsion, nothing of obligation!' (Kant 1991: 81). For him, this absence of a sense of duty has the consequence that it is

---

[1] These writers generally overlooked the large number of working-class women who did work outside their homes.

impossible for women to be morally worthy agents. It is very hard to see this as not implicitly taking women to be inferior to men. So even though Kant claims to value the ways in which women differ from men, we miss something if we classify him simply as claiming that women are complementary to men. This sort of slippage between complementarity claims and inferiority claims is a common one. It may in fact be very difficult to make claims of difference without some sort of ranking slipping in.

Quite naturally, many feminists (both early and recent) have fought to gain women greater freedom and more opportunities by attacking claims of psychological differences between men and women that destined them for different roles. One way to attack these ideas is simply to argue that women *don't* think differently from men. Unsurprisingly, this argument was not often made when women's upbringing, education, and lives were almost entirely different from men's. It is difficult to imagine such differences not producing differences in thinking. This idea—that differences in upbringing might produce significant differences that would not otherwise be present— is a commonplace and obvious one to us now. But this nature/nurture distinction has not always been a standard one. In fact, it is often exceptionally hard to sort out what sorts of claim thinkers like Kant and Hegel are making about women. Sometimes, they appear to be making assertions about women's unchangeable nature. At other times they discuss the need to educate women in the right way in order to maintain or inculcate this nature—a need that would not arise if the nature really were unchangeable. The second way to attack claims like Kant's or Hegel's turns crucially on a careful drawing of the nature/nurture distinction. This line of attack, used by many early feminists, holds that we know absolutely nothing of what women might be if they were not so carefully socialized into their feminine roles.

> I deny that anyone knows, or can know, the nature of the two sexes, as long as they have only been seen in their present relation to one another ... What is now called the nature of women is an eminently artificial thing—the result of forced repression in some directions, unnatural stimulation in others.
>
> (Mill 1986 [1861]: 27)

This line of argument continues with the claim that women should be allowed to develop whatever capacities they may have without the artificial restrictions imposed by sexist laws. The one element of this line which may come as a shock to modern readers is that early feminists such as John Stuart Mill and Harriet Taylor often accepted claims that women's thinking *as it was then* was inadequate. They argued that women should be improved by being educated in the same way as men. It is important to note, however, that Mill and Taylor also held men of their time to be psychologically and morally inadequate, and felt that both sexes would be greatly improved by equality of opportunity: 'Thus the position is corrupting equally to both [sexes]; in the one it produces the vices of power, in the other those of artifice' (Taylor 1970[1851]: 114).

Not all feminists, however, have contested claims that women's thinking is different from men's and should or must remain so. Some have in fact based their arguments for women's rights on precisely such claims. Consider the following quotations:

> The head and the arm of humanity, that is man; the heart of humanity, that is woman.
>
> (*Voix des femmes*, 16, 20 Apr., 22, 31 Mar. 1848, cited in Moses 1984: 132)

> We do not want women to be bad imitations of men; we neither deny nor minimise the differences between men and women. The claim of women to representation depends to a large extent on those differences. Women bring something to the service of the state different from that which can be brought by men.
>
> (Millicent Garrett Fawcett, 'Female Suffrage: A Reply', *The Nineteenth Century* (July 1889), cited in Pugh 1992: 3)

Both of these quotations are from advocates of women's suffrage and women's rights more generally. According to this line of reasoning, women should be given the opportunity to enter traditionally male areas of life—like the political arena, traditionally male workplaces, and higher education—because of the uniquely feminine virtues that they can bring to these endeavours. The world will be improved, proponents maintain, by women adding their very different talents to those of men. This line of argument, then, not only endorses but indeed depends upon claims of sex differences.

It is quite natural that feminists should have adopted both of the strategies I have outlined above. It is a tremendously powerful strategy to agree with widely accepted claims of fundamental differences but argue that these differences don't justify the subordination of women. It has the advantage of starting from widely accepted views, that makes it perhaps more likely to get a hearing than arguments which start by denying the common wisdom. But it also has some disadvantages. As already suggested, it can be hard to avoid sliding from claims of difference to claims of inferiority; and while feminists may manage to avoid this slippage, their audiences may have more trouble. In addition, it runs another important risk: many will gain new support for their sexist views. Those who remain convinced that sex differences justify the subordination of women will be able to point to even feminists as agreeing that the sex differences exist.

Those who deny the claimed differences or argue that they result merely from socialization don't run this risk. But they run others. One is that their arguments won't sway those who are firmly convinced of the unchangeable reality of sex differences. Many believed very strongly (as many still do today) that women's thinking is innately different from men's. An argument for women's rights which turns on denying this is likely to do little to convince such people that women should have rights. Another problem is that some of those who argue for the elimination of socialized differences slip all too easily into denigrating the lives and accomplishments of women in more traditional roles. Take, for example, Harriet Taylor's comment, a part of her argument that motherhood should not be assumed to be every woman's proper role: 'There is no inherent reason why all women should voluntarily choose to devote their lives to one animal function and its consequences' (Taylor 1970[1851]: 104).

By the end of the 1970s, feminism that began from the thought that women were importantly different from men psychologically had virtually disappeared from public discourse in the US and the UK (although of course there were still feminists who held this view). Some feminists denied that there were any psychological differences at all between women and men, while others accepted that there were currently differences but called for their elimination—much as Mill and Taylor did over a century earlier. The feminism that had become dominant at this time came to be seen as calling for women to become like men and as dismissing any potential value in traditionally feminine roles and lives.[2] So it came as a shock when, in 1982, Carol Gilligan, a feminist psychologist, argued that women's thinking about morality is different from men's, but in a way that deserves appreciation. In her book, *In a Different Voice*, Gilligan argued that empirical research did show women to have the very traits for which they had so often been criticized—being emotional rather than rational, concerned more with people than anything else, and not interested in abstractions. But she also argued that only sexist assumptions had prevented the realization of just how valuable these traits were.

The idea that a feminist might praise ways in which women differ from men had by this time come to seem startlingly new. Feminists (and others, as we shall see) seized on it with fervour. Although Gilligan had only suggested a difference in men's and women's thought about morality, feminists quickly began exploring the possibility that women's voices might offer new approaches to politics, science, business, and other male-dominated fields. Since women had only recently begun to enter these fields in noticeable numbers, the ideas derived from Gilligan's book held out the promise that the very presence of women would lead to almost unimaginable transformations. Outside academia, the idea took hold perhaps even more strongly. Women reported feeling that reading Gilligan made them feel for the first time as if someone had finally understood—and *appreciated*—how they think. More generally, Gilligan's work allowed all those who had been shy of making gender difference claims for fear of seeming sexist to begin exploring possible differences between men and women. And they did, with great popular success: in best-selling books like

---

[2] This is not to say that feminism really was so uniform. There were, even at this point, feminists who assigned value to traditionally female roles. But the focus during this period was on eliminating the assumption that women should automatically be confined to the home, and on demonstrating how damaging this assumption was to women; so little energy was devoted to drawing out positive elements of women's traditional roles. Nonetheless, we can see a genuine appreciation for women's traditional child-rearing tasks even in Germaine Greer's call for reform of traditional assumptions about the family: 'The family understood not as a necessary condition of existence in a system but as a chosen way of life can become a goal, an achievement of a creative kind' (Greer 1970: 234).

John Gray's (1992) *Men are from Mars, Women are from Venus* and in the press. To this day, stories about women's inroads into business rarely fail to discuss the different management styles resulting from women's different way of thinking, and stories about women's inroads into politics rarely fail to contain predictions of the different sort of world they will create, due to their different way of thinking. We can even see this in a recent discussion of the Women's National Basketball Association in the US.

> Many WNBA defenders, meanwhile, feel compelled to assert that women's basketball is not just as good as the NBA, but better. The league, they declare, is basketball the way it should be—an emphasis on team play and solid fundamental skills—while the men's game has degenerated into showboating, trash-talking and clashes under the basket by superstars with super-sized egos. To WNBA defenders, the league's signature absence of dunking becomes a virtue: A slam-dunk, after all, has no purpose but to show off and to humiliate the opponent. Women, as we all know, are too nice for such things.
>
> (Young 2000)

One reason Gilligan's claims had such an impact was that similar claims of women's special virtues from feminists of the past had been largely forgotten. Another was that, as we will see, she brought to light a shocking but almost unconscious form of sexism in psychological theory, which was quickly seen to have parallels elsewhere, even in some feminist thought—the idea that what men do is what humans are meant to do, and that where women deviate from this they just aren't measuring up. This was a form of sexism that very much needed exposure, and Gilligan exposed it beautifully. Finally, she brought new resources to bear on old issues, arguing that scientific research supported the idea that women have a different approach to morality. In this chapter, we will explore the idea that women have a 'different voice' on matters of morality by way of Gilligan, its most famous recent propagator. We will carefully examine the nature of her claims, looking in detail at nuances that are all too easy to gloss over, and we will explore the impact of her work. But we will also take a close and critical look at the consequences of her claims, their consequences, and the research that has been taken to support them.

Women's moral thinking: justice vs. care

Context

Gilligan's work was a response to that of Lawrence Kohlberg, a psychologist whose claims about moral development were, and to a large extent still are, widely accepted (Flanagan 1991: ch. 8; Kohlberg and Kramer 1969; Kohlberg 1981). Kohlberg developed a six-stage scale for charting moral development. This scale was meant to be a universal scale for moral development, in that all human moral development could be understood as progress from a lower point on the scale to a higher one (even though not everyone would progress through all the stages). Each stage, according to Kohlberg, represented a better way of thinking about morality than the previous one.

Kohlberg's stages:

Preconventional:

Stage 1. A person at this stage is concerned only with securing rewards and avoiding punishments.

Stage 2. A person is mainly concerned with satisfying their own needs, though gives some thought to reciprocity ('You scratch my back, I scratch yours.')

Conventional:

Stage 3. A person takes good behaviour to be that which pleases or helps others.

Stage 4. A person considers respect for authority and the maintenance of social order to be central to morality.

Postconventional:

Stage 5. A person takes what is right to be upholding the basic rights and values of their society, even when they conflict with the concrete rules or laws of the group. (A good example of this is early feminists' use of the official founding principles of their countries to argue for equal rights, which involved changing their countries' actual laws.)

Stage 6. A person is guided by principles they have arrived at through reason alone, which they take to apply to all of humanity.

An example of such a principle is 'treat others as you would want to be treated': (A person at this stage is no longer guided in their moral thinking by either the rules or the basic values of their society.)

Kohlberg based his claim that all moral progress could be understood as progress along his scale on studies of eighty-four children (eventually adults) over a twenty-year period (Gilligan 1982: 18), arguing that these subjects' moral progress was, in fact, progress along his scale. He assessed their level of moral development by interviewing them about hypothetical moral dilemmas. A typical example is the Heinz dilemma:

Heinz's wife is dying. There is a medicine which could cure her, but Heinz cannot afford to buy it. Should Heinz steal the drug?

The moral development of each child was assessed not by which answer (yes or no) they gave, but by what sort of reasoning they used in considering the dilemma. A child concerned only with whether or not Heinz could be caught and punished for his action might score at stage one, while a child invoking principles regarding the value of human life might score at stage five or six.

Kohlberg's original study did not include any females—he only tested males. When girls and women were tested for level of moral development using Kohlberg's scale, researchers found that women tended not to progress as far as men. While men often progressed to stage four, women tended not to get beyond stage three. Kohlberg suggested that this might be because stage three, with its focus on pleasing others, was "functional in the lives of mature women insofar as their lives take place in the home", suggesting that women only become fully mature morally if they abandon traditional women's roles.

Criticisms of Kohlberg

Kohlberg's original study was based on an all-male sample from a single culture. Gilligan rightly attacked this as a poor basis for general claims about human moral development. Although it would of course be impossible to base universal claims on a sample of all people, it would be easy to find a more representative sample than that which Kohlberg used.

In addition, Gilligan noted that Kohlberg's choice of an all-male sample for his study placed him in a very long tradition, made up of embarrassingly prominent thinkers. The idea that men represent the norm for human development is a very old one and a very persistent one. Its age can be illustrated by Aristotle's claim: 'We should look on the female as being as it were a deformity, though one which occurs in the ordinary course of nature' (Okin 1992 [1979]: 82). Its persistence can be illustrated by a disturbing study conducted in 1972 (Gilligan 1982: 17). Participants were asked what qualities they deemed necessary for adulthood, and what qualities were masculine or feminine. It turned out that the traits considered necessary for adulthood, such as the capacities for autonomous thinking, clear decision-making, and responsible action were considered not only masculine but undesirable for women. Although it may seem an obvious point (once made) that views about what it is to be human should not be based on views about what it is to be male, it has been all too easy to overlook.

Gilligan also criticizes Kohlberg for an excessively limited view of moral thinking. She makes this case by asking us to look closely at how Kohlberg would rank two of her subjects, Jake and Amy (both age eleven), and to reflect on how we think they should in fact be ranked. Take, for example, these quotations from Jake and Amy, responding to the question, 'When responsibility to oneself and responsibility to others conflict, how should one choose?' (pp. 36–7).

> JAKE: You go about one-fourth to the others and three-fourths to yourself.
>
> AMY: Well, it really depends upon the situation. If you have a responsibility with somebody else, then you should keep it to a certain extent, but to the extent that it is really going to hurt you or stop you from doing something that you really, really want, then I think maybe you should put yourself first. But if it is your responsibility to somebody really close to you, you've just got to decide in that situation which is more important, yourself, or that other person, and like I said, it really depends on what kind of person you are and how you feel about the other person or persons involved.

Gilligan notes that on Kohlberg's scale Jake's answer would be judged far more morally mature than Amy's, because Jake had a rule to apply in every situation, while Amy refused to formulate any such rule. But this is, of course, by no means the most natural response to the quotations. Amy may be long-winded and a bit indecisive, but she seems far more aware of the complexities of actual moral decision-making than Jake. Gilligan argues from cases like this that Kohlberg has missed some important facets of moral thinking: Amy is exhibiting what is unquestionably a kind of moral maturity, but one that cannot be recognized by Kohlberg's scale. Clearly, Gilligan argues, there is more to moral thinking than Kohlberg supposed.[3]

Gilligan, then, has two main criticisms of Kohlberg.

1. He should not have tried to develop a universal scale of moral development by studying only one small group of males.

2. There is good reason to suppose that there is a great deal more to moral thinking than he supposed.

These criticisms come together in Gilligan's response to the claim that women are morally underdeveloped. It is wrong, she argues, to rank women on a scale developed exclusively with reference to men. To argue from low female scores on such a scale to the conclusion that women are morally underdeveloped only makes sense if we assume that there is one norm for all people, and that norm is the one exemplified by men. Once we give up this assumption, we make room for the possibility that women's thinking may be different but not inferior. This leads quite naturally into the next phase of Gilligan's work, wherein she articulates the different kind of thinking that she has noticed in her research on women and girls.

---

[3] Another way to arrive at this conclusion is to take a quick look at the history of philosophy. Kohlberg has chosen a single sort of view on morality, as solely a matter of reason, and placed it confidently at the pinnacle of his scale of moral development. This view of morality is a version of that developed by Immanuel Kant. But the best way to think about morality has been a contested subject for thousands of years. Kant's views on morality are far from widely accepted. In fact, one would be hard-pressed to find more than a handful of philosophers who would happily assent to the emphasis Kant places on duty, reason, and principles to the exclusion of all other possible moral attributes. So Kohlberg's placement of a Kantian moral outlook as the obvious pinnacle of moral development would strike any philosopher as very odd. There are clearly many alternative approaches.

Different thinking

We have seen that Gilligan criticizes Kohlberg's studies for focusing only upon one type of moral development. Those who approach moral questions in a different manner are seen as not developing properly. Gilligan suggests that such people—in her experience, women—might instead be seen as simply developing differently. She calls their approach to morality 'Care' thinking, and provides a scale of her own which charts the development of Care thinkers. She calls the kind of thinking Kohlberg was concerned with 'Justice' thinking.[4]

Justice thinking involves an emphasis on universal principles and reason. It is also characterized as emphasizing impartiality, rights, and justice. Care thinking, by contrast, is described as guided by emotions, context-sensitive, and concerned with particular individuals and situations rather than universality and impartiality. Within these situations, a Care thinker's primary concerns will be with maintaining existing connections and with responding to others' needs. Justice thinking and Care thinking are meant to be fundamentally different *all-purpose* moral outlooks: for the most part, when presented with a moral problem, Justice thinkers will approach it via Justice thinking, and Care thinkers will approach it via Care thinking.[5]

Justice thinking:
Universal principles, impartiality, reason, and rights.

Care thinking:
Particular individuals, maintaining existing connections, emotions, and response to needs.

Gilligan takes Jake and Amy, whom we met earlier, to be examplars of

---

[4] Gilligan does not capitalize 'justice' and 'care', and most discussions of these notions follow her lead. I have done so, however, to call attention to the fact that it is a special, technical sense of these words at work in the discussion. This is simply for the sake of clarity, and no other significance should be attached to it.

[5] More accurately, this is Gilligan's *initial* understanding. Later, as we will see, she revises her view to allow for individuals to regularly adopt different perspectives for different problems and at different times.

these two approaches. Below, we see their responses to the Heinz dilemma.

> JAKE: The dilemma is 'sort of like a math problem with humans. . . . a human life is worth more than money, and if the druggist only makes $1,000, he is still going to live, but if Heinz doesn't steal the drug, his wife is going to die . . .'
>
> AMY: 'I think there might be other ways besides stealing it, like if he could borrow the money or make a loan or something, but he really shouldn't steal the drug—but his wife shouldn't die either.' If the druggist were to see the consequences of his high price, he would realize that 'he should just give it to the wife and then have the husband pay back the money later'.

Jake is seen as a Justice thinker because he is invoking a universal principle ('a human life is worth more than money'), and applying it rationally to the case before him. Amy, by contrast, focuses on the individuals, suggesting a solution involving better communication between them. Importantly, she wants to flesh out the context and survey more options, rather than just find a principle and apply it.

Gilligan argues that the Care perspective represents a distinctive all-purpose moral outlook, one that is at least as viable as the Justice perspective. Sometimes she appears to suggest that it is a better approach to morality than Justice thinking, and some of her followers seem to claim this (Flanagan 1991: 235). Initially, Gilligan seemed to hold that Justice thinkers and Care thinkers are strongly distinct: one is either a Justice or a Care thinker, not a blend of both. Later, we will see, Gilligan modified this claim.

Women's thinking

Gilligan states in the introduction to her book that she is not making claims about differences between men and women.

> The different voice I describe is characterized not by gender but by theme. Its association with women is an empirical observation, and it is primarily through women's voices that I trace its development.
>
> (Gilligan 1982: 2)

Gilligan encountered this different voice more often in women than in men, she writes, but she is not claiming that it is distinctively female. However, throughout the rest of her book she writes of the way that 'men and boys' think and the way that 'women and girls' think. In addition, as we shall see, the explanation she suggests for how the two kinds of thinking come about turns crucially on differences in the situations of girls and boys. It seems, then, fair to characterize her as making gender difference claims—she may have begun her book cautiously, but she soon abandoned that caution. This interpretation is a standard one, and it has had a large impact on debates both within and outside philosophy (Moody-Adams 1991: 197). With that in mind, we will interpret her in this way.

Gilligan claims that Care thinking is the approach to morality favoured by women. She does not argue at length for any particular explanation of why women might favour this approach, but the main explanation she discusses approvingly is based upon Nancy Chodorow's work. According to Chodorow (1978), gender differences result from the fact that women tend to be the primary caregivers for young children. On this explanation, both boys and girls start life deeply attached to their primary caregivers, in the vast majority of cases their mothers. Once children establish their gender identities at around age three, Chodorow's theory continues, boys feel a need to define themselves as different from their mothers, while girls can persist in their attachment. The result of this, according to Chodorow, is that girls (and later, women) place great emphasis on empathy, attachment, and maintaining connections, while boys (and later, men) assign importance to separation and maintaining emotional distance. Gilligan suggests that this explains why women tend to be Care thinkers and men Justice thinkers.

The impact of Gilligan's work

It is hard to overestimate the influence of Carol Gilligan's work, either inside or outside academia. Our primary focus initially will be on the impact within philosophy.

Philosophical impact

In philosophy, Gilligan's work helped give birth to vast new literatures. The most obvious implications of her work are in ethics and political philosophy. Feminist philosophers drew upon her work both to criticize traditional approaches to moral and political philosophy and to build new theories based on Care thinking. Traditional theories were criticized for privileging reason over emotion, for seeking universally applicable principles, for viewing moral agents as autonomous individuals rather than beings thoroughly enmeshed in connections with and dependencies on others, and for focusing on individual rights rather than on responsibility to others. According to Gilligan's claims, women view themselves primarily as situated in a complex web of interrelationships, emphasize particular contexts over general principles, give emotions a central role in their thinking about moral and political issues, and focus on responsibilities rather than individual rights. As a result of Gilligan's work, feminist theorists began working to construct moral and political theories that reflected these features of women's thinking. They argued that traditional moral and political philosophy was male-biased, and that its replacement by or supplementation with Care thinking would both eliminate that bias and improve the theories. They claimed both that the new theories were better in general and that they were essential to accomplishing feminist goals.

We will use the work of Annette Baier (1987) as an example of this sort of philosophical theorizing. She argues that the history of liberal political philosophy exhibits several importantly linked forms of male bias. Liberal political philosophy is generally characterized as placing an emphasis on the freedom and equality of all. Thus, it is especially puzzling that liberal political philosophers of the past, with very few exceptions, were opponents of equal rights for women.

Baier's explanation for this begins from the fact that, historically, the vast majority of liberal political philosophers have been male, and the vast majority of them have had wives who took care of their children and all household matters, leaving them free to pursue their goals outside the home. These philosophers' theories of the optimal structure for society varied in many ways. But, Baier notes, they shared some important features.

1. They began from the assumption that people are, in some important and basic sense, free and independent of one another.

2. They assumed that the realm of the family was essentially private, and not to be interfered with by the state or even discussed by political philosophers.

The first assumption is, Baier claims, false: all people begin life extremely dependent, and most have periods of illness and incapacitation during which they require a great deal of care from others. If nobody took care of us during these times of dependency, we would not only fail to flourish, but die. How could this obvious fact have been ignored? Only, she argues, because those doing the theorizing were not themselves involved in providing this care (they had wives to do that for them); and because they had already ruled that the realm in which such care took place was not a fit topic for discussion (because it was a private matter). This neglect of the family was also important to preserving the subordination of women. Women lacked many of the rights accorded to men and were legally subordinated to their husbands—a situation strongly inconsistent with these theorists' advocacy of equality and freedom. Only by not discussing the family at all could they avoid noticing that women's situation was at odds with their theories. Since women (at least those who the theorists knew well) were confined to the family, however, their situation was not a part of the accepted subject matter of political philosophy.[6]

Political theorists, Baier claims, constructed theories that only made sense if people were autonomous, rather than fundamentally interdependent.[7] These theories, with their emphasis on reason, principle, and protection of one's rights, were, moreover, ill-suited for application to the realm the theorists had ignored: the family. Indeed, the

---

[6] Chapter 1 also discusses political theorists' lack of attention to the family, as well as consequences of paying attention to the family, and Chapter 8 discusses ways in which one's social position affects what issues one is likely to consider.

[7] This is a contentious claim. But my concern here is with the workings of Baier's argument itself, not with whether or not Baier's representation of liberal political philosophy is accurate.

thought of responding to loved ones by applying reasoned principles and ignoring emotional reactions does seem rather bizarre. If women had been moral and political theorists, Baier argued, moral and political theories would look very different. Women would start from an awareness of the fact that people are interdependent, and they would not ignore the role of emotion in guiding thought about how people should relate to one another. In addition, they would assign greater importance to responding to the needs of others, as opposed to simply protecting one's own rights. And this is just what Gilligan's work seemed to show—women are more attuned to interrelationships, and place a higher priority on emotion and responsibility to others, than men.

Gilligan's work also profoundly affected philosophical thinking outside ethics and political philosophy. To take just one example, feminists in epistemology (the study of knowledge and justification) argued that:

1. Emotion has a vital role to play in theories of reasoning, hitherto widely unnoticed.

2. Seekers of knowledge should be viewed not as isolated individuals, but as members of knowledge-seeking communities.

3. Context, particularly social context, is central to understanding the workings of science.

Some of these claims stem directly from Gilligan's work on moral thinking. Other claims, though not always explicitly derived from her work, echo the same themes.[8]

Even more generally, Gilligan's work played an important role in shaping the rebirth of a feminism that emphasizes what is special or different about women's lives and experiences. This strand of feminism holds that it is a mistake for feminists to strive for access to traditionally male ways of life. Proponents of this view argue that striving for such traditionally male ways of life is implicitly recognizing them as better, or more valuable, than traditionally female ways of life. They suggest instead that the project of feminism should be that

---

[8] I discuss some of these claims, and ways that they can be motivated independently of Gilligan's work, in the next chapter.

of celebrating what is special and wonderful about women's lives—close relationships, care and responsiveness, and connection to one's emotions.

Worries and criticisms

Not all philosophers (feminist or otherwise) have embraced Gilligan's work. We will focus on three important sorts of criticism from philosophers.

1. The ways of thinking Gilligan claims to identify are not as distinct as she and her followers have thought.

2. Finding a way of thinking to be common among women is not a good reason to endorse that way of thinking.

3. Gilligan's claims serve (however unintentionally) to perpetuate damaging stereotypes of women.

Are Justice and Care distinct?[9]

The contrast between Justice and Care thinking is fundamental to the work of Gilligan and her followers. Yet it is not so clear that Justice and Care thinking are really distinct from one another. We will look at just a few reasons for questioning their distinctness. First, take the contrast Gilligan draws between a morality based on rights and one based on responsibilities. The notion of rights doesn't really make much sense without some corresponding notion of responsibilities—if I have a right to be free from violent attack, for example, then others have a responsibility not to attack me. Similarly, Gilligan contrasts application of universal principles with attention to context. But this contrast is, if anything, even more problematic. One cannot apply principles blindly: principles can only be applied by looking closely at a context. To see this, consider the universal principle 'Help those most in need'. To act on this principle, one needs to determine exactly who is most in need and what should be done to help them. But this requires close attention to the details of the particular situation. One

---

[9] The ideas in this section are discussed in Blum (1988), Kymlicka (2002), Sher (1987), and Tronto (1993).

also won't get very far by only attending to context without any recourse to principles. After all, in any situation there are a multitude of facts and details—one has to decide which ones matter and in what ways, and it is hard to see how this can be done without some kind of principle.

Even if we set aside these worries, it is unclear whether one would *want* a sharply distinct ethic either of Justice or of Care. Each ethic seems to suffer from clear limitations. Take the case of Justice first. When we vividly imagine one who deals with all moral issues via reason alone, we find such a person rather disturbing. There is, most of us suppose, something deeply wrong with someone who assigns no role to emotion in their reflections on how to deal with their close friends' or relatives' problems. (Imagine, if you can, determining your response to a close friend's suicidal depression via a carefully reasoned assessment of your moral obligations.) This is part of what lends appeal to the idea of Care as an approach to morality.

The ethic of Care revolves around responding caringly to the needs of those with whom one is connected. This may seem an appealing way to think about personal relationships. But on its own it also leads to a rather unappealing view of morality. Consider what it means for impersonal relationships—it seems to place no constraints on one's behaviour. For a somewhat gruesome example, suppose that my daughter needs a new liver or she will die. Billy, the boy next door, has a perfectly good liver that (I have learned) would be completely compatible with my daughter's body. I know neither Billy nor his family. It is far from obvious what in an ethic of Care could convince me that it is wrong to harvest Billy's liver to save my daughter—after all, I would simply be responding to a great need of one to whom I'm closely connected.

One can answer this worry by citing a Care thinker discussed by Gilligan, who says that 'the stranger is still another person belonging to that group, people you are connected to by virtue of being another person' (Gilligan 1982: 57). Care thinkers, then, may—and should, according to this line—care about everyone. This helps to explain why the perfect Care thinker is not the perfect nepotist, and why I should not harvest Billy's liver. But it also helps to dissolve what was meant to be a crucial difference between Justice and Care. It no longer looks as though Care thinkers have forsaken universality in favour of connections to particular others. Care thinkers care about everyone, which is about as universal as one can get.

So it is not entirely clear that Justice and Care are sharply distinct and incompatible, and it is also not clear that we would find either morality very appealing if we took them to be sharply distinct and incompatible. Rather, it seems likely that the best sort of moral thinking will combine elements of each ethic. We will return to this thought later.

Should we endorse 'women's thinking?'

It is by no means obvious that feminists should eagerly embrace whatever sort of thinking women are shown to engage in. Women have traditionally been far less educated than men, and limited in the experiences that they were permitted to have. Either of these factors alone could have brought it about that women's thinking *was* in fact less good than men's. Assuming that feminists want to think as well as possible, they should not simply accept uncritically whatever modes of thinking women happen to use. Uncritically to accept that women's thinking must be good is not very different from the more traditional mistake of uncritically accepting that men's thinking must be good.

It is also important to remember that rights-based Justice thinking has done a lot of good in the world, playing an important role in bringing about democracy, ending slavery, creating state-run educational systems, and so on. It played an extremely important role in bringing about the feminist victories of the last 150 years. Indeed, it is hard even to state the nature of these victories without using the (Justice-based) language of rights: the right to vote, the right to own property, the right to an education ... So it would be a mistake, it seems, for feminists to reject Justice thinking entirely.

Moreover, Barbara Houston (1987) and Claudia Card (1993) have pointed out that women's moral thinking, as characterized by Gilligan, is just the sort of thinking that one would expect subordinates to display—a concern with meeting others' needs, maintaining connections, and making people happy. This sort of morality is a natural one for those who are powerless, and one that may well be ill suited to ending that powerlessness. This thought gains support from studies cited by Carol Tavris showing that the traits women are meant to have—like empathy and sensitivity to the needs of others—are ones that show up in people of either sex when they are placed in subordinate roles (Tavris 1992: 65). Houston and Card suggest that feminists should not uncritically accept a mode of thinking shaped under conditions that they are committed to changing. This line of thought applies to women's lives and experiences more generally. While there is much to value in traditional women's lives, such lives have not always been freely chosen from a wide range of options. Traditionally, women's lives have been ones of subordination and dependence, and it is a mistake to accept uncritically all features of these lives and reject all features of traditionally male ones.

These worries are very important ones. They become even more important when we reflect on the fact that Gilligan does not take the gender difference she discusses to be innate, but rather suggests that it is the result of upbringing. If it is not innate, then it seems far more open to change. Feminists who conclude that women's thinking perpetuates powerlessness should be working to change the child-rearing arrangements that give rise to it and training women to adopt a mode of thinking more suited to gaining power. But even many of those who do not think there is anything wrong with the way women think have reason to be hesitant about endorsing it. We have already seen that Gilligan takes the gender difference in moral thinking to be the result of children being raised almost exclusively by their mothers. Feminists who hold that parenting should be shared (and many feminists do believe this) should think twice about endorsing a moral framework taken to arise from unshared parenting.[10] If we think Care thinking is the best way to approach moral issues, and we believe that it results from female parenting, then it becomes more difficult to argue that parenting should be shared (a key strand in feminist thought, as we saw in Chapter 1).

---

[10] It may be worth noting that Nancy Chodorow, from whom Gilligan takes her views on gendered development, takes her work to show shared parenting to be an important and worthwhile goal: she views current gender differences in thinking as problematic.

Perpetuation of stereotypes

A very serious worry about Gilligan's work and the work it has inspired is that it fits so well with traditional stereotypes of women. (The quotations with which this chapter began illustrate this nicely.) However much feminist proponents may value women's thinking, very similar claims about 'women's thinking' have been used for centuries as a way of limiting women's opportunities. Whatever the intentions of such feminists, their endorsement of gender difference claims can easily be used for anti-feminist ends. One illustrative example demonstrates that this worry is a real one. The American department store Sears was sued for sex discrimination because they were not allowing women to work in the electronics department, a competitive atmosphere where more money could be earned than elsewhere. In their defence they called a psychologist who, citing Carol Gilligan's work, argued that women wanted connection rather than competition, and therefore did not want to work in electronics. Sears won the case in 1986 (Pollitt 1994: 49–50). This case is one where, arguably, Gilligan's work was misused: she almost certainly would not take her claims to support such a defence of Sears. It is not fair to criticize a view simply because it can be distorted and used to further sexist ends,[11] but the degree to which Gilligan's view seems to fit stereotypical images of women is worrying.

Nonetheless, the fact that a view may perpetuate stereotypes is not a sufficient reason to reject it: if gender difference claims are true, they should be accepted as such. While feminists might then go on to argue about the proper reaction to these claims, rejecting them should not be a live option. It turns out, however, that Gilligan's claims do not seem to be supported by the empirical evidence.

---

[11] If it were, we could criticize feminist proponents of equality for the distortion of this goal which led to the US Supreme Court ruling that concern for equal treatment could not be used as an objection to denying women pregnancy benefits, since men are denied these benefits as well. (This criticism has been made. See Okin (1992 [1979]: 323–4) for an excellent discussion of the criticism and its weaknesses.)

Empirical evidence

General methodological concerns

There have been many methodological criticisms made of Kohlberg's and Gilligan's work. I have already discussed Gilligan's criticisms of Kohlberg's methodology. One of her most important criticisms was that Kohlberg's studies were based on a very limited sample, and that Kohlberg therefore erred in generalizing from this sample. But Gilligan herself can be criticized on similar grounds.[12] Michele Moody-Adams notes, for example, that 'few if any of the women interviewed in Gilligan's study seem to have undergone either the economic hardships or the racial and ethnic exclusion . . . that are constants of some women's experience' (Moody-Adams 1991: 205), and wonders whether women who had faced such problems might give more priority to concerns of justice and rights. She also speculates that deeply religious women might well understand morality in quite distinctive ways. More generally, one might wonder how reasonable it is to expect there to be *a* women's voice at all, given the many differences between various groups of women (Lugones and Spelman 1983).

Another problem common to both Gilligan and Kohlberg is that it is not entirely clear what is being tested in their experiments. Both Kohlberg and Gilligan assume that what people say to an interviewer about moral problems is a legitimate indicator of their level of moral development. But this is at least questionable. Honest reflection on our own lives and those of our friends is enough to convince most of us that there is a difference between what we say we would do (or think others should do) and what we actually do. Certainly one learns something from interviews like Kohlberg's and Gilligan's, but whether that something is level of moral development is another matter (Nails 1983; Flanagan 1991).

There is also a worry specific to Gilligan's methodology. Debra Nails has argued (drawing on full transcripts of Gilligan's interviews) that Gilligan is highly selective in her editing of quotations from the

---

[12] Gilligan's writing combines cautions about the unrepresentativeness of her sample with rather broad claims about 'women and men'.

women that she studied, and that she omitted important passages from the interviews without giving any indication of this (Nails 1983). What Gilligan writes in her book, according to Nails, is not an accurate reflection of what she found in her interview subjects. For example, Nails contrasts Gilligan's version of what one of her subjects, Betty, said, with what the full transcript reveals Betty to have said. (Bracketed questions are from the interviewer.)

Betty, Gilligan's version

Given her expectation that if she went to bed with him, he would continue to meet her needs, her disappointment with him was great when she discovered that 'after I went to bed with him, he just wanted me to do everything he wanted to do. I was more like a wife than a girlfriend, and I didn't like that.' Describing the relationship as one of exchange, she concludes that he 'was really one way,' seeking only to meet his needs and disregarding 'the fact that I wanted more freedom.'

Betty, full quotation

At first he treated me really nice, but then he started to change . . . [Because?] Because after I went to bed with him, he just treated me like shit. He was too possessive with me, he just wanted me to do everything that he wanted to do. Telling me to clean the house, to do this and telling me not to go here or there. I was more like a wife than a girlfriend. I didn't like it . . . I talked with him, but he was ignorant. He didn't quite understand. He was really a one-way person. [He didn't understand what?] The fact that I wanted more freedom.

The impression of Betty left by the full version is very different from that left by Gilligan's version. Nails finds this worrying, since Gilligan's quotation from Betty is used to illustrate an early, selfish stage in Care moral development. Betty does not seem nearly so selfish in the full version as in the one that Gilligan uses.

These worries are extremely important ones. However, I want now to set them aside, and to ask what the data show *even if* we assume them to be accurate indicators of subjects' moral development and outlooks.

Are there gender differences?

The first important fact for us to note is that Gilligan's book, *In a Different Voice*, does not contain any systematic study of gender differences in moral thinking. Instead, it is a compellingly written collection of extracts from mostly women's and girls' reflections on morality in general and on particular moral issues. It makes no pretence of being a systematic comparison of male and female thinking, and indeed really could not serve this function: one of the key studies on which it draws consists of interviews with women considering whether or not to have an abortion (not a study that could ever be repeated with males). At first, it may therefore seem remarkable that such a book has served as catalyst for so much work based on a presumption of gender differences. It is important, however, to remember the context in which it was published: it was a response to comparative studies done using the Kohlberg scale of moral development, studies that seemed to show a clear and striking difference between women and men. In this context, it is surely reasonable for a researcher to simply assume that such differences exist.

But the context did not remain this way for long. In response to Gilligan's work, researchers began to look again at the studies that seemed to show a difference between men and women on Kohlberg's scale. They found that the only studies that showed a gender difference were those in which the women participants had received significantly less formal education than the men. It also turned out that the single best predictor of how high an individual would score on Kohlberg's scale was level of educational attainment. The surest way to raise one's score on Kohlberg's scale is to get a university degree.[13] Further study of the data revealed that the differences between women's and men's scores on Kohlberg's scale are completely explained by level of educational attainment. When men and women with the same level of formal education are compared, their scores are

[13] This fact fits well with the first methodological criticism we examined: if we assume, as seems reasonable, that level of education is not linked to genuine level of moral development, then it suggests that Kohlberg's scale is not in fact measuring moral development.

indistinguishable. So the only difference these studies revealed was one due to level of formal education. Studies using Kohlberg's scale showed no genuine gender difference.[14]

These findings, however, by no means settle the issue of gender differences in moral thinking. If Gilligan is right (as seems likely) that there is more to moral thinking than Kohlberg believed, there might well be gender differences that simply don't show up on Kohlberg's scale. A large number of studies have now been done with the explicit aim of testing for gender differences in moral orientation (Justice or Care). One of the most significant findings to emerge from this work is that nearly all people, male or female, in fact use *both* moral orientations, sometimes at the same time. In addition, nearly all will quite readily switch from one orientation to the other, often with a prompt as simple as, 'Can you think of another way to approach this problem?' Gilligan's original picture, then, is in error. People do not simply have one moral orientation, which gets applied to every moral problem. Gilligan has acknowledged that this shows her original claims to be in need of revision. She has now shifted her claim, stating that Care thinking is more readily available and natural to women, while Justice thinking is more readily available and natural to men.[15]

This new claim, too, turns out to be unsupported by the data—*for the most part*. The vast majority of studies comparing preferred moral orientation reveal no statistically significant gender difference. Men and women are, according to these studies, equally likely to use either moral orientation (Flanagan 1991; Walker et al. 1987).

However, some studies do show a gender difference. According to these studies, women are more likely to choose Care thinking and men more likely to choose Justice thinking. So why do some studies show a gender difference while others do not? The answer lies in the fact that those studies showing gender differences are ones in which participants are asked to choose a moral problem from their own lives to discuss. In these studies, men and women choose to discuss very different sorts of problem. Women tend to choose personal problems

[14] The data discussed in this paragraph are taken from Walker (1993) and Flanagan (1991).

[15] For more on these findings, see Flanagan (1991), Gilligan (1988), and Johnston (1988).

involving their families, while men choose more impersonal problems involving work. This is highly significant, since studies also show that both sexes prefer Care thinking when discussing problems involving close relationships and both prefer Justice thinking when discussing more impersonal problems. (This makes perfect sense, after a little reflection: we are far more likely to give priority to emotions, think about the needs of particular others, and work to maintain connections when considering those to whom we are close.) Choice of problem type, it turns out, completely explains all the observed gender differences. If choice of problem is controlled for, there is no gender difference at all. Given the same sort of problem to discuss, women and men use the same moral orientation. The only difference between women's and men's moral thinking, then, is this: when asked to choose a moral problem for discussion, women are more likely than men to choose personal problems (Flanagan 1991; Walker et al. 1987).

The upshot of all this is that the popular claims about gender differences in moral thinking seem to be false. Women and men do not have completely opposed all-purpose moral outlooks which they apply to every moral problem. When presented with a moral problem, women are no more likely than men to choose Care thinking. Care thinking is no more accessible or natural to women than it is to men. Men are not from Mars and women are not from Venus (at least so far as moral thinking goes).

A puzzle

This leaves us with an important puzzle to be explained. Both men and women insist that Gilligan's gender difference claims ring true. There is something immensely natural and appealing about them. How could this be the case, if there really *isn't* a gender difference? Marilyn Friedman has suggested that the answer to this lies in the fact that Gilligan's claims fit so well with our deeply held stereotypes of male and female thinking (Friedman 1987). Care thinking represents not only how men take women to think, but how women take *themselves* to think. Gilligan's claims fit not only with each sex's ideas about the other, but with each sex's self-conception. Such assumptions and self-conceptions, even if false, have a profound influence on our thinking. Reflect, for example, on a response like one we saw earlier, which discusses caring about everyone. It is really quite difficult to classify such responses as Justice or Care. The same seems likely to be true of the sorts of thinking we encounter in everyday life—most people we know will exhibit both orientations, possibly even at the same time. In reflecting on the moral thinking of those we know, we have choices to make about which elements to focus on. And here is where our stereotypes may have their strongest effects. When we read Gilligan and reflect on men's moral thinking, we notice the Justice thinking, because it is what we expect. When we read Gilligan and reflect on women's thinking, we notice the Care thinking, because it is what we expect. Our self-conceptions are also affected by the stereotypes we have learned. A woman who 'knows' that women's moral thinking gives priority to emotion rather than reason may focus on this element of her thinking when she reflects on gender differences. And when she picks up *In a Different Voice*, what Gilligan says will ring true. So one reason that claims of men's and women's moral thinking may ring true is simply that they reflect those kinds of thinking that we stereotype as male and female.

This is not the only explanation possible. One gender difference claim, after all, seems to be true. When asked to choose a moral problem from their own lives for discussion, women are more likely than men to choose a personal problem. Since these are the problems that people tend to consider via Care thinking, there is a sense in which Care thinking is female: it is the kind of thinking most natural to the kind of problems women tend to raise if asked to present a moral problem from their own lives. But we cannot know what this means until we know why it is that women tend to choose such problems. There are several explanations available. The most obvious explanation for women's choice of personal problems would be that the women studied do not work outside the home, and so spend their lives concerned almost exclusively with close personal relationships. But this cannot be right—for it turns out that the women who were *most* likely to choose personal problems to discuss were those who worked *outside* the home (Flanagan 1991: 232).

There is, perhaps, a simpler explanation. It might be that women presented personal problems because these were most on their minds. There are at least two highly plausible reasons why women who work outside the home might tend to have personal problems on their minds. The difficulty of combining work outside the home and child-care (discussed in Chapter 1) could well lead them to spend more time worrying about their families; alternatively, they might raise issues concerning their families due to societal pressures which make them feel guilty for working outside the home. This explanation offers us a way in which Care thinking might be seen as genuinely (rather than stereotypically) female, and a way to explain why Gilligan's book rings true to so many women. If women do indeed spend more time considering personal problems, and everyone is more likely to employ Care thinking when considering personal problems, women spend more time employing Care thinking. No wonder, then (if this is right), that Gilligan's work strikes them as an accurate description of their thinking.

A very different—and intriguing—sort of explanation for women's choices of moral problem might be that women have different views from men about what counts as a moral problem. (Flanagan (1991) explores this sort of explanation.) We have already seen (in our discussion of Baier) that decisions as to what gets classified as moral or political have important, far-reaching effects. It is entirely possible that women have different views from men about which issues are moral issues. Women may take family issues to be central or paradigmatic examples of moral issues, and men may not. This would explain why women are more likely than men to raise family issues when asked to describe a moral problem. Further, if women consider family issues paradigmatic of the moral domain, then they will consider Care thinking to be paradigmatic of moral thinking. As a result of this, Gilligan's descriptions will seem like good descriptions of women's moral lives. So we have yet another way in which Care thinking could be seen as genuinely female, and yet another way to explain the appeal of Gilligan's claims.

Impact of the empirical findings

Gilligan's original claims led to a major shift in feminist thinking, and gave rise to re-examinations of assumptions both within and outside feminism. Ideas inspired by Gilligan have appeared in nearly every area of discourse to which gender differences could conceivably be relevant. But now it seems that the gender differences are not nearly what they at first appeared to be. Does this mean that all of this work should be abandoned? It seems to me that it does not. The reason for this is simply that claims of gender differences are not really essential to much of the work Gilligan has inspired.

Claims that women and men approach all moral problems in fundamentally different ways cannot be maintained, as we have seen. Some arguments for an ethic of Care begin from the thought that feminists should support such an ethic simply because this represents the way that women approach moral issues. These arguments must be abandoned, as there is no one way that women approach moral issues. Women, like men, use Justice thinking for impersonal problems and women, like men, use Care thinking for personal problems. So Care thinking cannot lay claim to being women's general approach to morality. We cannot then argue that Care thinking is good because it is women's thinking. But we have already seen that these arguments are open to strong criticism even if we assume Care thinking to be women's thinking. The fact (if it were one) that women think in a certain way does not give feminists sufficient reason to endorse that way of thinking. The discovery, then, that women don't have a special way of thinking only serves to make weaker an already weak argument.

Other arguments, like Baier's, do not in fact turn on claims of gender differences in moral thinking.[16] Her argument for Care thinking is that it is a better way of thinking about areas of life that have been traditionally considered female, and traditionally neglected by male philosophers. This argument fits very nicely with the empirical

---

[16] She makes frequent reference to gender difference claims, but they do not play a role in her arguments.

evidence, which indicates that both men and women find Care think-ing most natural to the traditionally female realm of the family. It is important, then, to pay close attention to the role that claims of gen-der difference play—and do not play—in feminist arguments. Rejec-tion of Gilligan's gender difference claims need not cause us to reject all the work that has been inspired by them.

Conclusion

One lesson we can draw from the work we have surveyed in this chapter is that it is immensely difficult to think clearly about differ-ences between women and men. It is difficult to discern what the differences are—differences in life experience, differences in patterns of thought, differences in ability, or differences in priorities; it is dif-ficult to discern what the causes of these differences are—biology, early childhood experience, or education; and it is difficult to discern what consequences follow from these differences—for men, for women, for feminism, and for philosophy.

Some points, however, seem to have emerged with clarity from the debate. First, it is wrong either to praise or to condemn traditionally female traits and activities simply on the grounds that they are *trad-itionally* female. It is equally wrong to praise or condemn them on the grounds that they actually represent what women are like. This latter sort of move is doubly problematic: first, we cannot infer anything about the value of a trait from the fact that women have it; second, we have seen that it is extremely hard to arrive at empirically supportable claims about what women are like. We should always move with great caution in this area. And we should always bear in mind an additional reason for caution: claims about male and female nature have a very long and often ugly history. Although they have some-times been used to improve the lot of women, they have a much longer history as a means of confining women's lives and opportun-ities. Feminists, then, should exercise great caution in making any claims about differences between women and men—especially since many of the feminist arguments that have been inspired by such claims do not really depend on them.

SUGGESTIONS FOR FURTHER READING

Background, overview

Flanagan, O., *Varieties of Moral Personality*. Cambridge, Mass.: Harvard University Press, 1991.

Friedman, M., 'Feminism in Ethics: Conceptions of Autonomy', in M. Fricker and J. Hornsby (eds.), *The Cambridge Companion to Feminism in Philosophy*. Cambridge: Cambridge University Press, 2000, 205–24.

Gilligan, C., *In a Different Voice*. Cambridge, Mass.: Harvard University Press, 1982.

Kymlicka, W., 'An Ethic of Care', in *Contemporary Political Philosophy: An Introduction*. Oxford: Oxford University Press, 2002, 398–430.

Tong, R., *Feminist Thought: A More Comprehensive Introduction*. Boulder, Colo.: Westview Press, 1998, ch. 4.

Moral and political philosophy building on Gilligan's work (a very few examples)

Baier, A., 'The Need for More than Justice', *Canadian Journal of Philosophy* supplementary vol. 13 (1987): 41–56.

Benhabib, S., *Situating the Self*. New York: Routledge, 1991.

Ruddick, S., *Maternal Thinking: Toward a Politics of Peace*. London: Women's Press, 1989.

Tronto, J., *Moral Boundaries: A Political Argument for an Ethic of Care*. New York: Routledge, 1993.

Philosophical criticism of ethics of care

Card, C., 'Gender and Moral Luck', in O. Flanagan and A. Rorty (eds.), *Identity, Character, and Morality*. Bradford, Mass.: MIT Press, 1993, 200–18.

Friedman, M., 'Beyond Caring: The De-moralization of Gender', *Canadian Journal of Philosophy*, supplementary vol. 13 (1987): 87–110.

Houston, B., 'Rescuing Womanly Virtues: Some Dangers of Moral Reclamation', in *Canadian Journal of Philosophy*, supplementary vol. 13 (1987): 237–62.

Okin, S. M., 'Thinking like a Woman', in D. Rhode (ed.), *Theoretical Perspectives on Sexual Difference*. New Haven, Conn.: Yale University Press, 1990, 145–59.

Discussions of empirical data on justice and care

Flanagan, O., *Varieties of Moral Personality*. Cambridge, Mass.: Harvard University Press, 1991.

Gilligan, C., Ward, J. V., and Taylor, J. M., *Mapping the Moral Domain*. Cambridge, Mass.: Harvard University Press, 1988.

Moody-Adams, M., 'Gender and the Complexity of Moral Voices', in C. Card (ed.), *Feminist Ethics*. Lawrence: University of Kansas Press, 1991, 195–212.

Nails, D., 'Social-Scientific Sexism: Gilligan's Mismeasure of Man', *Social Research* 50 (1983): 643–64.

Tavris, C., *The Mismeasure of Woman: Why Women are Not the Better Sex, the Inferior Sex, or the Opposite Sex*. New York: Touchstone, 1992, ch. 2, 57–92.

Walker, L. J., 'Sex Differences in the Development of Moral Reasoning', in M. J. Larrabee (ed.), *An Ethic of Care*. London: Routledge, 1993, 157–76.

—— de Vries, B., and Trevethan, S. D., 'Moral Stages and Moral Orientations in Real-Life and Hypothetical Dilemmas', *Child Development* 58 (1987): 842–58.

8

Feminism, Science, and Bias

There has been a lot of bad science in history (as most of us are already aware). In particular, poorly designed scientific research has served to reinforce false stereotypes that have been used to justify discriminatory behaviour against women, and people of whatever ethnicity or colour have been considered (in a particular time and place) to be inferior. A very clear example of this is intelligence tests given to US army recruits during the First World War, which seemed to confirm the prevailing prejudice that those of southern European origin were less intelligent than those of northern European origin. As it turns out, those from northern Europe had generally been in the US longer than those from southern Europe, and the test contained questions that could only be correctly answered by one who had been in the US for a while. One such question was, roughly, 'What is Crisco?' ('Crisco' is the brand name of a cooking fat popular in the US) (Gould 1992: 200). Steven Jay Gould's *The Mismeasure of Man* (from which the above example comes) is a classic study of the ways in which intelligence testing was used to give scientific credibility to prejudices, and it contains extensive discussion of ways that this has been used to discriminate against both non-whites and those whites that were considered inferior.[1]

There has been similar research with respect to women. Many nineteenth-century anthropologists took brain size to be a good indicator of intelligence. This theory was taken to confirm that women,

---

[1] IQ tests are still used to support racial prejudices. One recent example of this involved the work of Herrnstein and Murray (1994) and responses from those who embraced it. For critical discussion of this book, see Devlin et al. (1997) and Kincheloe et al. (1996).

whose heads tended to be smaller than men's, were indeed less intelligent than men. Many continued to stick with this theory even when it had been pointed out that elephants had much larger heads than men (Russett 1989).

How should one react to the discovery that science has been deeply affected by, and done much to reinforce, prejudice of many sorts? To some, it has seemed obvious that there must be something wrong with science as a discipline that has led to this. Others think that science is fine, but that its practitioners have been corrupted into doing bad science by their own prejudices and biases. Feminists have reacted in a wide variety of ways. This chapter will explore feminist discussions of science, focusing especially on the role of biases in scientific theorizing. We will begin with an extended case study that makes it clear just how deeply every aspect of a scientific endeavour can be affected by the scientists' biases and assumptions.

An example

Elisabeth Lloyd argues that scientists' biases may play an important role at all stages of scientific inquiry (Lloyd 1993). A bias can be understood, for our purposes, as a belief or interest that the investigator possesses prior to beginning research.[2] So, for example, we say that a scientist testing the link between smoking and cancer who is already convinced that smoking cannot cause cancer is biased due to a prior belief; and one being paid to produce results showing that smoking does not cause cancer is biased due to her interest in the results of the experiment.

Lloyd's particular example concerns attempts by evolutionary biologists to explain why it is that women have orgasms. She chronicles several such attempts, and the nature of the research that they took to support their theories. Lloyd argues that scientists' biases may play an important role at all stages of scientific inquiry. She specifically discusses:

---

[2] I take this definition from Antony (1993: 188). Antony offers it as a strict empiricist understanding of 'bias'.

1. the formulation of the problem to be explained;
2. the decisions about which data are relevant;
3. the collection of data; and
4. the interpretation of data.

Female orgasm has been viewed as a puzzle in a way that male orgasm has not. Male orgasm needs little explanation from an evolutionary perspective. It is an obvious aid in reproduction, and the desire for orgasm quite reasonably motivates men to engage in sexual intercourse,[3] as it is a reliable means of attaining orgasm for men. It is easy to see, then, how male orgasm has what evolutionary theorists call 'adaptive value'—that is, it is easy to see why men who have orgasms will be more likely to pass on their genes than men who do not have orgasms. This, then, means that we can easily explain how it is that male orgasm would come to evolve. Female orgasm, however, is a different matter. The problem is traditionally posed thus: why is it that women, unlike other female primates, should have orgasms? Why should it be that orgasms are of adaptive value for women, but not for other female primates? After all, women certainly don't need to have orgasms in order to reproduce. Further, it is not obvious what important difference there is between women and other female primates that would lead orgasms to have adaptive value for women but not for other female primates.

Interestingly, this traditional way of formulating the problem of female orgasm is simply mistaken. As it turns out, women are not the only female primates to experience orgasms. Lloyd points out that many female non-human primates experience orgasms.[4] These orgasms went unnoticed, however, because they did not tend to occur during sexual behaviour with *male* primates. In fact, in some species they occur most frequently during sexual behaviour with other *female* primates. Experimenters assumed that female orgasms would occur during heterosexual sex, so they missed (or at least misunderstood) the orgasms that occurred at other times. Moreover, they assumed

---

[3] I am using 'sexual intercourse' as it is commonly used in discussions of this kind, to refer to penetrative genital sex.

[4] It turns out that it is not only female *primates* that experience orgasms, but other female animals as well (Bagemihl 1999).

that all sexual behaviour would be heterosexual behaviour, so they often entirely failed to notice that there *was* any sex taking place between members of the same sex.

Lloyd suggests that an important assumption at work in the above is that female sexuality must be understood as centred on reproduction: since homosexual behaviour could not result in reproduction, it could not be sexual.[5] One might suppose that this assumption is required for any effort to explain women's sexuality from an evolutionary perspective. However, evolutionary explanations do not require this. First, an evolutionary explanation could invoke some advantage other than a directly reproductive one. Next, as Lloyd herself argues, not every trait need be taken to have adaptive value. A trait may, for example, be simply a by-product of one that has adaptive value. (In fact, this is the sort of explanation she ultimately prefers for female orgasm.)

We can also see the flawed research as related to a broader tendency—whether or not based on the assumption Lloyd pinpoints— to overlook the existence of non-heterosexual sexual activity.[6] Both the assumption that female sexuality must be based around reproduction and the tendency to overlook the existence of non-heterosexual sex are biases. The effects of these assumptions on research were dramatic. Orgasms that took place during non-heterosexual sex were simply not classified as orgasms. Indeed, the sex acts themselves were not recognized as such: instead, they were described in non-sexual terms. For example, bonobos engage in a practice called 'genitogenital rubbing', in which a female 'wraps her legs around another female, rubbing her own clitoris against her partner's while emitting screams of enjoyment'. This behaviour has been variously described as:

> 'greeting' behaviour, or 'appeasement' behaviour, or 'reassurance' behaviour, or 'reconciliation' behaviour, or 'tension-regulation' behaviour, or 'social bonding' behaviour, or 'food exchange' behaviour— almost anything, it seems, besides *pleasurable sexual* behaviour.'
>
> (Bagemihl 1999: 106)

---

[5] Male homosexual behaviour was often also described as non-sexual.

[6] Marilyn Frye (1983b) discusses some ways in which the existence of lesbians is obscured.

The problem of female orgasm, then, was misdefined from the beginning. No one should be asking why women differ from other female primates by having orgasms. There is, however, still a question in need of answer: why do women *and* other female primates have orgasms? Our focus here, though, is on attempts to answer the original, flawed question: *why do women, as opposed to other female primates, have orgasms?*

A truly stunning answer to this question was put forward by Desmond Morris (1967).[7] According to this explanation, women have orgasms because women walk upright. To see how this explanation works, first consider the position of the body when a woman walks, and compare it to the position of the body when a non-human primate walks. A woman's body is perpendicular to the ground, while a non-human primate's body is closer to parallel. Morris claims that if women walked around after having sex, they would lose seminal fluid and fail to get pregnant. This is not a risk when a female monkey walks around after having sex, because her body is tilted in such a way that fluid will not leak out. Fortunately, however, according to Morris, women have orgasms during intercourse with men, and this has just the desired effect. After an orgasm a woman collapses, exhausted, as her sexual excitement vanishes and fatigue sets in. Because the woman has collapsed, she doesn't get up and walk around, and this aids in reproduction.

Lloyd points out that Morris's explanation goes wrong at just about every stage. First, it turns out that after sex female baboons go off and squat for ten to fifteen minutes, invariably leaving behind large pools of semen. If positioning oneself perpendicularly to the ground and thereby losing seminal fluid were truly maladaptive, there would be a real problem for the baboons. (There doesn't seem to be one.) Second, as many readers may be aware, women don't always have orgasms during sexual intercourse with men. In fact, studies indicate that only 25–30 per cent of women regularly experience orgasms during sexual intercourse with men. Many readers were probably also puzzled by

---

[7] This explanation still has currency: I saw it put forward in a 1998 television documentary.

Morris's description of female orgasm.[8] Morris cites research in support of his claim, but the material he cites actually only claims that *men* are exhausted by orgasm. According to this research, women's sexual excitement does not vanish immediately, and women do not collapse with exhaustion. Instead, women often remain aroused and experience, or at least desire, more orgasms (Lloyd 1993: 146).[9] So female orgasm cannot possibly play the role that Morris ascribes to it—that of making women collapse, exhausted, after having sex with men.

Detailed study of theories like Morris's, Lloyd argues, show that experimenters' biases may infect every stage of the research process. They affect what problem the scientist sets out to answer, possibly causing them to ask inappropriate questions: Why do women, but no other female primates, have orgasms? They affect collection of data: when looking for female orgasms in non-human primates, scientists looked only at sexual behaviour between female and male primates. They affect decisions about what data are relevant: scientists who did observe female orgasms did not realize that they were observing orgasms. Finally, they affect interpretation of data: behaviour like genito-genital rubbing was considered food exchange behaviour!

The problem of biases

Case studies like Lloyd's make it clear just how much impact scientists' biases can have on research. Some feminists argue that work of this sort does not show any reason to change our thinking about science, except for a need to acknowledge that many of its practitioners have been biased—and therefore bad scientists (Haack 1993). After all, our common-sense notion of the scientific ideal is that it demands impartial, unbiased research. If it can be shown that some particular research was affected by experimenter bias, this shows that it was bad science. The scientists Lloyd discusses are bad scientists,

---

[8] The first time I taught this material, a male student blurted out, 'But that's what blokes do!'

[9] According to Hite (1976), cited by Lloyd (1993: 146) but not Morris, about 47% of women are unsatisfied and want more orgasms.

then, by science's own standards. This is of course a problem, according to this line of thought, but it does not show anything wrong with science or the way that we think of science.

This is a reasonable response, but some argue that it is still inadequate. In particular, it does not explain how scientists could have failed to see the problems caused by their biases, and it offers no guidance as to how these problems could be avoided in the future. Surely, the evolutionary scientists thought that they were not biased—they thought they were simply responding to the evidence before them objectively. The same is true of Lawrence Kohlberg, who (as we saw in Chapter 7) studied *human* moral development through experiments only involving males. Kohlberg's conviction that this was adequate came from the assumption that males can be taken as the norm for humanity. Lynn Hankinson Nelson insists that it is vital to realize just how difficult it has been to notice the presence and effects of certain sorts of biases:

> if the problem with an empirical base limited to males—a common limitation in developmental psychology—was obvious, then *why*, prior to the advent of feminist science criticism, had developmental psychologists *not* recognized it?
>
> (Nelson 1996: 286)

When convictions are deeply held by individual researchers and widely shared by the research community, the effects of those convictions on research will go unnoticed. This, according to Nelson, is one of the most important things that feminist philosophy of science has to teach us.

What, then, should be done about such robust unnoticed biases and their effects? One answer is that we should simply work harder to search out and eliminate biases. But this seems unduly optimistic—why should we think we will do any better in the future? Another answer, perhaps strangely, begins from acknowledging that bias is inevitable: we all have background beliefs and interests, and they *will* influence the ways that we make sense of the world.[10] Scientists are

---

[10] Indeed, the definition of 'bias' given earlier should make it clear that biases are unavoidable. How could anyone begin research without *any* prior beliefs or interests?

no different from the rest of us in this respect. The problem, then, is to make sure that our biases don't lead to error. In what follows, I will canvass three approaches to this problem. Each of these responses proposes as part of its solution the importance of women and/or feminists being involved with science.

The idea that involving women and/or feminists in science could be part of the solution to this problem is, at first, a puzzling one. Suggesting that women should be involved requires accepting that *who one is* could have an impact on how research proceeds; and suggesting that feminists should be involved requires, it would seem, actively seeking out particular prior beliefs and interests—that is, particular biases. Both of these ideas are very strange if we think that science should be done by impartial researchers who have eliminated all of their biases. But if this goal is in fact far from attainable, as it seems likely to be, the situation is different.

Many feminist epistemologists insist that case studies like Lloyd's show that certain background beliefs and interests are beneficial to science. Lloyd, and those whose work she draws on, are feminists: they are not free of bias. Their feminism may lead them to assume, for example, that reproduction is not (or may not be) central to women's sexuality; or to look for often-ignored non-heterosexual activity. These assumptions and tendencies affect the research that they do. If any influence of biases means *bad science*, then this science, too, must be written off as bad.[11] Yet the research they have done seems *good*. Indeed, it seems as though these biases *helped* them to do good research—by leading them to notice things that had previously been missed, for example. Reflections of this sort have led many feminists to suggest that biases can actually sometimes help to improve science. One version of this idea, standpoint theory, holds that some biases are better than others, and that feminists are especially well suited to gaining knowledge (at least) about certain areas. The next proposal, which focuses on scientific communities, holds that the usefulness of certain biases is due to the importance of researchers with a wide

---

[11] The problems involved in condemning some research as flawed due to bias, while supporting the role of biases in research, are well described in Louise Antony's discussion of what she calls the Bias Paradox (Antony 1993: 188–91).

variety of *different* biases working together. The final proposal, feminist naturalized epistemology, is a bit more complex, insisting that careful study is required to determine precisely which biases are helpful in which circumstances—and that feminists have done important work in coming to understand the workings and effects of certain biases.[12]

Standpoint theory

One way of making sense of the manner in which science can be improved when feminist women get involved is to suggest that there is something about *women* that allows this improvement. Sometimes this gets expressed as the idea that women have access to a special standpoint that makes them 'epistemically privileged'. What this means is (very roughly) that women are more reliable, insightful, or likely to be right than men are, when it comes to certain topics. Thus, they have an important contribution to make to research in these areas. This may sound odd initially but, as Elizabeth Anderson points out, this kind of claim is actually fairly ordinary:

> Many claims to epistemic privilege on behalf of particular perspectives are commonplace and uncontroversial. Auto mechanics are generally in a better position than auto consumers to know what is wrong with their cars. Practical experience in fulfilling the social role of the mechanic grounds the mechanic's epistemic privilege, which lays a claim to greater reliability than the judgments of auto consumers.

> (Anderson 2001)

The idea that women have access to a privileged standpoint in certain areas of study has its origins in Marxism. Marx argued that workers, or proletariats, are in a unique and privileged position to see the truth about the organization of society. Miranda Fricker, explaining this idea, writes:

> Whereas from the capitalist standpoint society appears to be made up of individuals each pursuing self-interest, from the standpoint of proletarian wage labor it can be seen that what is really going on is the systematic

---

[12] Although I have divided my discussion into sections, there is in fact substantial overlap in thinking between those advocating the views that I discuss.

exploitation of one class by another. Only one of these groups is in a position to see social reality for what it is.

(Fricker 1999: 194)

Marx did not hold that workers would automatically be able to see society for what it is. Indeed, he believed that workers would need to put in considerable effort to overcome the capitalist ideology that they had been taught. However, their social position gave them access to a standpoint from which they would be able to perceive social reality better than capitalists could. A key reason for this was that their labour was especially central to the functioning of society: they were more in touch with the concrete reality of the workings of the world than their capitalist employers.

The original formulations of feminist standpoint theory hold that women's labour, like workers' labour, gives them access to a privileged perspective on social reality (see e.g. Hartsock 1983). Women, even more than male workers, are said to be in touch with the concrete reality of life. Their work in giving birth to and raising the next generation, and in supplying the basic necessities of daily life for themselves and their families, makes them especially central to society's functioning. (It is worth noting that this view doesn't depend on the idea that women's labour is *confined* to the household—women who work outside the home but in addition carry out most of the household labour would also count as central in this way.) As a result, women were said to have access to a privileged standpoint for understanding the world. But—like workers for Marx—women would not automatically have this standpoint. They could only attain this *feminist standpoint*[13] by moving beyond the ideologies that they had been taught, and coming to understand the world in a new way. Women who successfully took up the feminist standpoint might come to realize that women's contributions to the world had been systematically overlooked or underestimated. This realization might, for example, lead them to question the standard economic definition of 'labour' as paid employment outside the home, thus allowing them to attain a

---

[13] It is worth noting at this point that the term 'women's standpoint' is also often used to describe the privileged standpoint available to women. This should not be taken to suggest that all women automatically have this standpoint.

more accurate picture of the world. The idea of a feminist standpoint, then, would offer a way of explaining how feminist biases could improve science.

Feminist standpoint theory can also be motivated independently of the Marxist story suggested above. This is a good thing, since the view above assumes a uniformity to women's experiences that just isn't the case—well-off women may spend substantially less time meeting the day-to-day needs of their families, childless women are not generally involved in reproducing the next generation, and a sex-linked division of labour simply isn't possible for lesbian couples—to name just a few examples. Here I will discuss just two alternative ways of understanding what makes certain standpoints privileged. First, women's status as outsiders might position them well to notice errors in standard scientific frameworks. Second, women's relative lack of power might give them an interest in discovering certain truths that the more powerful do not wish to pursue. If these claims are right, then one can still (without Marxism) defend the idea that women have access to a special standpoint that makes them especially able to discern at least certain sorts of truths.[14]

Outsider status

One explanation for women's ability to improve science comes from the fact that men have (predominantly) been the ones formulating scientific theories for a very long time. This means that women, as outsiders to the scientific world, are in a better position to notice blind spots, errors, and things that have been left out. So, for example, women are better situated to realize that a great deal of labour is overlooked when 'work' is defined as paid employment outside the home; or that women do not collapse immobile after having orgasms. Because women typically live different lives from men, they are able to notice ways in which theories formulated by men fail to

[14] Some standpoint theorists also argue that women have a special way of thinking about the world that gives them a privileged standpoint. However, attempts to establish that women and men think differently in this sort of way have not been very successful. Some of the relevant empirical research is discussed in Chapter 7 of this book.

accommodate wider spheres of experience. So, theorists like Smith (1996) argue, better science can be done from a woman's standpoint—women are more likely to notice mismatches between theory and reality.

Powerlessness

Women also have (in general) less power than men in society, and some have argued that those with less power will have a less distorted perspective on society. Those with more power will have an interest in maintaining systematically biased understandings of society that legitimate the status quo as just and appropriate. The powerless lack this motivation, and will thus be more able to discern the ways in which the status quo is damaging. They will have an interest in asking and investigating questions that might reveal problems in society. Further, the less powerful in society are forced, by their relative lack of power, to develop a good understanding of not only their own position but also the position of the more powerful. After all, if one lacks power, success in life may well depend on one's ability to understand those who hold power:

> ... because the ruling class has an interest in concealing the way in which it dominates and exploits the rest of the population, the interpretation of reality that it presents will be distorted in characteristic ways. In particular, the suffering of subordinate classes will be ignored, redescribed as enjoyment or justified as freely chosen, deserved, or inevitable.
>
> The standpoint of the oppressed is not just different from that of the ruling class; it is also epistemologically advantageous ... Whereas the condition of the oppressed groups is visible only dimly to the ruling class, the oppressed are able to see more clearly the ruled as well as the rulers and the relation between them. Thus, the standpoint of the oppressed includes and is able to explain the standpoint of the ruling class.
>
> (Jaggar 1988: 370–1)

Since women tend to have less power in society than men, women are able to improve scientific research by bringing their perspectives to bear on scientific issues. This provides a nice example of ways that prior interests might be said to be beneficial to the conduct of science: women who have taken up the feminist standpoint have a desire to help women gain more power in the world, and this prior interest leads them to seek an understanding of the ways that women are denied power.

Other 'outsiders', other groups lacking in power

Both of these considerations suggest that it is not just *women* who could improve science by getting involved with it. Indeed, they suggest that one shouldn't settle for simply involving women in science. Women are not the only group to have traditionally been outsiders to science, and women are not the only group to suffer powerlessness. Moreover, the women who are most likely to be involved in science are white middle-class women. While such scientists may be outsiders in terms of their gender, they are not outsiders in terms of their race or social class—scientists are predominantly white and middle-class. Similarly, while such women may lack power relative to white middle-class men, they tend to be quite powerful relative to black working-class women. So if oppression and outsider status lend a useful vantage point on scientific endeavours, white women may not have as much to offer as other groups. Patricia Hill Collins gives a vivid example of the ways that the perspectives of black women might change social science:

> Take, for example, the differences between how US Black women interpret their experiences as single mothers and how prevailing social science research analyzes the same reality. Whereas Black women stress their struggles with job discrimination, inadequate child support, inferior housing, and street violence, far too much social science research seems mesmerized by images of lazy 'welfare queens' content to stay on the dole.

(Collins 2000: 255)

Reflecting on these ideas leads to problems for the notion of a feminist standpoint that is particularly available to *women*. Women differ enormously from one another, and in ways that are very relevant to the contributions that they might be able to make to knowledge. Black women's lives are very different from white women's lives, and they would be likely to notice different problems with existing theoretical frameworks from those noticed by white women. Moreover, if lack of power increases one's ability to make a useful contribution to science, then black women may be *better* able to do this than white women.[15] Once we realize this, however, we might also notice that black women differ from one another. Middle-class black women will have different insights to offer from less well-off black women. Lesbian black women will have different experiences from heterosexual black women. Once we appreciate worries like these, it becomes somewhat more difficult to imagine a single privileged standpoint.[16]

Multiple standpoints for each thinker

Sandra Harding's solution to this problem is a complicated one. First, it is important to note that, for her, access to a standpoint does not depend on one's social location or identity. For Harding, a person has taken up a feminist standpoint if they manage to 'start their thought' from women's lives. It is not only women who are capable of doing this, according to her, although it comes more easily to women. Harding maintains that it is possible for men to take up a woman's standpoint, or for whites to take up a black standpoint. In addition, Harding thinks that valuable insights can come from the kind of understanding that can be achieved by one who has managed to take up (at least partially) the standpoint of others. She uses John Stuart Mill, a nineteenth-century proponent of women's suffrage and women's rights[17] more generally, as an example of this kind of thinker, suggesting that he developed

[15] This has led some to suppose that standpoint theorists should advocate the standpoint of whoever is most oppressed. (Hekman (1997) takes this to be a consequence of standard understandings of standpoint theory.) This sets up a worrying potential for a 'who's most oppressed' competition (Harding 1997). It would also undermine the claims of most standpoint theorists, since they themselves are unlikely to be maximally oppressed. Standpoint theorists themselves deny that they are committed to this (ibid.).

[16] Some have taken these considerations to indicate that the category 'woman' should be abandoned (see e.g. Nicholson 1990; Spelman 1988).

[17] For his general support of women's rights, see Mill (1986 [1861]). For his support of women's suffrage, see pp. 57–8.

a particular view that speaks partially from the position of women but partially also from his own life as a man. If you read *The Subjection of Women*, you kind of see him walking around in the world and looking at it differently from how he would have looked at it before he got feminism.

(Harding, quoted in Hersh and Olson 1995: 17)

There is much to this idea. Mill's writing does indeed seem to show a dual awareness that comes from being a man and from reflecting deeply on the situation of women.[18]

> Think what it is to be a boy, to grow up to manhood in the belief that, without any merit or any exertion of his own, though he may be the most frivolous and empty or the most ignorant and stolid of men, by the mere fact of being born a male he is by right the superior of all and every one of an entire half of the human race: including probably some whose real superiority to himself he has daily or hourly occasion to feel; but, even if in his whole conduct he habitually follows a woman's guidance, still, if he is a fool, he thinks that of course she is not, and cannot be, equal in ability and judgment to himself; and if he is not a fool, he does worse—he sees that she is superior to him, and believes that, notwithstanding her superiority, he is entitled to command and she is bound to obey.

(Mill 1986 [1861]: 86)

Harding generalizes this point, to cover not just the standpoints of women, but also those of other marginalized groups. Harding holds that the best theorizing will come from those who are able to 'start their thought' from multiple lives (Harding 1993: 66). She maintains that attempting to do this helps her to do better work as a white woman, and that she has an obligation to work in this way.

There's been a tendency to think that only the dominated, only the

---

[18] John Stuart Mill worked very closely with Harriet Taylor, who eventually married him. Although the extent of Taylor's contributions to work published as Mill's remains uncertain, *The Subjection of Women* was written after Taylor's death. Taylor undoubtedly played a role in shaping Mill's views on women (he credits her with shaping his views on much else besides). This does not, however, pose problems for understanding Mill as managing to 'start his thought' from women's lives. In fact, listening to women is one technique that Harding recommends for achieving this end.

marginal lives can use their social location as an instrument of the production of knowledge. They certainly *can* use it and *do* use it, but it's also the case that the people in the dominant groups can learn how to use their position (as a white woman in my case; for another, say, as a white man) to ask the kinds of questions and think the kinds of thoughts that would make use of the resources of that particular position. For example, I am very familiar with Western philosophy . . . if I do turn a critical lens on it, I can learn; I'm in the place to be able to do that.

(Harding, quoted in Hersh and Olson 1995: 16)

A part of Harding's motivation for insisting that standpoints are available to anyone willing to work hard enough is that she thinks it is self-defeating to maintain, for example, that only women can attain the right standpoint for knowledge.

> I suggest that feminists should find it inappropriate both to criticise male scholars and researchers for ignoring women and gender and also to insist that they are incapable of conducting research which satisfies feminist requirements.

(Harding 1987: 12)

To see this vividly, suppose that feminist scientists point out the errors in a male scientist's research, and the male scientist thanks them and asks what he should do differently in the future. If only women can attain the appropriate standpoint, all he can do is to simply give up on doing research. This seems wrong, and also a bad way to go about improving science. It is important, then, to allow for the possibility of men 'starting their thought' from women's lives.[19]

Helen Longino worries that it would be very difficult to put Harding's proposal into action. If Harding is right, then one should take most seriously those views expressed by people who have managed to start their thought from the most lives (Longino 1999). But it is very difficult to know when one has managed to take up the standpoint of even a single group. Suppose that you, whatever sex you are, and

---

[19] There is, however, a response to this argument available. Taking up a woman's standpoint may be an especially good way to gain knowledge, but it may not be the *only* way. So male scientists might still be able to acquire knowledge even without being able to take up a woman's standpoint.

whatever race you are, are trying to take up the standpoint of a black woman. Even if you are *yourself* a black woman, you can never be sure that you have succeeded in taking up a black woman's standpoint. What is required is that you 'start your thinking' from black women's lives; but Harding offers no recipe for discerning when you have managed to do this. Moreover, she really wants you to do something even more challenging than this: to start your thinking from as many privileged standpoints as possible. This seems a daunting (and potentially confusing) task, and one that might well leave you forever in a state of worry over whether you had attained a legitimate position from which to begin to do science. Alternatively, you might become convinced all too easily that you had successfully taken up the necessary standpoints. Since it is so difficult to know when you have managed to start your thinking from others' lives, you may well leap to the conclusion that you have done so when you are in fact very far from managing it. Harding's proposal, then, faces serious practical difficulties.

Multiple standpoints, multiple thinkers

One particularly appealing feature of Harding's proposal is that it offers a way of maintaining something like the idea that there is a particular best position to be in for obtaining knowledge, while at the same time abandoning the idea that there is *a* woman's standpoint. For Harding, the best position to be in is that of starting one's thought from as many marginalized lives as possible. We have seen, however, that this faces difficulties.

Patricia Hill Collins maintains that there are a variety of privileged standpoints that each provide privileged yet partial knowledge—a black lesbian, a Latina heterosexual, and an Asian man all have different standpoints available to them, and each such standpoint is epistemically privileged in its own way (Collins 2000). None of these standpoints can be considered *the best* for obtaining knowledge, but each should instead be considered vital for providing at least part of the truth.

Each group speaks from its own standpoint and shares its own partial, situated knowledge. But because each group perceives its own truth as partial, its knowledge is unfinished. Each group becomes better able to consider other groups' standpoints without relinquishing the uniqueness of its own standpoint or suppressing other groups' partial perspectives.

(Collins 2000: 270)

Miranda Fricker (1999) suggests that, despite the enormous differences to be found in women's experiences, there are still sufficient commonalities to ground the idea of a feminist standpoint that is particularly available to women. For example, black and white women may have very different experiences of discrimination on grounds of sex. Nonetheless, there is *something* in common between these experiences that makes it appropriate to categorize them as experiences of discrimination on grounds of sex. Fricker suggests that this sort of commonality, thin though it is, may be sufficient to allow for the idea that we can speak of a feminist standpoint.[20] Women will have access to a privileged standpoint on certain issues: she suggests, for example, marital rape, stalking, and glass ceilings. Fricker does not deny that other groups (including subcategories of women, like black lesbians or Latina heterosexuals) will also have privileged standpoints on particular issues. Indeed, she seems committed to this. She argues that the key source of epistemic privilege for oppressed groups is that they have not had much say in forming the concepts and theories used by dominant groups to make sense of reality. Important aspects of reality, those relating to the experiences of oppressed groups, will therefore have been left out or misunderstood. Oppressed groups have epistemic privilege in that they can provide a better understanding of these issues.

On both Collins's and Fricker's views, diversity matters. If, as for Collins, each standpoint only gives partial knowledge, the fullest knowledge can only be obtained by those from various groups working together. If, as for Fricker, different standpoints will be privileged with respect to different subject matters, then again, multiple standpoints

---

[20] Although Fricker holds that women's experience of sex discrimination contains enough commonalities to ground the idea that there is a standpoint distinctively available to women, she notes that what is common to women's experience may in many cases not be the most illuminating subject matter. Much will be missed, for example, if one fails to attend to the ways that race, class, sexual orientation, and the like can affect the nature of sex discrimination.

will lead to a fuller understanding. Harding's theory also incorporates diversity among researchers, calling for dialogue as a means of learning to think from one another's lives. The next theory we will turn to rejects the idea of privileged standpoints altogether and focuses on the importance of diversity.

Scientific communities

Helen Longino (1990; 1993) rejects feminist standpoint theory. She finds elements of its motivation compelling, but thinks that they can be accommodated in a different way, one that is free of the sorts of problems that confront standpoint theories. What she finds compelling is the idea that the biases and assumptions of feminist scientists (like those Lloyd draws on) *helped* them to do good science, rather than hindering them. In addition, she finds it plausible that features which standpoint theorists have identified—outsider status and powerlessness—might help women to notice important problems with existing science, and thus enable them to improve it.

Longino, however, takes all of this to show simply a need for scientific communities to be diverse. No individual scientist can (or should) free herself completely of biases and assumptions. But a group of scientists with a wide variety of different biases and assumptions will be able to notice when one or another of their biases has a detrimental effect on research. And this is one reason that feminists, carrying with them their own assumptions, improved science: they noticed that previous scientists' different assumptions had caused them to overlook important data and misformulate their questions. Because the researchers had shared the problematic assumptions, they had failed to notice their detrimental impact. But new scientists, with different biases, were in a position to point out errors.

For Longino, scientific inquiry is a fundamentally social endeavour. This is contrary to the stereotypical image of a lone scientist working away in his laboratory late into the night in a passionate quest to uncover truths. But this image has always represented a rather distorted view of the way that scientific inquiry takes place—especially today. Most laboratories are filled with communities of researchers (scientists, students, and assistants) who—in ideal circumstances any-way—confer with each other, debate what they are doing, and share ideas and questions about research projects. Moreover, a very tradi-tional demand in science is that experiments should be replicable. That is, if one scientist's laboratory produces a result, other laborator-ies had better be able to produce the same result. If they cannot, researchers will be less likely to accept the first result. This demand for replicability is a key way that scientists criticize and evaluate each other's research; and, Longino claims, it absolutely requires that one conceive of science as a social endeavour.

According to Longino, objectivity in science can *only* be achieved via diversity in the scientific community. Indeed, she takes objectivity to be a property of scientific communities rather than individuals. It is, according to her, simply a mistake to talk about an individual researcher being objective. This, for Longino, follows naturally out of recognizing that science is communal; and that individual scientists are inevitably influenced by their own biases and assumptions. She can be seen as expanding upon the traditional demands for repeat-ability, and free interchange of ideas in the scientific community. She adds to this (1) the thought that repeatability and free interchange of ideas will not do much to correct errors that are based on assumptions shared throughout the scientific community, and (2) the idea that we cannot even speak of individuals being objective.

We will now turn to some potential problems for this view, begin-ning with the least worrying and progressing to the most problematic.

Making sure that various perspectives are heard

Longino's objectives would not be achieved by a scientific community that merely added some women and minorities to its membership. A diversity of perspectives is not on its own sufficient for achieving objectivity. It does no good to have a diversity of people in the scien-tific community if those with power are not willing to listen to the insights of those from different backgrounds. Many feminists have written of the difficulty of getting marginalized perspectives taken seriously (see e.g. Fricker 1998). Longino hopes to address this problem by maintaining that the scientific community must view the facilitation of diverse criticism as essential to its success. It must value the publication of criticism, be responsive to it, and help people from a wide range of backgrounds to find their way into the scientific community (Longino 1993).

These proposals may not, however, be sufficient. Those from 'outsider' groups may have developed their own ways of expressing themselves, ways that are different from those used by the more powerful. Patricia Hill Collins writes of the fact that black women have often expressed themselves in song and poetry, rather than in writing of the sort that would be easily accessible to social scientists:

> Investigating the subjugated knowledge of subordinate groups—in this case a Black women's standpoint and Black feminist thought—requires more ingenuity than that needed to examine the standpoints and thought of dominant groups. I found my training as a social scientist inadequate to the task of studying the subjugated knowledge of a Black women's standpoint. This is because subordinate groups have long had to use alternative ways to create independent self-definitions and self-valuations and to re-articulate them through our own specialists.
>
> (Collins 1997: 198)

If there are opposing perspectives to be found *outside* the scientific community (perspectives that could be important for revealing the influence of scientists' biases)—and it seems nearly certain that there are—then Longino's proposals are not enough. She urges a diverse scientific community, so one solution might be to try to bring some of those of whom Collins speaks into the scientific community. But if those with important insights to offer are poets, this amounts to a proposal to turn poets into scientists. This seems unlikely to be wildly successful, and would probably not be strongly supported by the poets themselves.

So, scientists must do more than ensure diversity within their communities. They must find a way to listen to the insights of those outside the scientific community. They must also make sure (at least in the social sciences) that the research they do involves effectively listening to and understanding those who are the subjects of the research, even when they may communicate in ways that are not familiar to the scientists.

What research can we accept?

Most scientific research, in fact, has not come out of very diverse communities. Most of the scientific claims we accept today could be criticized from Longino's perspective for not having been subjected to criticism from a diverse enough range of people. After all, the scientific community is still mainly white, middle-class, and male—and was even more so in the past. And this would seem to run the risk of undermining a good deal of what we accept today as scientifically established.

It might also seem that, if Longino is right, we shouldn't be accepting the results of research if we don't know the social identity of the experimenters. Consider the experiments I discussed in the previous chapter. Some of those experiments you know to have been done by women. Some of them you know to have been done by men. Others you probably don't know about—you've only been given initials for the first names of their authors. Should you have looked up the names of those authors in an attempt to discern their sex before being willing to accept their claims? Even if you did this—which does seem an odd thing to do—Longino would, one might think, maintain that you should do more than that. You should find out about their racial and socioeconomic backgrounds. And you should find out about the backgrounds of those in the psychological community that have accepted their research. If the research community was not a diverse enough group, this alone should give you pause. But this seems very strange.

However, these concerns may not be as worrying as they sound. Longino would not advocate simply rejecting research because it was not done by a diverse enough group of scientists. For her, the only reasons for rejecting or criticizing scientific theories are traditional ones such as misinterpretation of evidence. What she claims is that problems like this are more likely to be noticed by a diverse group of scientists. How would Longino react, then, to research carried out and evaluated by, for example, a group known to be comprised exclusively of white, heterosexual, middle-class men? First, she would not reject it out of hand. She would not reject the results unless she, or someone else, found errors in it. But she would maintain that errors would be more likely to be spotted if the research were subjected to critique by scientists from other backgrounds. Moreover, she would insist that the research had not been carried out objectively. As long as the scientific community is not diverse, for Longino, it is not objective.

Repetition vs. repeatability

Longino makes much of the scientific community's demand for repeatability of research, claiming that it requires a conception of science as social. But, Louise Antony argues, this is not quite right (Antony 1995). A demand that experiments be repeat*able* is simply a demand that it be *possible* to repeat the experiments and get the same results. If the scientific community demanded that experiments actually be repeat*ed* before their results could be accepted, this would indeed ground the thought that science is fundamentally social. But it is very difficult to secure funding for repetition of experiments, and very difficult to publish the results, except in unusual cases. Thus, not much repetition of experiments actually goes on. The presumption that experiments should be repeat*able* is present, but on its own this does little to make science social. A lone experimenter, working in isolation, might well take her results to be repeatable. (And they might well be so.) The community only gets involved if there is actually a demand for *repetition* to take place.

Communities, individuals, and objectivity

Antony also argues that Longino is too quick to give up on the idea of objectivity as a property of individuals (Antony 1995). Perhaps individuals cannot obtain perfect objectivity, but they can certainly be more or less objective. Although diverse communities can be very helpful in minimizing the destructive effects of individual biases, so can individual actions. Longino's view of objectivity seems to suggest that no individual should work to correct her own biases, but that each should instead go ahead and work *from* her biases in order to maximize the objectivity of science through a pooling of a wide variety of perspectives. But this seems plainly wrong. As Antony notes, we certainly think that scientists can become *more* objective through simple actions like not having a financial stake in the outcome of their experiments. To make sense of this idea, we need a notion of *individuals* being more or less objective.

Feminism and naturalized epistemology

Some, such as Louise Antony (1993) and Elizabeth Anderson (1995), argue that we can make sense of the ways that feminists have improved science without such radical moves as employing the idea of a privileged standpoint, or formulating a new notion of objectivity. They suggest making use of what is by now a well-established strand of contemporary philosophy of science. This is the approach known as naturalized epistemology.[21] The term 'epistemology' refers to the study of knowledge, and the term 'naturalized' suggests that we should approach the study of human knowledge-seeking in the way that we approach any other elements of the natural world: we should study it using the techniques of science.[22]

When we do this, Antony notes, one of the first things we can see is that biases are inevitable, and that often they are even helpful. Humans have innate predispositions that help us to make sense of the world, innate assumptions about how things we encounter will be— and these are in fact essential to our functioning. Commonplace examples of this are psychological mechanisms that aid in language acquisition and face recognition. These ideas, then, fit well with the idea that biases are inevitable and sometimes good.

The approach of naturalized epistemology, Antony argues, can also help us to develop a much more subtle and sophisticated approach to biases. Standpoint theorists argue that certain perspectives are conducive to good biases; Longino urges simply accepting the presence of

---

[21] Nelson (1990; 1993) also argues that naturalized epistemology is important to feminism. But she combines this with the Longino-like claim that only communities can be seen as knowers.

[22] This calls for a sort of bootstrapping approach. One uses science as a tool for investigating science, perhaps revising some portions of one's methodology in light of discoveries.

biases and seeking research groups with a diversity of biases. Naturalized epistemology allows us to move beyond simply branding some
perspectives as conducive to good or bad biases, while still accom-
modating the idea that some biases (for example, the desire to keep
women 'in their place') are bad. It does so by offering a way of pursuing the question of which biases are good and which bad. The good
biases, Antony quite reasonably suggests, are those that reliably lead
us to truth, while the bad biases are those that tend to lead us to
falsehood.[23] We cannot know in advance which—or whose—biases
will be good or bad. Instead, this is something deserving of study.

Building on ideas like these, Anderson suggests that feminists have
been particularly good at uncovering certain sorts of bias that lead to
error (Anderson 1995). I will discuss only one of Anderson's
examples, what she calls 'androcentrism'. According to Anderson, 'A
knowledge practice is androcentric if it reflects an orientation geared
to specifically or typically male interests or male lives' (1995: 70). One
sort of androcentric practice is that of taking specifically male experiences as the norm. This bias (along with many others) is at work in
our initial example of Morris's explanation for female orgasm. A key
move in Morris's argument involves the claim that women collapse,
exhausted and unable to move, after orgasm. We saw that this
description of the after-effects of orgasm was actually drawn from
descriptions of male orgasm. Male experiences of orgasm, then, were
falsely taken to apply to women as well. Lawrence Kohlberg, discussed in the previous chapter, also fell victim to this bias: he
attempted to confirm that his scale of moral development was accurate by testing it only on males. When females later turned out not to
progress as he had predicted humans should, Kohlberg inferred that
there was a problem with women. Rather than that, he should have
tested both males and females initially to learn whether his scale was
accurate. This inference is an indication of the strength of Kohlberg's
assumption that males represent the norm for humanity.

Anderson also describes a different sort of androcentric bias:
'Another way in which the content of theories can be androcentric is

---

[23] Actually, her picture is more complicated than this: a bias that is helpful in
one situation may be damaging in another. Really, then, we need to study *when*
particular biases are good and bad.

in describing or defining phenomena from the perspective of men or typically male lives, without paying attention to how they would be described differently if examined from the point of view of women's lives' (1995: 71). The example that she offers of this bias at work also seems to me to show the influence of at least one other significant bias. Anderson's example focuses on the fact that productive labour has traditionally been defined by economists as including only labour done for pay outside the home. Other labour, in particular house-work, is classed as unproductive—and often as leisure. When study-ing countries where a large proportion of labour is actually the domestic labour involved in subsistence agriculture and the like, economists faced a problem. They felt the need to designate some of these household activities as productive and others as not productive, just as they have traditionally done when studying Western economies. So, writes Anderson,

> economists apply the concept of 'housework' to whatever productive activities a society essentially assigns to women . . . The result is that in Africa, where women do 70 percent of the hoeing and weeding of subsistence crops, 80 percent of crop transportation and storage, and 90 percent of water and fuel collecting and food processing, these vital activities rarely appear in the national income accounts.

> (p. 72)

The neglect of women's labour as productive has not just distorted research, but also had devastating effects on policies.

> In Malawi and Lesotho, where women grow most of the food for domestic consumption, foreign aid projects have provided agricultural training to the men who have no use for it, and offered only home economics education to women.

> (p. 74)

Anderson takes androcentric bias to be at work in the initial desig-nation of unpaid activities inside the home as 'unproductive', and this is surely right. If attention had been paid to how women viewed their own lives, household labour would be counted as productive. But it is equally important to note that it is not just androcentric bias that is at work in the view that 'housework' should refer to whatever women do. We have seen already (in Chapter 1, for example), that enormous numbers of Western women work outside their homes for pay, and have done so for a very long time. Only women in relatively privileged economic positions have even had the possibility of being full-time homemakers. Those who assume that women do not work outside the home seem to be taking a privileged socioeconomic position as the norm for humanity. There is, then, also a bias at work that relates to socioeconomic position.

SUGGESTIONS FOR FURTHER READING

General

Alcoff, L., and Potter, E., *Feminist Epistemologies*. London: Routledge, 1993.

Anderson, E., 'Feminist Epistemology and Philosophy of Science', in E. N. Zalta (ed.), *The Stanford Encyclopedia of Philosophy*. Stanford, Calif.: Stanford University Press, 2001. http://plato.stanford.edu/archives/win2001/entries/feminism-epistemology/ Consulted 27 Nov. 2002.

Keller, E. F. and Longino, H. E. (eds.), *Feminism and Science*. Oxford: Oxford University Press, 1996.

Longino, H., 'Feminist Epistemology', in J. Greco and E. Sosa (eds.), *The Blackwell Guide to Epistemology*. Oxford: Blackwell, 1999, 327–53.

Tanesini, A., *An Introduction to Feminist Epistemologies*. Oxford: Blackwell, 1999.

Wylie, A., 'Feminism in Philosophy of Science: Making Sense of Contingency and Constraint', in M. Fricker and J. Hornsby (eds.), *The Cambridge Companion to Feminism in Philosophy*. Cambridge: Cambridge University Press, 2000, 166–85.

Feminist criticism of scientific practice

Bleier, R., *Science and Gender: A Critique of Biology and Its Theories on Women*. New York: Pergamon Press, 1984.

Fausto-Sterling, A., *Myths of Gender: Biological Theories about Women and Men*. New York: Basic Books, 1992.

Hubbard, R., *The Politics of Women's Biology*. New Brunswick, NJ: Rutgers University Press, 1990.

Lloyd, E., 'Pre-theoretical Assumptions in Evolutionary Explanations of Female Sexuality', *Philosophical Studies* 69 (1993): 139–53.

Martin, E., 'The Egg and the Sperm: How Science has Constructed a Romance Based on Stereotypical Male-Female Roles', in E. F. Keller and

H. E. Longino (eds.), *Feminism and Science*. Oxford: Oxford University
Press, 1996, 103–17.

Russett, C. E., *Sexual Science: The Victorian Construction of Womanhood*.
Cambridge, Mass.: Harvard University Press, 1989.

Tavris, C., *The Mismeasure of Woman*. New York: Touchstone, 1992.

Thompson, L., *The Wandering Womb: A Cultural History of Outrageous Beliefs
About Women*. Amherst, NY: Prometheus, 1999.

Standpoint theory

Collins, P. H., *Black Feminist Thought: Knowledge, Consciousness, and the Politics
of Empowerment*, 2nd edn. New York: Routledge, 2000.

Fricker, M., 'Epistemic Oppression and Epistemic Privilege', *Canadian
Journal of Philosophy*, supplementary vol. 25 (1999); also known as
C. Wilson (ed.), *Civilization and Oppression*. Calgary: Calgary University
Press): 191–210. (*This is an especially clear and accessible discussion of
standpoint theory.*)

Harding, S., 'Rethinking Standpoint Epistemology: What is "Strong
Objectivity"?', in L. Alcoff and E. Potter (eds.), *Feminist Epistemologies*.
London: Routledge, 1993, 49–82.

Hartsock, N., 'The Feminist Standpoint Theory: Developing the
Ground for a Specifically Feminist Historical Materialism', in
S. Harding and M. B. Hintikka (eds.), *Discovering Reality*. Dordrecht:
Reidel, 1983.

Smith, D., 'Women's Perspective as a Radical Critique of Sociology', in
E. F. Keller and H. Longino (eds.), *Feminism and Science*. Oxford: Oxford
University Press; 1996, 17–27.

Scientific communities

Longino, H., 'Essential Tensions—Phase Two: Feminist, Philosophical,
and Social Studies of Knowledge', in L. Antony and C. Witt (eds.),
A Mind of One's Own. Boulder, Colo.: Westview Press, 1993,
257–72.

——*Science as Social Knowledge: Values and Objectivity in Scientific Inquiry*.
Princeton, NJ: Princeton University Press, 1990.

Nelson, L. H., *Who Knows: From Quine to Feminist Empiricism*. Philadelphia:
Temple University Press, 1990.

Feminist naturalized epistemology

Anderson, E., 'Feminist Epistemology: An Interpretation and a Defence',
Hypatia 10 (3) (1995): 50–84.

Antony, L., 'Quine as Feminist', in L. Antony and C. Witt (eds.), *A Mind of One's Own*. Boulder, Colo.: Westview Press, 1993, 185–225.

Nelson, L. H., *Who Knows: From Quine to Feminist Empiricism*. Philadelphia: Temple University Press, 1990.

9

Feminism and 'Respect for Cultures'

February 1991: a village 40 kilometers north of Udaipur city, Rajasthan, India. Metha Bai, an upper-caste widow with two minor sons, describes her plight as a young widow from a caste which prohibits women from working outside the homestead. Before her husband's death two years before, she had not been allowed to work outside their homestead, even to fetch water or fuelwood (her husband performed all outside chores). Now, she helps her father cultivate the land she inherited from her husband and fetches water and fuelwood. However, her in-laws do not allow Metha Bai to engage in any outside gainful employment. Her only source of support is her father, who helps her till the land and brings regular gifts of food and clothing.

(Chen 1995: 37)

I may die, but still I cannot go out. If there's something in the house, we eat. Otherwise, we go to sleep.

(Metha Bai, India, 1991, quoted in Chen 1995: 37)

The traditional restrictions at work in Metha Bai's life place her in danger of starvation. To me, it seems absolutely clear that these restrictions are wrong, and that feminists have an obligation to oppose them. But many members of Bai's cultural community—some of whom are women—will defend these restrictions as central to their way of life, which they value very highly. They insist that outsiders to their community (like me) who criticize these practices are bound to be mistaken: outsiders cannot possibly understand or appreciate the lives of insiders. We should not, therefore, judge them or attempt to change them.

There is a serious quandary here. It seems wrong to care only about women of my own cultural group[1]—surely, if I care about the lot of women, I should care about the lot of women from other groups as well. Indeed, white middle-class Western feminists have been rightly and strongly criticized for focusing only on the situations of women like themselves, or for assuming that all women face exactly the same difficulties.[2] Moreover, it seems as though Western[3] feminists should try to *do* something to improve the situation of women from other cultural groups. On the other hand, it is also important to respect the cultures of others, and not simply to assume that ways of life that I easily understand are the only acceptable ones. There is a long and shameful history of Westerners arrogantly and ignorantly condemning other cultures as backward and inferior. There is also a long history of Westerners imposing their own views on others, to extremely damaging effect. Nussbaum describes the situation well:

> To say that a practice endorsed by tradition is bad is to risk erring by imposing one's own way on others who surely have their own ideas of what is right and good. To say that a practice is all right wherever local tradition endorses it as right and good is to risk erring by withholding critical judgment where real evil and real oppression are surely present. To avoid the whole issue because the matter of proper judgment is so fiendishly difficult is tempting, but perhaps the worst option of all.

(Nussbaum 1995a: 1)

The problem Nussbaum describes is not specific to feminism, but applies to all cross-cultural judgments. Nonetheless, it is arguably an

---

[1] It also seems wrong to care only about women. This chapter focuses on women; but many of the issues considered here arise also in considering the situation of men or children of another culture.

[2] See e.g. hooks (1984); Lugones and Spelman (1983); Harris (1993); Spelman (1988).

[3] Although there are both Western and non-Western outsiders to any culture, I will often focus on problems specific to *Western* outsiders' views of other cultures. I am following a common usage by casting these difficulties in terms of 'Westerners' and 'non-Westerners', or, sometimes 'Third World' cultures. This usage is itself very problematic: there are people in the West from many different cultural, religious, and racial backgrounds; and some of those cultures that are commonly called 'Third World'—such as those in South and Central America are actually *in* the West. This latter issue has led some to prefer to contrast 'Northerners' with 'Southerners'. I am not happy with any of the terminological options, but have chosen to follow the most common usage for convenience.

especially acute one for feminists. Indeed, some feminists have gone so far as to wonder just how far feminism is compatible with respect for cultures—either one's own or those of others.[4] Katha Pollitt summarizes this tension:

> Feminism and multiculturalism . . . are very far apart. In its demand for equality for women, feminism sets itself in opposition to virtually every culture on Earth. You could say that multiculturalism demands respect for all cultural traditions, while feminism interrogates and challenges all cultural traditions.
>
> (Pollitt 1999: 27)

In this chapter I will argue that it *is* possible to be a feminist while respecting cultural traditions. My strategy will be to begin with two crude approaches to the problem above, showing what is wrong with each of them. Next, I will turn to the increasingly and justifiably popular suggestion that cross-cultural dialogue is the key to proper cross-cultural judgement. We will see that the internal complexity of cultures poses difficulties for each of the approaches considered—effectively demolishing the first two, and making it clear that the last is far from simple. But we will also see that proper appreciation of the complexity of cultures helps to dissolve the problem described above.[5] As many of the problems under discussion are applicable not just to feminism, but to cross-cultural judgments more generally, our discussion will sometimes turn to issues that are not specifically *feminist* ones; it will always return, however, to specifically feminist concerns.

---

[4] A good source for this worry—and for a variety of responses to it—is Okin (1999).

[5] In fact, by the end of this chapter we will see that these complexities also make it difficult to understand the notion of a culture. However, many of the concerns discussed in this chapter are generally posed simply in terms of 'cultures'. In order to discuss these concerns, I will proceed as though the notion of culture was unproblematic, only raising worries about it later in the chapter.

Do what seems right

One (overly) simple answer is that Western feminists should simply trust the judgements that seem right to them. If a practice seems wrong to me, I should judge it as wrong. I should trust my instincts, and not worry about what members of other cultures might think about the practices that I am judging. They may be unable to see the wrongness of practices that they take for granted. They may be brainwashed. And they may simply be ill-educated and unable to imagine other possibilities. Thus, I should rely only on my own judgements. What I should do next is a different matter: I might simply quietly make judgements in the privacy of my own mind, or I might attempt to change those practices that seem wrong to me. In this section, we will examine problems concerning both Westerners' judgements of other cultures and their interventions. Initially, we will concentrate on judgements of acceptability of practices, but we will also examine analyses of practices and issues of priority.

Before we begin our examination of Western judgements, however, it is important to be reminded that Western nations, especially those who have colonized other lands, have in general not hesitated to impose their own cultural standards on others[6]—often to devastating effect. To make matters worse, they have often used their own cultural standards as an excuse for colonizing other nations, arguing that the values and practices of these other countries— especially, as it happens, concerning their treatment of women—showed their people to be unsuited for self-government. The following quotation from a 1927 article in the *London New Statesman and Nation* cites a book by Katherine Mayo,[7] that (it says) reveals:

---

[6] There have, of course, been exceptions to this. For example, the British in India were very concerned about the possibility that attempting to stamp out particular Indian practices might lead to instability or rejection of British rule. As a result, they devoted considerable resources to attempting to discern how central these practices really were to Indian traditions. These investigations, Uma Narayan reports, were sometimes hampered by false assumptions about the right ways to investigate the nature of Indian traditions (Narayan 1997).

[7] Katherine Mayo's book *Mother India*, published in 1927, argued against Indian independence from Britain.

the filthy personal habits of even the most highly educated class is in India—which, like the degradation of Hindu women, are unequalled even among the most primitive African or Australian savages . . . Katherine Mayo makes the claim for Swaraj [self-rule] seem nonsense and the will to grant it almost a crime.

(Narayan 1997: 198, n.37)

In these justifications for colonization, Western powers often took practices that were relatively rare or localized, and attributed to them great significance for the entire country (Ahmed 1992; Narayan 1997). They also often claimed to be staunch defenders of women's rights when discussing the rights of women of other countries, while opposing feminist efforts (such as suffrage) back home. In some cases, even their judgements about a single culture revealed them to be less committed to women's rights than they claimed to be. Leila Ahmed, for example, notes that Lord Cromer, a British leader in Egypt, accused Egyptians of degrading women through veiling and seclusion, while simultaneously doing his best to put an end to the pre-existing Egyptian practice of training women to be doctors (Ahmed 1992: 153). This sort of history quite reasonably makes those in non-Western countries suspicious of Western judgements of their cultures, and should also give Westerners pause.[8] In this section, I will mainly leave aside concerns about insincerity and hypocrisy, as my goal is to show that problems arise even for sincere, non-hypocritical judgements by Westerners. However, the history noted above will be relevant to some of the examples discussed.

---

[8] Using treatment of women as an excuse for accomplishing other goals, some suggest, is by no means a vanished tactic. The US, which had previously shown little interest in the status of women in Afghanistan, began to express far more concern for the rights of Afghan women when they had *other* reasons (the events of 11 Sept. 2001) to work for the downfall of the Taliban. Nor is hypocrisy on women's issues a thing of the past, some argue. The US condemned the treatment of women in Afghanistan while continuing to support the Saudi Arabian regime, which—as we'll see shortly—is also extremely repressive toward women; in addition, unlike 170 other countries, the US has not ratified the UN Convention on the Elimination of All Forms of Discrimination Against Women (CEDAW). For more on CEDAW, see www.un.org/womenwatch/daw/cedaw. Consulted 20 Nov. 2002. For discussion of differences in US reaction to the treatment of women in various countries, see Jefferson (2002); Kristof (2002); Viner (2002).

Potential for error

I'll begin with a case study of mistaken Western judgements—that of Islamic women's veiling. This practice has historically been widely misunderstood and oversimplified, and continues to be so today. Westerners often take Islamic women's veiling to have one simple meaning: the subordination of women to men. This idea leads them to condemn the practice of veiling, and often both Islam and Islamic cultures. In such criticisms, all sorts of garments—from headscarves that cover only the hair to the tent-like burqas of Afghanistan[9] that cover the entire body, with only a mesh panel for the eyes—are generally dealt with together under the simple label 'veil'.

There are many problems with this sweeping condemnation. First, there are no distinctions drawn between various sorts of veil. Next, it falsely assumes that veiling has the same significance for all women in all cultures at all times. Relatedly, it fails to consider the different motivations women may have for veiling in various cultural contexts. Finally, it takes both Islam and the cultures it is found in to be monolithic, and does not even attempt to distinguish between cultural and religious influences.

There are an enormous variety of garments that are called 'veils'. I have already noted that they range from headscarves to the burqas of Afghanistan. But things are much more complicated than even this suggests. Different varieties of veil, for example, may carry different messages in terms of class or social status within a single culture (Soueif 2001). This alone indicates that their significance is more complicated than the simple condemnation would suggest—indicating social class is a very different matter from indicating subordination to men.[10] Considering the *effects* of various 'veils' is also revealing: while a woman in a burqa has impaired vision and mobility and is unable to carry out a wide variety of tasks, a woman in a headscarf suffers no such impairment. To view all 'veils' on the confining model of the burqa is a serious distortion.

[9] Burquas were legally required by the Taliban, and are still worn in many parts of Afghanistan.

[10] Though class and gender issues may of course interact in a variety of complicated ways.

Next, it is important to distinguish between reasons for veiling. In Saudi Arabia and Iran (as in Taliban-era Afghanistan), women are legally required to wear veils, a requirement enforced by religious police. In Saudi Arabia, the required garment is especially restrictive, while in Iran a gradual liberalization of dress codes has been taking place. The enforcement of these dress codes is often violent. Women who wear veils in these countries, then, may be doing so simply out of compliance with the law. (They may also be doing so for other reasons, of course.) Criticisms can be made of these legal requirements, and the ways that they are enforced, which do not apply to the wearing of veils where it is legally optional.[11] Veiling is generally not legally required,[12] and many Muslim women do not wear veils (Hirschmann 1988). Among those who do, veils are worn for many different reasons. The most commonly cited is modesty, but many other reasons are important as well. Sometimes, a veil is simply a sign of Islamic faith or pride—it is worn in much the same way that many Christian women wear crosses. Sometimes, a veil is worn for beautification, as Westerners wear makeup (Hoodfar 1993). In many countries, veils are worn as a sign of nationalism or rejection of Western culture, and this message may be more important to their wearers than any other (Hirschmann 1988; Hoodfar 1993; Soueif 2001). Leila Ahmed writes that veiling has allowed professional Islamic women to function comfortably in a sexually integrated urban public world, where they would otherwise be uncomfortable. She notes that this is especially important for those who come from rural backgrounds, who are not used to a great deal of public interaction between the sexes (Ahmed 1992). Some young women wear veils as a way of reassuring their families that, although they are pursuing advanced education or careers, they are still loyal Muslims (Hoodfar 1993). Others maintain that their veils enable them to achieve the familiar

---

[11] Such criticisms, however, are not quite as simple to make as it might at first appear. The mere fact of requiring a particular sort of clothing, for example, is not considered objectionable by most—only a small minority of people in Western countries, for example, object to laws forbidding women's toplessness.

[12] It is important to bear in mind, however, that legal requirements are not the only means of forcing or coercing. The lack of a legal requirement does not automatically make an activity genuinely voluntary. Detailed investigation of specific circumstances is important to these issues.

feminist goal of avoiding sexual objectification. One British Muslim who adopted a headscarf and modest attire reports, 'The attention I got from the other sex changed. Instead of a sexual approach, they had to take an interest in what was in my head and in my personality, rather than my body' (Bunting 2001: 3). This woman's motivation should be a very familiar one to Western feminists: the desire to be taken seriously as a person and not merely considered a sex object. Most Western feminists would not adopt her method for achieving this goal, but, as Azizah Al-Hibri asks, 'Why is it oppressive to wear a head-scarf but liberating to wear a miniskirt?' (Al-Hibri 1999: 40). Given the range of reasons for wearing veils, it is clearly wrong to assume that all women who veil do so in order to signify their subordination to men.

Finally, cultures, religions, and their interactions are tremendously complicated. We have seen that veiling customs and motivations vary greatly from culture to culture (as well as from woman to woman). One key to understanding all this is realizing that Islam, like Christianity or Judaism, comes in many forms. What holds true of one Islamic tradition need not hold true of others. Islam contains within it many traditions, and these traditions take importantly different attitudes toward women (see Ahmed 1992; Mernissi 1987; Stowasser 1996; Wadud 1999). Another important part of the explanation is the fact that Islam is found in many different cultures. These cultures have their own traditional practices, and the influence of these cultures is often mistaken for the influence of Islam.[13] So—even if the blanket condemnation of veiling *was* acceptable (as we've seen it isn't)—it would still be unacceptable to move from this to a blanket condemnation of 'the Islamic view' of women. Moreover, cultures are not so simple. Any culture contains many conflicting traditions and views, including in many cases well-established feminist movements. Blanket condemnations of cultures then, are no more acceptable than blanket condemnations of religions. These complexities will

---

[13] Islam, according to Azizah Al-Hibri, explicitly celebrates diversity by allowing Islamic countries to retain any local customs that are not inconsistent with Islam. The local customs of many Islamic countries are often mistaken for Islamic traditions (Al-Hibri 1999: 43).

turn out to be very important to our discussion throughout this chapter.[14]

Effects of Western judgements

Whether or not their interest in liberating women was sincere, we have seen that colonizing powers have used women's liberation as a justification for their actions. They condemned colonized cultures as backward on the basis of their treatment of women. This had two presumably unintended effects that were detrimental to women in these cultures. First, the focus on treatment of women served to make women's treatment emblematic of the colonized cultures, not just to the colonizers but also to many of the colonized. Defenders of these cultures against colonizers, then, tended to focus especially on preserving traditions relating to women.

> [I]n these conflicts, Western colonial powers often depicted indigenous practices as symptoms of the 'backwardness and barbarity' of third-world cultures in contrast to the 'progressiveness of Western culture.' The figure of the colonized woman became a representation of the oppressiveness of the entire 'cultural tradition' of the colony. Male-dominated Third-World elites often responded by constructing these very practices as sacred and longstanding traditions that were constitutive of their values and worldviews, and as practices that were tied to the spiritual place of, and respect for, women in their cultures.
>
> (Narayan 1997: 17)

Thus, the ways of treating women that came under particular attack by colonizers began to seem especially crucial to defend—even if these practices were in fact relatively rare. And, in general, opposition grew to the idea of changing anything related to women and their role. This contrasted sharply with attitudes in other areas: Western technology was happily adopted, for example, as was Western clothing *for men*.

Others, however, reacted in a different way to Western criticism. Some of those seeking independence from, or the respect of, the West,

---

[14] For good discussions of cultural complexity, see Al-Hibri (1999), Bhabha (1999), Honig (1999), Mohanty (1991b), Narayan (1997), Parekh (1999), Tamir (1999).

sought to prove their worthiness by making sudden and visible changes to the lives of women. While, of course, improving the lives of women was an eminently worthy goal, we will see that trying to achieve this simply by responding to criticisms of colonial powers was not the best method. Moreover, often the changes made did not stem from a thoroughgoing commitment to women's rights. Leila Ahmed notes that Qassim Amin, a key advocate of changes to seclusion customs[15] and women's dress, and often viewed as a very important Islamic feminist, also argued that women's and girls' educations should be substantially reduced (Ahmed 1992: 144–68).

The mandatory unveiling of women in Iran provides a good example of the way that opposition to veiling could have detrimental effects on women's lives (Hoodfar 1993). In 1936, as part of a modernization/Westernization plan, the Shah of Iran made it illegal for women to wear any sort of veil whatsoever, including any 'kind of a head covering except a European hat' (p. 10). The law was enforced by policemen who were required to remove and rip up any such covering. Although the law was not enforced in rural areas, it was enforced in cities. Before the law came into force, women in cities often left their houses to socialize, to learn marketable skills like carpet weaving, to manage their finances, and to do what was needed for the upkeep of their homes. Most of these women considered it indecent to leave the house without a veil. As a result of the law, women no longer felt that they could leave the house in the ways that they had done before. They grew isolated, and came to lead more restricted lives of much greater dependence on men.

Errors in analysis of customs

So far, our focus has been mainly on judgements of whether a particular practice is morally or politically objectionable. But even those who agree that a practice is objectionable may disagree over the proper way to understand that practice, and outsiders are prone to error on this topic as well. These errors, what I call 'errors in analysis', may

---

[15] By 'seclusion customs' I mean customs like those mentioned in our discussion of Metha Bai, which involve restricting women's mobility.

have damaging effects. Uma Narayan provides a useful illustration of this with her extended discussion of the rare and now nearly extinct practice of *sati*—widows throwing themselves, or being thrown,[16] on their husband's funeral pyres.[17] *Sati* has been practised very infrequently by some Hindus in some parts of India. It is clear that *sati* is to be condemned, and few (if any) feminists would disagree. However, this judgement alone gives little real-world guidance. In particular, it does nothing to suggest the most effective strategy for fighting it. Westerners have often gone badly wrong in their discussions of *sati*, in ways that have made it more difficult for Indian feminists to fight the practice. External opponents of *sati* have often portrayed it as a central Hindu tradition. This has played into the hands of Hindu fundamentalists who also wrongly represented *sati* as a central Hindu tradition, and it has worked against the efforts of Indian feminists to fight *sati*. Indian feminists have preferred to fight *sati* through careful attention to the historical and contemporary facts. By highlighting these facts, they are able to take a two-pronged approach to *sati*, arguing (a) it would be unacceptable even if it were a central Hindu tradition, and (b) that it in fact has no such status. Western feminists who attack *sati* as 'a central Hindu tradition' not only add their voices to inaccurate fundamentalist efforts to claim *sati* as such a tradition, but also help to perpetuate the idea (already very damaging to Indian feminists) that fighting *sati* (or being a feminist) requires the rejection of Hinduism and the denigration of Indian culture.[18]

A close look at discussions of *sati* can also reveal other ways that analysis of practices go wrong. Uma Narayan notes that Westerners, both feminist and otherwise, have tended to view the two practices of *sati* and dowry murder (to be explained shortly) as instances of a single Hindu tradition: the burning of women. *Sati*, we have already noted, is a nearly extinct practice, which was always rare, and only

---

[16] There are many complex issues regarding women's 'consent' to *sati*. See Narayan (1997: 74–6).

[17] The discussion in this section concerning *sati*, dowry murder, and domestic violence draws heavily on Narayan (1997), esp. ch. 3.

[18] This view gains even more strength when Western feminists objecting to *sati* do so by approvingly citing racist, colonialist works like Katherine Mayo's. Narayan criticizes Mary Daly for her blindness to the problems with such works (Narayan 1997: ch. 2).

practised by *some* Hindu groups. Dowry murder is, on the contrary, increasingly common in India. In dowry murder, women are killed, most commonly in purported 'kitchen accidents', as the culmination of campaigns of harassment and violence to extract additional dowry.[19] It is a very recent phenomenon, and religious justifications have never been claimed for it. Treating these two practices as part of a single Hindu tradition then, is an important mistake. It also impairs one's ability to properly assimilate new information. Narayan cites the example of one writer who describes these practices as instances of a single Hindu tradition, even while illustrating the practice of dowry murder through the example of a Sikh woman—not a Hindu woman—who managed to survive a murder attempt (Narayan 1997: 107).[20] Other errors are more subtle. Narayan writes that when she describes dowry murder as domestic violence, Westerners are startled. Because they see it as part of a foreign religious tradition, it does not occur to them to place it in the more familiar context of domestic violence.

Similarly, the exotic idea that Hinduism gives a special significance to the burning of women prevents Westerners from recognizing the significance of the fact—even, sometimes, as they cite it—that burning is a popular and convenient murder method in India (Narayan 1997: 111–12). It has this popularity because there is a great deal of unsafe cooking equipment, which means that it is easy to pass off a deliberate fire as an accidental one, and because it disposes of much of the evidence. The fact that dowry murders generally take place by burning does not necessarily point to a special religious or cultural significance to the burning of women.

The inability to see connections between practices in foreign cultures and practices in one's own is often an instance of a more general tendency to *exoticize*—to see cultures other than one's own as *very*

[19] Although dowry is traditionally given at the time of marriage, further dowry is now often extracted after the marriage takes place (Narayan 1997: 111).

[20] Although one might try to argue that historical connections might lead to Sikhs being affected by—or sharing—some of the same traditions as Hindus, this would still mean that the traditions could not properly be described simply as 'Hindu'. Substantial argument would also be needed for such claims, and Narayan notes that the writer she discusses apparently fails even to notice the significance of the fact that she is discussing a Sikh woman.

different, and to fail to see resemblances between other cultures and one's own. For Westerners reflecting on non-Western cultures, this often takes the form of attributing deep religious or cultural significance to practices or events that may have more mundane, practical explanations. Focusing on the notion that Hinduism assigns special significance to burning women and failing to consider more mundane explanations for the role of fire in Indian murders is a form of exoticizing; exoticizing also plays a role in the failure to see dowry murder as domestic violence.

Another problematic tendency is that of *assimilating* other cultures to one's own—failing to see important differences. Much has been written recently of ways that white, middle-class Western feminists have failed to see that other women's situations differ from theirs.[21] If Western feminists saw dowry murders *simply* as domestic violence, to be dealt with in the same ways as domestic violence in Western countries, they would miss much and go badly wrong. The institution of dowry is important for understanding this particular form of domestic violence; and the shelters that have been so important to Western campaigns against domestic violence would be less effective in an Indian context, as not many women would have the material resources to leave abusive relationships, even if shelters were provided (Narayan 1997: 94). Consideration of this example, then, shows how the very different errors of exoticizing and assimilating can each have important effects.

It is important to note, however, that difficulties in understanding do not always stem from either exoticizing or assimilating. Understanding can be impeded in a variety of ways. For example, Western activism against domestic violence has tended to focus on cases in which the violence falls short of murder. (One reason for this is the use of shelters as a way of helping women escape from violent relationships before violence escalates.) Indeed, Narayan could not find statistics specifically on domestic violence *murder* in the United States. However, Indian feminists have tended to focus on dowry murders: domestic violence that does result in death. These differences in focus—resulting simply from different practical and political imperatives in different contexts—can serve as cultural barriers to connecting the two phenomena.

Priorities

Westerners may also go wrong in their prioritizing of issues. Western feminists are often criticized, for example, for the degree of attention they pay to female genital mutilation (FGM).[22] The practices most often criticized under this name are a range of procedures, from removing part of the clitoris to removing the clitoris and the labia minora, and stitching together the labia majora (Nussbaum 1999: 119).[23] FGM is usually performed on young girls, and it can lead to a variety of extremely severe health problems, and even to death. Removing all or part of the clitoris, naturally, has—to put it mildly—damaging effects on women's capacity for sexual pleasure. Although some, including some women, defend FGM, most feminists agree that it should be fought.[24] However, many feminists from countries in

[22] It is widely though falsely believed that FGM is either soley an African or solely an Islamic custom. Neither of these claims is right: many Africans and Muslims do not practise FGM and many non-Africans and non-Muslims do. Leila Ahmed notes, for example, that in Egypt FGM is as common among Christians as Muslims (Ahmed 1992: 175–6); and Lana Thompson discusses the use of FGM in nineteenth-century England (Thompson 1999: 137). For more on FGM, see El Saadawi (1980: 33–43), Gunning (2000), Nussbaum (1999: 118–29), Obiora (2000).

[23] There is substantial controversy both over which practices should be categorized together and over what these practices should be called. Although Nussbaum claims that opponents of FGM are in agreement that the practices they oppose are only the severe ones described above, Obiora (see next footnote) takes opponents of FGM to be opposed even to symbolic nicking of women's genitalia. In part because Obiora is concerned to highlight this arguably non-mutilating procedure, she prefers to use the term 'female circumcision'. Nussbaum opposes this term, as the procedures *she* is concerned with are not analogous to male circumcision. As she notes, the male equivalent of the least severe of *these* procedures would be removal of part of the penis. One confusing feature of this literature, then, is that it may seem at first that Nussbaum and Obiora disagree over what name should be given to a single collection of practices. However, they also disagree over what practices should be categorized together under the name that each advocates.

[24] Obiora maintains that there are acceptable forms of what she calls 'female circumcision' (see previous footnote), in particular symbolic nicking of genitalia. Whether or not this counts as defending FGM depends on whether or not one classifies this as FGM. Obiora insists that this is non-mutilating, and that

which FGM takes place object to the emphasis that Western feminists place on it. Angela Gilliam, for example, notes that Nawal El Saadawi (an Egyptian opponent of FGM) has written 'that Western women often go to countries such as the Sudan and "see" only clitoridectomy,[25] but never notice the role of multinational corporations and their exploited labour' (Gilliam 1991: 218). More generally, non-Western feminists often object to the tendency of Western feminists to focus on sexual issues to the exclusion of others. They may agree with Westerners' views on these issues, but they may at the same time hold that others—poverty, health, employment, and education, for example—deserve at least as much (if not more) attention.[26]

Stay out!

Reasons for staying out

After considering the worries above, one might be tempted to conclude that outsiders should never make judgements about other cultures, and should certainly never try to change the cultural practices of others.[27] We have already seen some reasons for this: the likeliness of errors, and the history of misguided, damaging, and often hypocritical interventions. These might give reason enough to suppose that the best course of action for Westerners is to simply mind their own business and neither judge nor interfere with other cultures.

One might also hold that respecting other cultures is important, and that such respect demands that outsiders refrain from judgement or

it is usually classified together with more severe procedures as FGM. (Nussbaum claims that it is not usually considered FGM.) Obiora maintains that the more severe procedures discussed in the text above should be fought.

25 Clitoridectomy is a form of FGM in which part or all of the clitoris is removed (Nussbaum 1999: 120).

26 The focus on *sati* in the face of all the other problems faced by Indian widows has also drawn criticism (Narayan 1997: 65).

27 It is worth noting that the categories of insiders and outsiders are something of an oversimplification. Many people are hard to classify into such crude categories: immigrants, children of immigrants, and members of minority communities within a culture, to name a few examples. Nonetheless, the simplified categories are useful for discussing the issues of this chapter.

intervention. Often, this idea is accompanied by a commitment to what is known as cultural relativism, the view that moral judgements can only be made relative to particular cultures. On this view, it is a mistake to judge that some type of action is simply wrong. It may be wrong for one cultural group, but right for another. So, for example, one might judge that cannibalism is wrong for an American but right for someone from a culture that condones cannibalism. A cultural relativist might argue that if a practice is condoned by a particular culture, then no outsider can legitimately question it: it is right for that culture, even if it is wrong for others.

In the context of the current discussion, one particularly important form of cultural relativism is the claim that the language of rights is only appropriate to a Western context. According to this view, non-Western cultures do not have the concept of rights, and this concept is therefore inappropriate to use when discussing these cultures. So if, in discussing a non-Western culture, we say things like 'forbidding women to work is a violation of their rights' we are making a grave error. Using this notion in discussing such cultures is an arrogant imposition of Western standards on the rest of the world.

Problems with staying out

Although cultural relativism holds a great deal of initial appeal for those who want to respect cultural differences, in fact most people would be unwilling to accept the full consequences of the view once they are made clear. To see this, imagine a culture in which women are not permitted to leave their houses for any reason. In this culture, widows simply starve to death once they have exhausted the resources in their homes, unless relatives help them. Nobody in this culture resists or questions this tradition. They all believe that it is right. Indeed, they insist that these rules have allowed their culture to thrive through the centuries.[28] How would we react to this culture? If

---

[28] It will be apparent that this imaginary culture is inspired by the example of Metha Bai described at the start of this chapter. The key difference—for our purposes—between this imaginary culture and real ones is the total uniformity of attitudes toward the practices in the imaginary culture. As this chapter emphasizes, real cultures are not like this.

there were a culture like this, would we really think that is acceptable to simply let widows starve? It seems to me that we would not. Instead, we would think that great wrongs are taking place. If I am right that we would be outraged by this situation, whether or not anyone within the society was, then we seem committed to something less than full deference to cultural insiders. In at least some cases, we think that we are entitled to our judgements regardless of what insiders say. Deep down, we are not really willing to accept cultural relativism.[29]

Even if cultural relativism were true, however, the claim that rights are a Western imposition does not seem to be accurate. There is clear evidence for this in the history and reception of the Universal Declaration of Human Rights. This document, which lays out rights that every human being is taken to have, was adopted by the United Nations without a dissenting vote in 1948, and 'it has been estimated that the declaration has inspired or served as a model for the rights provisions of some ninety constitutions' (Glendon 2001: 228). Moreover, the countries endorsing this document were not merely going along with a document imposed upon them by powerful Westerners. Some of the most influential members of the committee that wrote the Declaration were Filipino, Indian, Chilean, and Chinese.[30] There were very few objections to the document that finally emerged. For example, when Saudi Arabia argued that 'freedom to marry and to change one's religion are Western ideas ill-suited for universal application' (Glendon 2001: 222), no other country agreed. The idea that the very notion of rights is antithetical to many cultures, then, seems mistaken (see also Narayan 1993).

Even if we now set aside worries that stem from cultural relativism, there are still reasons that seem to favour a policy of 'staying out'.

---

[29] Some feminists, such as Laurie Shrage (1994) and Lorraine Code (1998), have worked to develop versions of relativism that avoid this sort of problem. Other cultural relativists would respond by claiming that our outrage shows only how strongly we adhere to our culture's morality. They would insist that we are wrong to apply this morality to those of other cultures, but that our desire to do so is just what they would predict.

[30] It was, in fact, an Indian woman who pushed most strongly for inclusive language, worrying that 'men' would be interpreted as a gender specific term. For more on concerns over usage of 'man' and 'men', see Chapter 6 above.

First, respect for other cultures might still motivate a preference for refraining from judgement or action. Second, outsiders are, as we have seen, prone to important errors.

There are, however, some problems with simply 'staying out'. First, it may simply not be possible. The UK and the US are multicultural nations. As a result, laws in each country affect people from many different cultural groups. Citizens of either country, then, cannot avoid being faced with issues that call for judgements of the sort that 'staying out' would forbid. To name a few examples: such countries must decide whether to permit FGM or polygamy, and whether to teach children that their sex need not determine their role in life (Okin's proposal from Chapter 1 above). How to deal with these issues is an important, difficult, and timely topic.[31] Many Western countries have undergone or are undergoing fierce debates over the extent to which laws should be reformed to accommodate, or to ban, particular practices of cultural groups other than the dominant ones.

Another reason that staying out is often not possible is that Western countries like the US have relationships with other countries.[32] The US makes decisions about which countries to help financially and politically. At the moment, for example, it is especially supportive of the Saudi Arabian regime. In Saudi Arabia, women are forbidden to drive, unable to vote, and legally required to wear black abayas (garments that cover them completely except for a slit for eyes) in public. In one recent incident in Saudi Arabia, fifteen schoolgirls burned to death when religious police refused to let them leave a burning school because they were not wearing abayas (BBCi: 2002). Westerners cannot view concerns over the treatment of women in Saudi Arabia as local matters, in which they should not involve themselves. They are, by virtue of their governments' actions, *already* involved in the affairs of other countries. Everyone who pays taxes to the US government is already playing a role in Saudi Arabian affairs.[33]

However, there is something that Westerners could do that might

---

[31] A variety of views on these issues, with specific reference to feminist concerns, can be found in the various essays in Okin (1999).

[32] For more on this line of thought, see Narayan (1997: 153).

[33] Western multinational corporations also play an important role in non-Western cultures (Mohanty 1991a).

seem to be the next best thing to staying out, given the degree of involvement that is inevitable: 'stay out' as far as possible. The US government, for example, could stay out by not letting judgements about the practices of other cultures influence its policies, and by doing everything it can to accommodate the practices of the various cultural groups within the US.[34]

But is it really acceptable to respond to the school fire incident described above by saying, 'Well, that's what they do in Saudi Arabia, and I should just respect their different way of life'? It is hard to resist the thought that 'staying out' can be a terrible thing to do in some cases, and that Americans should at least consider whether they want their government to support a government that engages in such actions.

Moreover, the idea that we should simply respect the practices of 'another culture' greatly oversimplifies the situation. Any American or British person knows that their own culture is not monolithic: each contains many sub-groups with different beliefs, goals, traditions, and priorities. To assume that other cultures are not like this is to make a grave yet common error. Other cultures, like our own, are internally diverse. Most relevantly for our purposes, they contain groups with a wide variety of views on practices relating to women. Feminism is not, contrary to many misconceptions, a Western import that outsiders have sought to impose on cultures that they dominate.[35] Instead, there are feminist groups to be found in nearly every culture. Moreover, feminist groups are resilient, even in the face of great adversity. Even, for example, in Taliban-era Afghanistan, feminist groups ran secret schools for girls, and secretly filmed the reality of women's lives for broadcast abroad to help organize resistance to the Taliban.[36] They did this despite grave risks to their own lives. Given such internal diversity, the idea that respecting a culture dictates a

[34] Interestingly, the cultural practices most frequently claimed to be so crucial to traditions that they must be accommodated are those involving women and the family. Very few would even attempt to argue, as Katha Pollitt notes, that an Algerian should be exempted from paying their credit card bill because Islam forbids interest on borrowed money (Pollitt 1999).

[35] For a history of Islamic feminism, see Ahmed (1992).

[36] One key group was the Revolutionary Association of the Women of Afghanistan (RAWA). For more on RAWA, see www.rawa.org (consulted 14 Sept. 2002).

particular policy really makes no sense. There is no one policy that could be dictated by a desire to respect *the* culture. Simply staying out, or encouraging the status quo, amounts to supporting whatever groups happen to be in power in the culture at that time.

Outsiders often take cultures not their own (especially those of the 'Third World') to contain timeless traditions that have been passed down, unchanging, through generation after generation. They worry that any alterations might represent disrespect for these timeless traditions. Again, this is an error. Other cultures, like our own, undergo large changes over time. Many of these changes are the result of internal struggles between various groups with their own agendas— just what one would expect, given the cultural diversity noted above. The idea that the timeless traditions of a culture should be preserved unchanged is a very useful one, however, for those in power who have managed to define their own views as timeless traditions. Uma Narayan writes,

> We need to move away from a picture of national and cultural contexts as sealed rooms, impervious to change, with a homogenous space inside them, inhabited by 'authentic insiders' who all share a uniform and consistent account of their institutions and values. Third-world national and cultural contexts are as pervaded by plurality, dissension, and change, as are their 'Western' counterparts. Both are often replete with unreflective and self-congratulatory views of their 'culture' and 'values' that disempower and marginalize the interests and concerns of many members of the national community, including women. We need to be wary about all ideals of 'cultural authenticity' that portray 'authenticity' as constituted by a lack of criticism and lack of change.
>
> (Narayan 1997: 33)

Often, what is propagated as 'timeless tradition' is simply the perspective of those who happen to hold power at a particular time. And—even more problematically for those defending 'tradition' from outside influence—Westerners have in many cases had a considerable impact on which traditions the powerful endorse as 'timeless' and central to their way of life. We have already seen some indirect ways that this has happened: traditions that Westerners opposed came to be seen as especially important, often to the detriment of women. However, sometimes the influence is more direct. During the 1980s, the

United States gave substantial support to fundamentalist Islamic groups because of their involvement in fighting the Soviets in Afghanistan (AbuKhalil 2000; Hiro 1999). An important result of this has been the strengthening of particular strains of Islamic fundamentalism. This means that more areas are controlled by those who claim these particular traditions to be the 'timeless traditions' of their lands. (One particularly stark example of this was the Taliban control of Afghanistan.)

Once we realize that cultures are diverse, containing many different traditions that may be struggling against each other, we can no longer view 'respecting *the* tradition' as a viable option. This means that cultural relativism is actually not a coherent view. Cultural relativism insists that practices within a culture should be judged by that culture's own values. But if no one set of values can be identified as those of 'the culture', this makes no sense. When we consider cultures other than our own, we are actually confronted with a wide range of conflicting traditions and views, just as in our own culture. And sometimes we are confronted with practices that are doing a great deal of harm. To ignore these harms on the spurious grounds of respecting 'the tradition' is clearly wrong.

Dialogue

We have seen that Westerners simply do not have the option of 'staying out' of other cultures—they are already involved. We have also seen that cultures are so complex and varied that it makes no sense to call for respecting 'the tradition'. We even imagined a fictional, monolithic culture lacking this complexity; and we saw that we would not always think it right to defer to the culture's traditions. We need, then, to find a way to avoid the sorts of arrogance and error that have historically been so common—while not giving up on the possibility of cross-cultural judgments. It has become increasingly popular to maintain that cross-cultural dialogue is the key to adequate cross-cultural judgement. Many difficult issues arise, however, over exactly what form this dialogue should take.

Internal complexity

The complexity of cultures was an important part of what made us reject the idea of simply supporting 'the tradition'. It also poses difficulties for some oversimplified ideas about how dialogue should proceed. In particular, it means that one cannot expect a single representative of a culture under discussion (or—worse yet—one representative of the 'Third World') to be able to represent the view of 'the culture' (or 'the Third World'). One representative is better than none, of course—but not so much better as one might have imagined. To properly understand and appreciate the situations of other cultures, it is important to acknowledge the diversity that exists within them. This requires acknowledging and attempting to come to grips with the multiplicity of views held by members of that culture. One American woman would not be able to represent the full range of views and concerns regarding some issue of her country,[37] and neither would one Indian woman (Narayan 1997: ch. 4).

With proper awareness of the internal diversity of cultures, it becomes impossible for a cultural outsider to expect an insider to simply dictate 'the right view' to outsiders. The diversity of perspectives within any culture means that *whatever* view an outsider might wish to hold (within reason), she will very likely find an insider who holds it. This means that outsiders cannot take a short-cut to finding the right view: they need to canvass the various options, do research, and think very carefully.

Automatic knowledge

The idea that one representative could offer 'the culture's' view is often also tied—if unconsciously—to the idea that any representative

---

[37] As an American living in Britain, I have frequently been asked to do such unfeasible things as explain 'why Americans are so into guns' (by many, many people that I meet), or to offer 'the American view' of the British elections (by BBC Radio Sheffield). I have no doubt that such experiences are far more common for those from non-Western countries, which tend to be viewed as monolithic and unchanging.

of that culture will do. Uma Narayan writes of frequently being asked to offer 'the Indian view' on issues far outside her areas of expertise. These invitations seem to stem from an underestimation of the difficulty of attaining knowledge about one's own culture's practices. This underestimation has several bad effects. First, to properly understand a cultural practice may require a great deal of knowledge of history, politics, and religion. It is by no means the case that every member of a particular culture possesses this knowledge. Moreover, insiders are (as we shall shortly see) by no means guaranteed to be free of false or distorted understandings of practices within their own cultures. Finally, one motivation for seeking insiders' views—respect for them and their culture—may be undermined by the implicit assumption that understanding of cultural practices is automatic.

> I have sometimes wondered with wry amusement whether 'Third-World individuals' were assumed to have a kind of 'knowledge by osmosis' about everything pertaining to their culture or to that internally complex entity, 'the Third World.' I am less amused when I wonder whether the part of my work that pertains to 'Third World issues' might seem like automatic knowledge seeping from my Third World pores, rather than the results of intellectual and political effort!
>
> (Narayan 1997: 145)

The 'automatic knowledge' assumption also makes it easy to manipulate a discussion. If *any* representative of a culture is considered sufficient for achieving genuine dialogue and understanding, one can easily bring about the result that one wants by picking the appropriate representative. Opponents of feminism, for example, need only find some internal female supporter of an oppressive practice in a particular culture. Proper awareness of the diversity within all cultures, and of the difficulty of attaining knowledge even about one's own culture, would help to protect against this sort of manipulation.[38]

Insiders may be wrong

Implicit (and occasionally explicit) in the above worries is the simple fact that insiders *can* be wrong about their own cultures. This should not really come as a great shock. To see why this should be so

[38] Narayan discusses related points in Narayan (1997: 213, n. 43).

unsurprising, think about your own culture, and all the various views people within it hold about some controversial issue or practice—such as abortion, drugs, sex, guns, or religious teaching in schools. Most likely, you think that some of these views are *wrong*. Moreover, you have probably frequently heard people say false things about your culture. (In all likelihood, you have said such false things yourself.) Now ask yourself: why should it be any different in another culture? Everyone makes mistakes, and to suppose that this is impossible for those of other cultures is absurd. In what follows, I look at some ways that people can go wrong in thinking about their own cultures.

One important way that errors may occur lies in the fact that those raised to accept an injustice can have difficulty perceiving it as an injustice.

> [W]e are not always enlightened about what is just by asking persons who seem to be suffering injustices what they want. Oppressed people have often internalized their oppression so well that they *have* no sense of what they are justly entitled to as human beings . . .

> (Okin 1994b: 19)

Those who are raised to believe they deserve a certain treatment may indeed have difficulty questioning it. Moreover, this treatment may be deeply bound up with their sense of themselves. At first, it might seem difficult to see how this could be the case—especially with respect to, for example, a tradition of giving women and girls proportionally less food than men and boys. But Hanna Papanek writes of an elderly Javanese woman who was taught from childhood that girls and women have an obligation to restrain themselves with respect to all pleasures in life, and even with respect to food. The reason for this, she was told, was that 'women set the norms for civilization because men cannot control themselves' (Papanek 1990: 172). One who holds this belief will not readily see it as wrong for women and girls to be less well nourished than men.

Internal sources can go wrong in other ways as well. One stems quite directly from the internal complexity of cultures. Chandra Talpade Mohanty discusses the fact that class divisions within a culture may mean that what is presented as applying to all members of a particular culture may only apply to some (Mohanty 1991b: 52).

Another problem stems from the simple fact that—as we've noted—acquiring knowledge, even about one's own culture, is difficult. Uma Narayan also notes that insiders may, like outsiders, simply fail to properly take account of the complex relationships between religions and cultures. Narayan writes,

> [F]ailing to be aware of the existence of such problematic modes of writing about 'Third World' cultures by 'native subjects' is an additional handicap to the project of mainstream Westerners 'understanding Other cultures' given that such writing then tends to be uncritically quoted, referenced, and 'assimilated' by some Western scholars.
>
> (Narayan 1997: 108)

Problems with subject matter of dialogue

Elizabeth Spelman takes a dialogue between Westerners and non-Westerners to have gone wrong if it includes only discussion of non-Western cultural practices. She praises Martha Nussbaum for spending a great deal of time talking to desperately poor Third World women before writing about them and their problems in her book, *Sex and Social Justice*; but she thinks Nussbaum errs by asking these women only about their own lives and their own needs. She suggests that 'you have not responded to the capabilities of others if you ignore or exclude consideration of how they see you' (Spelman 2000: 9). She suggests that Nussbaum should want to know 'not simply what they think about the theories in which they figure but what they think about the theorists, their struggles, their hopes'. If we do not try to learn such things, Spelman argues, we are not taking women from other cultures seriously as thinking, reflective subjects like ourselves. We are viewing our thoughts about them as valuable, but showing no interest in their thoughts about us. In this way, she maintains, we are merely using or objectifying them.

This criticism seems somewhat misplaced when applied specifically, as it is in this case, to Nussbaum's writings about the situation of extremely impoverished women. It seems to me that it would be grotesque for Nussbaum, after hearing about their struggles on the verge of starvation, to then ask them what they thought about her life as a philosophy professor and her own personal struggles and hopes.

Nonetheless, understood more generally, there is a worthwhile point here: it would be wrong to assume that those from other cultures can only contribute to theorizing about their own cultures. In particular, it is wrong to assume that outsiders to our culture could have nothing of value to say to us about our culture. Taking the perspectives of others seriously requires taking seriously their perspectives not only on themselves but also on others, including Westerners. In part, this is a matter of respect. But it is also more than this. First, quite generally, outsiders can offer a useful perspective to insiders, and those who are outsiders to Western cultures can offer much to insiders. However, there are also special reasons to take seriously what such people say. Westerners often get by in life without needing to understand anything about non-Western cultures. But non-Westerners do not really have the option of not learning about the West—its impact on them is great, and they are therefore likely to know much more about Westerners than Westerners know about them. Moreover, their perspective on Western culture will be one that attends to features that might not be so salient to Westerners, thus offering a fuller understanding.[39] (In the terminology of the previous chapter, we can see the standpoint of non-Westerners as especially valuable for understanding Western culture, due to their status as outsiders to it, and in many cases due to the ways that elements of Western cultures have served to oppress them.) To assume that the views of non-Westerners are only relevant to their own cultures is a grave error (Alexander and Mohanty 1997).

Failure to question or criticize

So far I have emphasized ways that Westerners can go wrong in thinking about other cultures, arguing for a need to listen to members of other cultures, and in fact *many* members of other cultures. Often, Westerners think that they should respond to those from other cultures simply by respectfully listening, and not judging, questioning, or criticizing any of the views expressed. Uma Narayan, however, raises

---

[39] For more on this sort of forced knowledge, see Lugones and Spelman (1983), Lugones (1989).

two important problems for this idea. The first is that simply listening, without criticism or questioning, may not be the best way to treat non-Westerners. Narayan focuses especially on the academic context, in which (she maintains) non-Western academics are often not subjected to the same sort of criticism and discussion as Westerners. While this is well intentioned in many cases, she notes that one effect of this is that non-Western academics do not get a chance to benefit from the same sort of critical discussion that helps Westerners to develop and improve their ideas.

> Being in such a situation feels like participating in some sort of 'ritual of diversity', where the 'Insider' has the instrumental role of 'speaking difference' but is not seen to have her own stakes in hearing a rich range of responses and criticisms that would enable her to refine, rearticulate, or defend her account.
>
> (Narayan 1997: 149)

One might suppose that such a discussion from Westerners could not be of any help, since Westerners do not share relevant experiences. But, Narayan notes, academic papers involve much more than first-hand experiences. They also involve analyses, and causal and historical claims, among many other features. While Westerners may be unable to offer useful first-hand experience, there is no reason to suppose that they would have nothing useful to say on these other matters.

Narayan also finds the idea of *not judging* problematic from a practical perspective (Narayan 1997: 150). She suggests that it is actually very difficult to refrain fully from making judgements about cultures other than one's own. When Westerners attempt not to pass judgement, she suggests, they probably all too often are merely not *expressing* their judgements. Because the judgements are not expressed, they are not subjected to critical scrutiny: they will not be revised and refined by the sort of questioning and criticism that might occur if they were expressed. So what may begin as an attempt to be respectful and deferential to others in fact results in protecting Westerners' own judgements from the critical scrutiny of non-Westerners. There is a common thread in these two worries of Narayan's: certain kinds of attempts to be respectful to non-Westerners may impair the development of the ideas of both Westerners and non-Westerners, and form a barrier to communication.

On the other hand, there are good reasons for Westerners to be cautious about questioning and criticizing. The views of non-Westerners have all too often not been taken seriously, and have simply been dismissed out of hand. Westerners must be wary of the sort of cultural arrogance that has done (and continues to do) so much damage. But there is a difference between dismissing and questioning (or even criticizing). Narayan suggests, in an earlier discussion, that those who are not the victims of a particular sort of oppression should conduct themselves carefully in discussion with those who are, behaving with what she calls 'methodological humility' and 'methodological caution'. To have methodological humility is to sincerely assume that one 'may be missing something, and that what appears to [the outsider] to be a "mistake" on the part of the insider may make more sense if [the outsider] had a fuller understanding of the context' (Narayan 1988: 38). To proceed with methodological caution is to make criticisms 'in such a way that it does not amount to, or even seem to amount to, an attempt to denigrate or dismiss entirely the validity of the insider's point of view'.

We have not managed to arrive at a simple recipe for accurate cross-cultural judgements and analyses. But this should not be surprising. There is no simple recipe for accuracy on these matters within a single culture. It can only be more difficult cross-culturally, with all the barriers to knowledge and communication that we have seen, and with all the history of arrogance and colonialism. Cross-cultural dialogue seems vital to proper understanding, but again there is no simple method for carrying this out properly. This emphatically does not mean, however, that it is not worth the effort. Women's lives are at stake, and turning away from these issues because they are difficult is not an acceptable response.

Dissolving the conflict between feminism and 'respect for cultures'

I ended my introductory section with a quotation from Katha Pollitt, suggesting a serious conflict between feminism and respect for cultures:

> Feminism and multiculturalism . . . are very far apart. In its demand for equality for women, feminism sets itself in opposition to virtually every culture on Earth. You could say that multiculturalism demands respect for all cultural traditions, while feminism interrogates and challenges all cultural traditions.
>
> (Pollitt 1999: 27)

Now we are in a position—through close reflection on the nature of cultures—to see what has gone wrong in Pollitt's positing of this conflict. Real cultures contain within them traditions of challenge and interrogation, and even traditions of feminism. A multiculturalism that demanded *endorsement* of every cultural tradition would indeed be at odds with feminism. But such a multiculturalism would make no sense—cultural traditions conflict, and endorsing every such tradition as right would be incoherent. Fortunately, however, respecting cultures does not require this. In fact, respecting cultures requires that we appreciate their genuine diversity and complexity, rather than seeing them as unchanging and monolithic. Speaking very loosely, we can take respect for a culture to require that we take it seriously—that we do not make blanket judgements of 'backwardness' or 'inferiority', for example, and that we engage in open, honest, and respectful dialogue with members of the culture. On this understanding, there need be no conflict between feminism and respect for cultures.

It might seem that this response overlooks something important. Even if feminist views are represented within a particular culture, it might still be that success of feminist proposals would mean the destruction of that culture. Surely, one might suppose, this is not compatible with respect for such a culture. The thought behind this is that a culture may contain features that are so crucial that any alteration to them would effectively destroy the culture. If this is right, then it is at least possible that changes desired by feminists might bring

about the end of a culture. In such a case, one could legitimately say
that feminism is incompatible with respect for the culture in question.

Suppose for the moment that there is a culture that would die out if
its feminist elements prevailed. Imagine, for example, a culture that
simply could not survive giving women and men equal entitlements
to the food and medical care that they need. In this fictional culture,
the idea that women's needs should not be taken seriously is so central that taking women's needs seriously would cause the culture to
disintegrate. If there *were* such a culture, it is not at all clear to me
that one should favour the survival of the culture over the victory of
feminism. At the very least, some argument would be needed that
a culture's survival is more important than its women's survival.

The case described above is, of course, an extreme and implausible
one. Once we turn to real cases, however, it becomes clear that this
sort of conflict really doesn't make much sense. In order to generate
a conflict like this, cultures need to have features that are essential
to them: features such that the culture simply couldn't survive their
removal. Particular practices are indeed often *claimed* to be essential,
and in fact this tends to happen particularly often with practices
relating to women. But cultures change, and competing traditions
within a culture have very different ideas about what features are
essential to the culture. At the very least, this makes it exceedingly
difficult to determine what, if any, traits really are essential to a
given culture. Moreover, proper attention to all the historical and
political factors involved in such claims casts doubt on the idea that
we can make intelligible sense of any particular features being genuinely essential to cultures. In fact, even the idea of sharply delineating one culture from another becomes problematic once we are
aware of all the complicated interactions between 'cultures'. Finally,
what groups we call 'cultures' will vary depending on our purposes—for some purposes, it will seem appropriate to speak of
'American culture', but for other purposes it will make more sense
to speak of 'Black American culture', 'Black American middle
-class culture', 'Black Christian American culture', or 'Black Muslim
American culture', and so on. We do not have pre-existing entities
that are cultures, that can be destroyed by changing certain key
features. This worry, then, cannot succeed: the conflict between

feminism and 'respect for cultures' is based on a misunderstanding of the nature of cultures.[40]

SUGGESTIONS FOR FURTHER READING

Criticism of Western feminists' discussions of 'Third-World' cultures

Hoodfar, H., 'The Veil in Their Minds and on Our Heads: The Persistence of Colonial Images of Muslim Women', *Review of Feminist Research* 22(3–4) (1993): 5–18.

Mohanty, C. T., *Third World Women and the Politics of Feminism*, Bloomington, Ind.: Indiana University Press, 1991.

Narayan, U., 'Working Together Across Difference: Some Considerations on Emotions and Political Practice', *Hypatia* 3(2) (1988): 31–47.

——*Dislocating Cultures: Identities, Traditions, and Third World Feminism*. New York: Routledge, 1997.

Obiora, L. A., 'Bridges and Barricades: Rethinking Polemics and Intransigence in the Campaign against Female Circumcision', in A. K. Wing (ed.), *Global Critical Race Feminism: An International Reader.* New York: New York University Press, 2000.

Okin, S. M., *Is Multiculturalism Bad for Women?* Princeton, NJ: Princeton University Press, 1999. (*Several essays in this book.*)

Criticism of idea that 'respect for cultures' should deter Western feminists from discussing 'Third-World' women's issues

Benhabib, S., 'Cultural Complexity, Moral Interdependence, and the Global Dialogical Community', in M. Nussbaum, and J. Glover (eds.), *Women, Culture and Development: A Study of Human Capabilities.* Oxford: Clarendon Press, 1995, 235–55.

Narayan, U., *Dislocating Cultures: Identities, Traditions, and Third World Feminism.* New York: Routledge, 1997.

——'Essence of Culture and a Sense of History', *Hypatia* 13(2) (1998): 86–106.

Nussbaum, M., *Sex and Social Justice.* New York: Oxford University Press, 1999, essays 1, 3, 4.

——'Human Capabilities, Female Human Beings', in M. Nussbaum and J. Glover (eds.), *Women, Culture and Development: A Study of Human Capabilities.* Oxford: Clarendon Press, 1995, 61–104.

[40] For more on worries about cultural essentialism, see Narayan (1998).

Okin, S. M., 'Feminism, Women's Human Rights, and Cultural Differences', *Hypatia* v. 13(2) (1998): 32–52.

——*Is Multiculturalism Bad for Women?* Princeton, NJ: Princeton University Press, 1999. (*Several essays in this book.*)

References

AbuKhalil, A. (2000), 'Women in the Middle East'. Foreign Policy in Focus
   Policy Brief, Vol. 5, No. 30, Sept. **www.fpif.org/briefs/vol5/**
   v5n30women_body.html, consulted 10 Aug. 2002.
ACLU (1997), 'Coercive and Punitive Governmental Responses to Women's
   Conduct During Pregnancy': www.aclu.org/issues/reproduct/coercive.html,
   consulted 12 Aug. 2002.
Ahmed, L. (1992), *Women and Gender in Islam*. New Haven, Conn. Yale
   University Press.
Alexander, M. J., and Mohanty, C. T. (1997), 'Introduction: Genealogies,
   Legacies, Movements'. In M. J. Alexander and C. T. Mohanty (eds.), *Feminist
   Genealogies, Colonial Legacies, Democratic Futures*. New York: Routledge, xiii–xlii.
Al-Hibri, A. (1999), 'Is Western Patriarchal Feminism Good for Third World/
   Minority Women?' In Okin (1999: 41–6).
American Society for Aesthetic Plastic Surgery (2002), 'Cosmetic Surgery
   Trends: Women Have over 7.4 Million Procedures, 88% of Total'. **http://**
   surgery.org/news_releases/feb2002statswomen.html, consulted 28 Nov.
   2002.
American Academy of Orthopaedic Surgeons (2002), 'Bunions'. **http://**
   orthoinfo.aaos.org/fact/thr_report.cfm?Thread_ID=204&topcategory
   =Foot, consulted 25 Sept. 2002.
Anderson, E. (1995), 'Feminist Epistemology: An Interpretation and
   a Defence'. *Hypatia* 10(3): 50–84.
—— (2001), 'Feminist Epistemology and Philosophy of Science'. In E. N. Zalta
   (ed.), *The Stanford Encyclopedia of Philosophy*. **http://plato.stanford.edu/**
   archives/win2001/entries/feminism-epistemology/, consulted 27 Nov.
   2002.
Antony, L. (1993), 'Quine as Feminist'. In L. Antony and C. Witt (eds.), *A Mind of
   One's Own*. Boulder, Colo.: Westview Press, 185–225.
—— (1995), 'Sisters, Please, I'd Rather Do It Myself: A Defense of Individualism
   in Feminist Epistemology'. *Philosophical Topics* 23(2): 59–94.

—— (1998), ' "Human Nature" and Its Role in Feminist Theory'. In J. Kourany (ed.), *Philosophy in a Feminist Voice*. Princeton, NJ: Princeton University Press, 63–91.

Austin, J. L. (1962), *How to Do Things with Words*. London: Oxford University Press.

Bagemihl, B. (1999), *Biological Exuberance: Animal Homosexuality and Natural Diversity*. London: Profile.

Baier, A. (1987), 'The Need for More than Justice'. *Canadian Journal of Philosophy*, supplementary vol. 13: 41–56.

Baron, D. (1986) *Grammar and Gender*. New Haven, Conn.: Yale University Press.

Bartky, S. (1990a), 'Foucault, Femininity, and the Modernization of Patriarchal Power'. In *Femininity and Domination*. New York: Routledge, 63–82.

—— (1990b), 'Narcissism, Femininity, and Alienation'. In *Femininity and Domination*. New York: Routledge, 33–44.

Bartlett, K., and Harris, A. (1998), *Gender and Law*. New York: Aspen.

BBC (2001), 'Abortion Law to be Reviewed'. http://news.bbc.co.uk/1/hi/northern_ireland/1385897.stm, consulted 21 Nov. 2002.

BBCi (2002), 'Saudi Police "Stopped" Fire Rescue'. http://news.bbc.co.uk/1/hi/world/middle_east/1874471.stm, consulted 5 Sept. 2002.

Benhabib, S. (1995), 'Cultural Complexity, Moral Interdependence, and the Global Dialogical Community'. In M. Nussbaum and J. Glover (eds.), *Women, Culture and Development: A Study of Human Capabilities*. Oxford: Clarendon Press, 235–55.

Bernstein, R. (2001), 'Guilty If Charged'. In L. LeMoncheck and J. Sterba (eds.), *Sexual Harassment: Issues and Answers*, Oxford: Oxford University Press, 187–93.

Bhabha, H. K. (1999), 'Liberalism's Sacred Cow'. In Okin (1999: 79–84).

Bleier, R. (1984), *Science and Gender: A Critique of Biology and its Theories on Women*. New York: Pergamon.

Blum, L. (1988), 'Gilligan and Kohlberg: Implications for Moral Theory'. *Ethics* 98(3): 472–91.

Bodine, A. (1998), 'Androcentrism in Prescriptive Grammar'. In D. Cameron (1998: 124–38).

Boonstra, H., and Sonfield, A. (2000), 'Revisiting Public Funding of Abortion for Poor Women'. Guttmacher Report on Public Policy, Apr. 2000, www.agi-usa.org/pubs/ib-funding00.html, consulted 12 Aug. 2002.

Bordo, S. (1993), *Unbearable Weight: Feminism, Western Culture, and the Body*. Berkeley: University of California Press.

—— (1999), *The Male Body: A New Look at Men in Public and in Private*. New York: Farrar, Straus & Giroux.

Bunting, M. (2001), 'Can Islam Liberate Women?' *Guardian*, 8 Dec. www.guardian.co.uk.weekend/story/0,3605,614357,00.html, consulted 21 Aug. 2002.

Bureau of the Census (1997), 'Census Brief: Children with Single Parents—How They Fare'. CENBR/97–1. Washington, DC: US Dept. of Commerce.

Buss, D. (1999), *Evolutionary Psychology*. Needham Heights, Mass.: Allyn & Bacon.

Butler, J. (1990), *Gender Trouble: Feminism and the Subversion of Identity*. New York: Routledge.

Califia, P. (1994), *Public Sex*. Pittsburgh, Penn.: Cleis.

Callahan, S. (1984), 'Commentary to Chapter 12'. In S. Callahan and D. Callahan (eds.), *Abortion: Understanding Differences*. New York: Plenum, 325–30.

Cameron, D. (1985), *Feminism and Linguistic Theory*. Basingstoke: Macmillan.

—— (1995), *Verbal Hygiene*. London: Routledge.

—— (ed.) (1998), *The Feminist Critique of Language*, 2nd edn. London: Routledge.

—— and Frazer, E. (2000), 'On the Question of Pornography and Sexual Violence: Moving Beyond Cause and Effect'. In D. Cornell (ed.), *Feminism and Pornography*. New York: Oxford University Press, 240–53.

Cannold, L. (2000), *The Abortion Myth: Feminism, Morality and the Hard Choices Women Make*. Hanover, NH: Wesleyan University Press.

Card, C. (1993), 'Gender and Moral Luck'. In O. Flanagan and A. Rorty (eds.), *Identity, Character, and Morality*. Bradford, Mass.: MIT University Press, 200–218.

Chen, M. (1995), 'A Matter of Survival: Women's Right to Employment in India and Bangladesh'. In M. Nussbaum and J. Glover (eds.), *Women, Culture and Development: A Study of Human Capabilities*. Oxford: Oxford University Press, 37–57.

Chodorow, N. (1978), *The Reproduction of Mothering*. Berkeley: University of California Press.

Christensen, F. M. (1994), ' "Sexual Harassment" Must Be Eliminated'. *Public Affairs Quarterly* 8(1): 1–17.

Christopher, K., England, P., McLanahan, S., Ross, K., and Smeeding, T. (2001), 'Gender Inequality in Poverty in Affluent Nations: The Role of Single Motherhood and the State'. In K. Vleminkx and T. M. Smeeding (eds.), *Child Well-Being, Child Poverty, and Child Policy in Modern Nations*. Bristol: Policy Press.

Clark, J. B. (1999), 'Plastic Surgery: Plain Truths'. *Kiplinger's Personal Finance Magazine*. www.Kiplinger.com/magazine/archives/1999/April/mmapr994.htm, consulted 17 Apr. 2002.

Clark, M. M. (2001), 'The Silva Case at the University of New Hampshire'. In L. LeMoncheck and J. Sterba (eds.), *Sexual Harassment: Issues and Answers*. Oxford: Oxford University Press, 194–206.

Code, L. (1998), 'How to Think Globally: Stretching the Limits of Imagination'. *Hypatia* 13(2): 73–85.

Cole, C., Hill, F., and Dayley, L. (1983), 'Do Masculine Pronouns Used Generically Lead to Thoughts of Men?', *Sex Roles* 9: 737–49.

Collins, P. H. (1997), 'Toward an Afrocentric Feminist Consciousness'. In S. Kemp and J. Squires (eds.), *Feminisms*. Oxford: Oxford University Press.

—— (2000), *Black Feminist Thought: Knowledge, Consciousness, and the Politics of Empowerment*, 2nd edn. New York: Routledge.

Cornell, D. (2000), 'Pornography's Temptation'. In D. Cornell (ed.), *Feminism and Pornography*. New York: Oxford University Press, 551–68.

Crawford, M. (1995), 'Daily Life on the Home Front: Women, Blacks, and the Struggle for Public Housing'. In D. Albrecht (ed.), *World War II and the American Dream: How Wartime Building Changed a Nation*. Washington, DC/Cambridge, Mass.: National Building Museum, MIT Press, 91–143.

Crittenden, A. (2001), *The Price of Motherhood*. New York: Henry Holt.

Crossthwaite, J. and Priest, G. (1996), 'The Definition of Sexual Harassment'. *Australasian Journal of Philosophy* 74(1): 66–82.

Crouch, M. (2001), *Thinking about Sexual Harassment: A Guide for the Perplexed*. Oxford: Oxford University Press.

Dahl, A. (1965), *Always Ask a Man*. London: Muller.

Daly, M., and Caputi, J. (1987), *Websters' First New Intergalactic Wickedary of the English Language*. Boston, Mass.: Beacon Press.

Davis, K. (1995), *Reshaping the Female Body: The Dilemma of Cosmetic Surgery*. New York: Routledge.

Department of Trade and Industry (2002a), 'Maternity Leave: Changes'. www.dti.gov.uk/er/matleafr.htm, consulted 5 Nov. 2002.

—— (2002b), 'Paternity: Leave and Pay'. www.dti.gov.uk/er/individual/paternity-p1514.htm, consulted 29 Aug. 2002.

—— (2002c), 'Parental Leave: Summary Guidance'. www. dti.gov.uk/er/intguid1.htm, consulted 5 Nov. 2002.

Devlin, B., Feinberg, S. E., Resnick, D. P., and Roeder, K. (eds.) (1997), *Intelligence, Genes and Success: Scientists Respond to the Bell Curve*. New York: Springer.

Dittrich, L. (2002), 'About-Face Facts on Socioeconic Status, Ethnicity, and the Thin Ideal'. www.about-face.org/r/facts/ses.html, consulted 28 Nov. 2002.

Donnerstein, E., Linz, D., and Penrod, S. (1987), *The Question of Pornography: Research Findings and Policy Implications*. New York: Free Press

Duarte, P. (1988), 'Older, but Not Invisible'. *Women's Center News* (Women's Center of San Joaquin County, Calif.) 12 (12): 1–2.

Dworkin, A. (1981), *Pornography: Men Possessing Women*. London: Women's Press.

Dwyer, S. (ed.) (1995a), *The Problem of Pornography*. Belmont, Calif.: Wadsworth.

—— (1995b), 'Legal Appendix'. In Dwyer (1995a: (ed.)), *The Problem of Pornography*. Belmont, Calif.: Wadsworth.

—— (2003), ' "Enter Here"—at Your Own Risk: The Moral Dangers of Cyberporn'. In R. Cavlier (ed.), *The Impact of the Internet on our Moral Lives*. Albany, New York: State University of New York Press.

Dyzenhaus, D. (1992), 'John Stuart Mill and the Harm of Pornography'. *Ethics* 102: 534–51.

Einsedel, E. (1992), 'The Experimental Research Evidence: Effects of Pornography on the "Average Individual" '. In C. Itzin (ed.), *Pornography: Women, Violence, and Civil Liberties*. New York: Oxford University Press, 248–83.

Elgin, S. (1985), *A First Dictionary and Grammar of Laadan*. Madison, Wis.: Society for the Furtherance and Study of Fantasy and Science Fiction.

Eller, T. J. (1996), 'Who Stays Poor? Who Doesn't?' US Census Bureau, Current Population Reports, June. Washington, DC.

El Saadawi, N. (1980), *The Hidden Face of Eve: Women in the Arab World*. London: Zed Press.

English, J. (1998), 'Abortion: Beyond the Personhood Argument'. In L. P. Pojman and F. J. Beckwith (eds.), *The Abortion Controversy: 25 Years After Roe v. Wade*. Belmont, Calif.: Wadsworth, 315–24.

Equal Employment Opportunity Commission (2002a), 'Policy Guidance on Current Issues of Sexual Harassment'. www.eeoc.gov/docs/currentissues.html, consulted 25 Oct. 2002.

—— (2002b), 'Dealing with Sexual Harassment'. www.eoc.org.uk/EOCeng/EOCcs/Advice/sexual_harassment.asp, consulted 24 Oct. 2002.

—— (2002c), 'Sexual Harassment: What the Law Says'. www.eoc.org.uk/EOCeng/EOCcs/Advice/sexual_harassment_the_law.asp, consulted 24 Oct. 2002.

Erlich, S., and R. King (1998), 'Gender-based Language Reform and the Social Construction of Meaning'. In Cameron (1998: 164–79).

Everywoman (1988), *Pornography and Sexual Violence: Evidence of the Links: The Complete Record of Public Hearings for Experts, Witnesses and Victims of Sexual Assault Involving Pornography*. London: Everywoman.

Faludi, S. (1991), *Backlash*. New York: Anchor.

Farley, L. (1978), *Sexual Shakedown: The Sexual Harassment of Women on the Job*. New York: McGraw-Hill.

Farrell, E. M. (1995), *Lost for Words: The Psychoanalysis of Anorexia and Bulimia*. London: Process Press.

Fausto-Sterling, A. (1992), *Myths of Gender: Biological Theories about Women and Men*. New York: Basic Books.

Feminists Against Censorship (1991), *Pornography and Feminism*. London: Lawrence & Wishart.

Flanagan, O. (1991), *Varieties of Moral Personality*. Cambridge, Mass.: Harvard University Press.

Forbes, G. B., Adams-Curtis, L. E., Rade, B., and Jaberg, P. (2001), 'Body Dissatisfaction in Women and Men: The Role of Gender-Typing and Self-Esteem'. *Sex Roles* 44(7–8): 461–83.

Forna, A. (1992), 'Pornography and Racism: Sexualizing Oppression and

Inciting Hatred'. In C. Itzin (ed.), *Pornography: Women, Violence, and Civil Liberties*. New York: Oxford University Press, 102–12.

Foucault, M. (1979), *Discipline and Punish*. New York: Vintage.

Fraser, L. (1999), 'The Hard Body Sell'. *Mother Jones* (Mar./Apr. 1999). www.motherjones.com/mother_jones/MA99/fraser.html, consulted 29 Sept. 2002.

Fredman, S. (1997), *Women and the Law*. Oxford: Clarendon Press.

Fricker, M. (1998), 'Rational Authority and Social Power: Towards a Truly Social Epistemology'. *Proceedings of the Aristotelian Society* 98(2): 159–77.

—— (1999), 'Epistemic Oppression and Epistemic Privilege', *Canadian Journal of Philosophy*, supplementary vol. 25 (also known as C. Wilson (ed.), *Civilization and Oppression*. Calgary: Calgary University Press), 191–210.

Friedan, B. (1997), *Beyond Gender*. Washington, DC: Woodrow Wilson Center Press.

Friedman, M. (1987), 'Beyond Caring: The De-moralization of Gender'. *Canadian Journal of Philosophy*, supplementary vol. 13: 87–110.

Frye, M. (1983a), 'Sexism'. In *The Politics of Reality: Essays in Feminist Theory*. Freedom, Calif.: Crossing Press.

—— (1983b), 'To Be and Be Seen'. In *The Politics of Reality: Essays in Feminist Theory*. Freedom, Calif.: Crossing Press.

Gastil, J. (1990), 'Generic Pronouns and Sexist Language: The Oxymoronic Character of Masculine Generics'. *Sex Roles* 23 (11/12): 629–43

Gates, H. L. (1992), 'To "Deprave and Corrupt" ', *The Nation*, 29 June. Cited in L. Williams, 'Second Thoughts on *Hard Core*'. In P. C. Gibson and R. Gibson (eds.), *Dirty Looks*. London: BFI, 1993.

George, S. (1988), 'Censorship and Hypocrisy: Some Issues Surrounding Pornography that Feminism has Ignored'. In G. Chester and J. Dickey (eds.), *Feminism and Censorship: The Current Debate*. Bridport, Dorset: Prism, 110–18.

Gillespie, M. A. (1998), 'Mirror Mirror'. In R. Weitz (ed.), *The Politics of Women's Bodies: Sexuality, Appearance, and Behaviour*. Oxford: Oxford University Press, 184–8.

Gilliam, A. (1991), 'Women's Equality and National Liberation'. In C. T. Mohanty, A. Russo, and L. Torres (eds.), *Third World Women and the Politics of Feminism*. Bloomington, Ind.: Indiana University Press, 215–36.

Gilligan, C. (1982), *In a Different Voice*. Cambridge, Mass.: Harvard University Press.

—— (1988), 'Prologue: Adolescent Development Reconsidered'. In C. Gilligan, J. V. Ward, and J. M. Taylor (eds.), *Mapping the Moral Domain*. Cambridge, Mass.: Harvard University Press, vii–xxix.

Ginsburg, F. (1989), *Contested Lives*. Berkeley, Calif.: University of California Press.

Glendon, M. A. (1991), *Rights Talk*. New York: Free Press.

—— (2001), *A World Made New*. New York: Random House.

Gould, S. J. (1992), *The Mismeasure of Man*. Harmondsworth: Penguin.

Gray, J. (1992), *Men Are from Mars, Women Are from Venus*. London: HarperCollins.

Green, K. (1986), 'Rawls, Women and the Priority of Liberty'. *Australasian Journal of Philosophy*, supplement to vol. 64, 26–36.

Greer, G. (1970), *The Female Eunuch*. London: MacGibbon and Kee.

Grimshaw, J. (1986), *Feminist Philosophers*. Brighton: Wheatsheaf.

—— (1997), 'Ethics, Fantasy, and Self-Transformation'. In A. Soble (ed.), *The Philosophy of Sex*. Lanham, Md.: Rowman & Littlefield, 175–87.

—— (1999), 'Working Out with Merleau-Ponty'. In J. Arthurs and J. Grimshaw (eds.), *Womens's Bodies: Discipline and Transgression*. London: Cassell, 91–116.

Gunning, I. R. (2000), 'Uneasy Alliances and Solid Sisterhood: A Response to Professor Obiora's "Bridges and Barricades" '. In A. K. Wing (ed.), *Global Critical Race Feminism: An International Reader*. New York: New York University Press.

Haack, S. (1993), 'Knowledge and Propaganda: Reflections of an Old Feminist'. *Reason Papers* 18: 31–43.

Hajdin, M., and LeMoncheck, L. (1997), *Sexual Harassment: A Debate*. Lanham, Md.: Rowman & Littlefield.

Hanigsberg, J. (1997), 'Glamour Law: Feminism through the Looking Glass of Popular Women's Magazines'. In M. Fineman and M. McCluskey (eds.), *Feminism, Media, and the Law*. Oxford: Oxford University Press.

Harding, S. (1987), 'Is There a Feminist Method?' In *Feminism and Methodology*. Bloomington, Ind.: Indiana University Press, 1–14.

—— (1993), 'Rethinking Standpoint Epistemology: What is "Strong Objectivity"?' In L. Alcoff and E. Potter (eds.), *Feminist Epistemologies*. London: Routledge, 49–82.

—— (1997), 'Comment on Hekman's "Truth and Method. Feminist Standpoint Theory Revisited": Whose Standpoint Needs the Regimes of Truth and Reality?' *Signs* 22(2): 385–6.

Harris, A. (1993), 'Race and Essentialism in Legal Theory'. In D. K. Weisberg (ed.), *Feminist Legal Theory: Foundations*. Philadelphia: Temple University Press, 348–58.

Hartsock, N. (1983), 'The Feminist Standpoint Theory: Developing the Ground for a Specifically Feminist Historical Materialism'. In S. Harding, and M. B. Hintikka (eds.), *Discovering Reality*. Dordrecht: Reidel.

Haslanger, S. (1993), 'On Being Objective and Being Objectified'. In L. Antony and C. Witt (eds.), *A Mind of One's Own*. Boulder, Colo.: Westview.

—— (1995), 'Ontology and Social Construction'. *Philosophical Topics* 23(2): 95–125.

—— (2000), 'Race and Gender: (What) Are They? (What) Do We Want Them to Be?' *Noûs* 34(1): 31–55.

Hegel, G. W. F. (1952 [1821]), *The Philosophy of Right*, trans. T. M. Knox. Oxford: Oxford University Press.

Hekman, S. (1997), 'Truth and Method: Feminist Standpoint Theory Revisited'. *Signs* 22(2): 341–65.

Herrnstein, N., and Murray, C. (1994), *The Bell Curve: Intelligence and Class Structure in American Life*. New York: Free Press.

Hersh, E., and Olson, G. A. (1995), 'Starting from Marginalized Lives: A Conversation with Sandra Harding'. *JAC* 12(2), http://jac.gsu.edu/jac/15.2/Articles/1.htm, consulted 27 Nov. 2002.

Hiro, D. (1999), 'The Cost of an Afghan "Victory". *The Nation*, 15 Feb. www.thenation.com/docprint.mhtml?i=19990215ands=hiro_wtc_19990215, consulted 9 Oct. 2002.

Hirschmann, N. (1988), 'Western Feminism, Eastern Veiling, and the Question of Free Agency'. *Constellations* 5: 345–68.

Hite, S. (1976), *The Hite Report*. New York: Macmillan.

Hochschild, A. R. (1997), *The Time Bind*. New York: Metropolitan.

Hofstadter, D. (1998), 'A Person Paper on Purity in Language'. In Cameron (1998: 141–8).

Holcomb, B. (2000), 'Friendly for Whose Family?' *Ms.* (Apr./May). www.msmagazine.com/apr2k/family.html, consulted 31 May 2002.

Honig, B. (1999), 'My Culture Made Me Do It'. In Okin (1999: 31–5).

Hoodfar, H. (1993), 'The Veil in Their Minds and on Our Heads: The Persistence of Colonial Images of Muslim Women'. *Review of Feminist Research* 22(3–4): 5–18.

hooks, b. (1982), *Ain't I A Woman? Black Women and Feminism*. London: Pluto Press.

—— (1984), *Feminist Theory: From Margin to Center*. Boston, Mass.: South End Press.

Horn, L., and Kleinedler, S. R. (2000), 'Parasitic Reference vs. R-based Narrowing: Lexical Pragmatics meets *He-Man*'. Paper presented to the Linguistic Society of America, Chicago, 6 Jan.

Hornsby, J. (1995), 'Disempowered Speech'. In S. Haslanger (ed.), *Feminist Perspectives on Language, Knowledge, and Reality*, special issue of *Philosophical Topics* 23(2): 221–59.

—— (2000), 'Feminism in Philosophy of Language: Communicative Speech Acts'. In M. Fricker and J. Hornsby (eds.), *The Cambridge Companion to Feminism in Philosophy*. Cambridge: Cambridge University Press, 87–106.

Houston, B. (1987), 'Rescuing Womanly Virtues: Some Dangers of Moral Reclamation'. *Canadian Journal of Philosophy*, supplementary vol. 13: 237–62.

Hrdy, S. B. (1999), *Mother Nature*. London: Chatto & Windus.

Hughes, M. (2002), 'Why Women Should Get Angry'. *Guardian*, 3 Aug. http://money.guardian.co.uk/pensions/story/0,6453,768395,00.html, consulted 28 Nov. 2002.

Hursthouse, R. (1987), *Beginning Lives*. Oxford: Blackwell Open University Press.

Itzin, C. (1992), 'Legislating against Pornography without Censorship'. In Itzin (ed.), *Pornography: Women, Violence, and Civil Liberties*. New York: Oxford University Press, 401–34.

Jacobson, D. (1995), 'Freedom of Speech Acts? A Response to Langton'. *Philosophy and Public Affairs* 24: 64–79.

Jaggar, A. (1973), 'Abortion and a Woman's Right to Decide'. *Philosophical Forum* 5: 347–60.

—— (1988), *Feminist Politics and Human Nature*. Savage, Md: Rowman & Littlefield.

—— (1997), 'Regendering the US Abortion Debate'. *Journal of Social Philosophy* 28(1): 127–40.

Jefferson, L. (2002), 'The War on Women'. *Wall Street Journal*, 22 Aug. at Human Rights Watch website, http://hrw.org/editorials/2002/women0822.htm, consulted 20 Nov. 2002.

Jervis, L. (2000), 'My Jewish Nose'. In O. Edut (ed.), *Body Outlaws: Young Women Write About Body Image and Identity*. Seattle: Seal Press, 62–7.

Johnston, D. (1988), 'Adolescents' Solutions to Dilemmas in Fables: Two Moral Orientations'. In C. Gilligan, J. V. Ward, and J. M. Taylor (eds.), *Mapping the Moral Domain*. Cambridge, Mass.: Harvard University Press, 49–71.

Kant, I. (1991 [1761]), *Observations on the Feeling of the Beautiful and Sublime*. trans. J. Goldthwaite. Berkeley, Calif.: University of California Press.

Kaw, E. (1997), 'Opening Faces: The Politics of Cosmetic Surgery and Asian American Women'. In M. Crawford and R. Unger (eds.), *In Our Words: Readings on the Psychology of Women and Gender*. New York: McGraw-Hill, 55–73.

—— (1998), 'Medicalization of Racial Features: Asian-American Women and Cosmetic Surgery'. In R. Weitz (ed.), *The Politics of Women's Bodies: Sexuality, Appearance, and Behaviour*. Oxford: Oxford University Press, 55–73.

Kelly, W. (2001), 'You, but Sexier: 18 Showoff Positions to Flatter Your Figure in Bed'. *Cosmopolitan* (Feb.): 98–101.

Kilbourne, J. (2000), *Can't Buy My Love*. New York: Touchstone.

Kimmel, M. (2000), *The Gendered Society*. New York: Oxford University Press.

Kincheloe, J. L., Steinberg, S. R., and Gresson, A. D. (eds.) (1996), *Measured Lies: The Bell Curve Examined*. New York: St. Martin's Press.

Kohlberg, L. (1981), *The Philosophy of Moral Development: Moral Stages and the Idea of Justice*. San Francisco, Calif.: Harper and Row.

—— and Kramer, R. (1969), 'Continuities and Discontinuities in Childhood and Adult Moral Development'. *Human Development* 12: 93–120.

Kristof, N. (2002), 'Bush vs. Women'. *New York Times* (16 Aug.). www.nytimes.com/2002/08/16/opinion/16KRIS.html, consulted 16 Aug. 2002.

Kurz, D. (1995), *For Richer For Poorer: Mothers Confront Divorce*. New York: Routledge.

Kymlicka, W. (2002), *Contemporary Political Philosophy: An Introduction*, 2nd edn. Oxford: Oxford University Press.

Langton, R. (1993), 'Speech Acts and Unspeakable Acts'. *Philosophy and Public Affairs* 22: 293–330.

Lea, R. (2000), 'Do Women Lose Out at Work Because of Maternity Leave?' *Guardian Saturday Review* (26 Aug.): 2.

LeMieux, D. (2002), 'Here's the Wrinkle on Botox'. *San Francisco Chronicle. Your Health Daily*, http://199.97.97.16/contWriter/yhdweek/2002/05/06/medic/2314–0063-pat_nytimes.html, consulted 29 Sept. 2002.

Levin, M. (1981), 'Vs. Ms.'. In Vetterling-Braggin (1981: 217–22).

Linz, D., and Donnerstein, E. (1989), 'The Effects of Counter-information on the Acceptance of Rape Myths'. In D. Zillman and J. Bryant (eds.), *Pornography: Research Advances and Policy Considerations*. Hillsdale, NJ: Erlbaum: 259–88.

—— and Penrod, S. (1987), 'The Findings and Recommendations of the Attorney General's Commission on Pornography: Do the Psychological "Facts" Fit the Political Fury?' *American Psychologist* 42(10): 946–53.

Little, M. O. (1999), 'Abortion, Intimacy, and the Duty to Gestate'. *Ethical Theory and Moral Practice* 2: 295–312.

Lloyd, E. (1993), 'Pre-theoretical Assumptions in Evolutionary Explanations of Female Sexuality'. *Philosophical Studies* 69: 139–53.

Longino, H. (1990), *Science as Social Knowledge: Values and Objectivity in Scientific Inquiry*. Princeton, NJ: Princeton University Press

—— (1993), 'Essential Tensions—Phase Two: Feminist, Philosophical, and Social Studies of Knowledge'. In L. Antony and C. Witt (eds.), *A Mind of One's Own*. Boulder, Colo.: Westview, 257–72.

—— (1995), 'Pornography, Oppression, and Freedom: A Closer Look'. In S. Dwyer (ed.), *The Problem of Pornography*. Belmont, Calif.: Wadsworth, 34–47.

—— (1999), 'Feminist Epistemology'. In J. Greco and E. Sosa (eds.). *The Blackwell Guide to Epistemology*. Oxford: Blackwell, 327–53.

Lovelace, L., with Grady, M. (1980), *Ordeal*. Seacaucus, NJ: Citadel Press.

Lugones, M. (1989), 'Playfulness, "World"-Traveling, and Loving Perception'. In A. Garry and M. Pearsall (eds.), *Women, Knowledge, and Reality*. Boston, Mass.: Unwin Hyman, 275–90.

—— and Spelman, E. (1983), 'Have We Got a Theory for You! Feminist Theory, Cultural Imperialism and the Demand for "The Woman's Voice" '. *Women's Studies International Forum* 6(6): 573–81.

McCurdy, J. A. (1990), *Cosmetic Surgery of the Asian Face*. New York: Thieme.

McDonagh, E. (1996), *Breaking the Abortion Deadlock: From Choice to Consent*. Oxford: Oxford University Press.

McElroy, W. (1995), *XXX: A Woman's Right to Pornography*. New York: St. Martin's Press.

McKeever, M., and Wolfinger, N. H. (2001), 'Reexamining the Economic

Costs of Marital Disruption for Women'. *Social Science Quarterly* 82(1): 202–17.

MacKinnon, C. (1979), *The Sexual Harassment of Working Women*. New Haven, Conn.: Yale University Press.

—— (1987), *Feminism Unmodified*. Cambridge, Mass.: Harvard University Press.

—— (1989), *Toward a Feminist Theory of the State*. Cambridge, Mass.: Harvard University Press.

—— (1992), 'Pornography, Civil Rights, and Speech'. In C. Itzin (ed.), *Pornography: Women, Violence, and Civil Liberties*. New York: Oxford University Press, 456–511.

—— (1993), *Only Words*. Cambridge, Mass.: Harvard University Press.

McLanahan, S., and Kelly, E. (1999), 'The Feminization of Poverty: Past and Future'. In J. S. Chavetz (ed.), *Handbook of the Sociology of Gender*. New York: Kluwer, 127–45.

McNaught, S. (1998), 'Deadly Diets'. *Boston Phoenix* (15–22 Oct.), www.bostonphoenix.com/archive/features/98/10/15/DEADLY_DIETS.html, consulted 25 Sept. 2002.

Maguire, D. C. (1993), 'A Catholic Theologian at an Abortion Clinic'. In R. M. Baird and S. E. Rosenbaum (eds.), *The Ethics of Abortion*, rev. edn. Amherst, NY: Prometheus.

Marquis, D. (1989), 'Why Abortion is Immoral'. *Journal of Philosophy* 86(4): 183–202.

Martin, E. (1996), 'The Egg and the Sperm: How Science Has Constructed a Romance Based on Stereotypical Male-Female Roles'. In E. F. Keller and H. E. Longino (eds.), *Feminism and Science*. Oxford: Oxford University Press, 103–17.

Martyna, W. (1978), 'What Does "He" Mean?' *Journal of Communication* 28: 131–8.

Maushart, S. (2002), *Wifework*. London: Bloomsbury.

Mercier, A. (1995), 'A Perverse Case of the Contingent A Priori: On the Logic of Emasculating Language (A Reply to Dawkins and Dummett)'. *Philosophical Topics* 23(2): 221–59.

Mernissi, F. (1987), *Beneath the Veil*. Bloomington, Ind.: Indiana University Press.

Mill, J. S. (1986 [1861]), *The Subjection of Women*. Buffalo, New York: Prometheus.

—— (1998 [1859]), 'On Liberty'. In J. Gray (ed.), *On Liberty and Other Essays*. Oxford: Oxford University Press, 5–128.

Miller, C., and Swift, K. (1976), *Words and Women: New Language in New Times*. New York: Anchor.

Mohanty, C. T. (1991a), 'Introduction'. In C. T. in Mohanty, A. Russo, and L. Torres, (eds.), *Third World Women and the Politics of Feminism*. Bloomington, Ind.: Indiana University Press, 1–47.

—— (1991b), 'Under Western Eyes: Feminist Scholarship and Colonialist

Discourses'. In C. T. Mohanty, A. Russo, and L. Torres (eds.), *Third World Women and the Politics of Feminism*. Bloomington, Ind.: Indiana University Press, 51–80.

Moir, A., and Moir, B. (1998), *Why Men Don't Iron*. London: HarperCollins.

Moody-Adams, M. (1991), 'Gender and the Complexity of Moral Voices'. In C. Card (ed.), *Feminist Ethics*. Lawrence: University of Kansas Press, 195–212.

Moore, N. (2002), 'Indirect Discrimination Not Just a Statistical Formula'. *Personnel Today* (16 Apr.).

Morgan, K. P. (1998), 'Women and the Knife: Cosmetic Surgery and the Colonization of Women's Bodies'. In R. Weitz (ed.), *The Politics of Women's Bodies: Sexuality, Appearance, and Behaviour*. Oxford: Oxford University Press.

Morris, D. (1967), *The Naked Ape*. London: Cape.

Moses, C. G. (1984), *French Feminism in the 19th Century*. Albany, NY: State University of New York Press.

Moulton, J. (1981), 'The Myth of the Neutral "Man" '. In Vetterling-Braggin (1981: 100–115).

—— Robinson, G. M., and Elias, C. (1978), 'Sex Bias in Language Use: Neutral Pronouns That Aren't'. *American Psychologist* 33: 1032–6

Munoz-Dardé, V. (1999), 'Is the Family to be Abolished Then?' *Proceedings of the Aristotelian Society*, vol. 99: 37–56.

Nails, D. (1983), 'Social-Scientific Sexism: Gilligan's Mismeasure of Man'. *Social Research* 50: 643–64.

Narayan, U. (1988), 'Working Together Across Difference: Some Considerations on Emotions and Political Practice'. *Hypatia* 3(2): 31–47.

—— (1993), 'What Do Rights Have to Do With It?' *Journal of Social Philosophy* 24(2): 186–99.

—— (1997), *Dislocating Cultures: Identities, Traditions, and Third World Feminism*. New York: Routledge.

—— (1998), 'Essence of Culture and a Sense of History'. *Hypatia* 13(2): 86–106.

National Committee on Pay Equity (2002), 'Little Progress on Closing Wage Gap in 2000'. www.feminist.com/fairpay/f_wagegap.htm, consulted 2 May 2002.

National Institute of Mental Health (2002), 'Facts About Eating Disorders and the Search for Solutions'. www.nimh.gov//publicat/eatingdisorder.cfm, consulted 25 Sept. 2002.

Nelson, L. H. (1990), *Who Knows: From Quine to Feminist Empiricism*. Philadelphia: Temple University Press.

—— (1993), 'Epistemological Communities'. In L. Alcoff and E. Potter (eds.), *Feminist Epistemologies*. New York: Routledge, 121–60.

—— (1996), 'Who Knows? What Can They Know? And When?' In A. Garry and M. Pearsall (eds.), *Women, Knowledge, and Reality: Explorations in Feminist Philosophy*, 2nd edn. New York: Routledge, 286–97.

Nicholson, L. (1990), *Feminism/Postmodernism*. New York: Routledge.

—— (1998), 'Gender'. In A. M. Jaggar and I. M. Young (eds.), *A Companion to Feminist Philosophy*. Malden, Mass.: Blackwell, 289–97.

Nielson, S. (1988), 'Books Bad for Women: A Feminist Looks at Censorship'. In G. Chester and J. Dickey (eds.), *Feminism and Censorship: The Current Debate*. Bridport, Dorset: Prism, 17–25.

Nussbaum, M. (1995a), 'Introduction'. In M. Nussbaum and J. Glover (eds.), *Women, Culture, and Development: A Study of Human Capabilities*. Oxford: Clarendon Press, 1–34.

—— (1995b), 'Human Capabilities, Female Human Beings'. In M. Nussbaum and J. Glover (eds.), *Women, Culture and Development: A Study of Human Capabilities*. Oxford: Clarendon Press, 61–104.

—— (1999), *Sex and Social Justice*. New York: Oxford University Press.

Obiora, L. A. (2000), 'Bridges and Barricades: Rethinking Polemics and Intransigence in the Campaign against Female Circumcision'. In A. K. Wing (ed.), *Global Critical Race Feminism: An International Reader*. New York: New York University Press.

Okin, S. M. ([1979], New edn. 1992), *Women in Western Political Thought*. Princeton, NJ: Princeton University Press.

—— (1981), 'Women and the Making of the Sentimental Family'. *Philosophy and Public Affairs* 11(1): 65–88.

—— (1989), *Justice, Gender, and the Family*. New York: Basic Books.

—— (1994a), 'Political Liberalism, Justice, and Gender'. *Ethics* 105: 23–43.

—— (1994b), 'Gender Inequality and Cultural Differences'. *Political Theory* 22(1): 5–24.

—— (1998a), 'Feminism and Political Theory'. In J. Kourany (ed.), *Philosophy in a Feminist Voice*. Princeton, NJ: Princeton University Press, 116–44.

—— (1998b), 'Feminism, Women's Human Rights, and Cultural Differences'. *Hypatia* 13(2): 32–52.

—— (ed.) (1999) *Is Multiculturalism Bad for Women?* Princeton, NJ: Princeton University Press.

Osman, S. (1988), 'Should It Be Unlawful to Incite Sexual Violence?' In G. Chester and J. Dickey (eds.), *Feminism and Censorship*. Bridport, Dorset: Prism, 151–60.

Paglia, C. (2001), 'No Law in the Arena'. In L. LeMoncheck and J. Sterba (eds.), *Sexual Harassment: Issues and Answers*. New York Oxford: University Press, 260–3.

Palac, L. (1995), 'How Dirty Pictures Changed My Life'. In A. Stan (ed.), *Debating Sexual Correctness*. New York: Delta.

Papanek, H. (1990), 'To Each Less than She Needs, from Each More than She Can Do: Allocations, Entitlements, and Value'. In I. Tinker (ed.), *Persistent Inequalities: Women and World Development*. Oxford: Oxford University Press, 162–81.

306 | REFERENCES

Parekh, B. (1999), 'A Varied Moral World'. In Okin (1999: 69–76).

Patai, D. (2001), 'Heterophobia'. In L. LeMoncheck and J. Sterba (eds.), *Sexual Harassment: Issues and Answers*. New York: Oxford University Press, 274–86.

Pateman, C. (1988), *The Sexual Contract*. Stanford, Calif.: Stanford University Press.

—— (1989), *The Disorder of Women*. Stanford: Stanford University Press.

Paul, E. F. (2001), 'Bared Buttocks and Federal Cases'. In L. LeMoncheck and J. Sterba (eds.), *Sexual Harassment: Issues and Answers*. New York, Oxford University Press, 245–8.

Penelope, J. (1990), *Speaking Freely: Unlearning the Lies of the Fathers' Tongues*. New York: Pergamon.

Petchesky, R. P. (1986), *Abortion and Woman's Choice*. London: Verso.

Pollitt, K. (1994), *Reasonable Creatures*. New York: Knopf.

—— (1999), 'Whose Culture?' In Okin (1999: 27–31).

Pugh, M. (1992), *Women and the Women's Movement in Britain 1914–1959*. London: Macmillan.

Purdy, L. (1981), 'Against "Vs. Ms." '. In Vetterling-Braggin (1981: 223–8).

Quin, C. (2002), 'Girly Phones'. iVillage.co.uk, www.ivillage.co.uk/computers/experts/gadget/articles/0,9439,181463_183871,00.html, consulted 14 May 2002.

Rahmanou, H. (2001), '*The Widening Gap:* A New Book on the Struggle to Balance Work and Caregiving'. Washington, DC: Institute for Women's Policy Research Publication C349.

Rawls, J. (1971), *A Theory of Justice*. Cambridge, Mass.: Harvard University Press.

—— (1999), *The Law of Peoples*. Cambridge, Mass.: Harvard University Press.

Reed, L. C. (2002), 'Eyeing my Career in a World without Mascara'. *Washington Business Journal* (2 Aug.). http://washington.bizjournals.com/washington/stories/2002/08/05/editorial4.html, consulted 14 Nov. 2002.

Renzetti, C., and Curran, D. (1992), 'Gender Socialisation'. In J. A. Kourany, J. P. Sterba, and R. Tong (eds.), *Feminist Philosophies*. London: Prentice-Hall, 31–48.

Rhode, D. (1997), 'Media Images/Feminist Issues'. In M. Fineman and M. McCluskey (eds.), *Feminism, Media, and the Law*. Oxford: Oxford University Press, 8–21.

—— (1998), 'The Politics of Paradigms: Gender Difference and Gender Disadvantage'. In A. Phillips (ed.), *Feminism and Politics*. Oxford: Oxford University Press, 344–60.

Richards, J. R. (1980), *The Sceptical Feminist*. London: Routledge.

Roiphe, K. (2001), 'Reckless Eyeballing: Sexual Harassment on Campus'. In L. LeMoncheck and J. Sterba (eds.), *Sexual Harassment: Issues and Answers*. New York: Oxford University Press, 249–59.

Rothman, B. (1986), *The Tentative Pregnancy: Pre-natal Diagnosis and the Future for Motherhood*. New York: Viking.

Rowbotham, S. (1973), *Woman's Consciousness, Man's World*. Harmondsworth: Penguin.

Royalle, C. (2000), 'Porn in the USA'. In D. Cornell (ed.), *Feminism and Pornography*. New York: Oxford University Press, 540–50.

Rozin, P., and Fallon, A. E. (1988), 'Body Image, Attitudes to Weight, and Misperceptions of Figure Preferences of the Opposite Sex: A Comparison of Men and Women in Two Generations'. *Journal of Abnormal Psychology* 97(3): 342–5.

Rubin, G. (1993), 'Misguided, Dangerous and Wrong: An Analysis of Anti-Pornography Politics'. In A. Assiter (ed.), *Bad Girls and Dirty Pictures*. London: Pluto Press, 18–40.

Ruddick, S. (1989), *Maternal Thinking: Toward a Politics of Peace*. New York: Basic Books.

Russell, D. (1993), 'Introduction'. In Russell (ed.), *Making Violence Sexy: Feminist Views on Pornography*. Buckingham: Open University Press, 1–22.

Russett, C. E. (1989), *Sexual Science: The Victorian Construction of Womanhood*. Cambridge, Mass.: Harvard University Press.

Sandler, L. (2002), 'Beauty Tips and Politics'. *The Nation* (2 Sept.) www.thenation.com/doc.mhtml?i=20020902ands=sandler, consulted 14 Sept. 2002.

Sayoc, B. T. (1974), 'Surgery of the Oriental Eyelid'. *Clinics in Plastic Surgery* 1: 157–71.

Scales, A. (2000), 'Avoiding Constitutional Depression'. In D. Cornell (ed.), *Feminism and Pornography*. New York: Oxford University Press, 318–44.

Schor, J. (1991), *The Overworked American*. New York: Basic Books.

Schroedel, J. R. (1986), *Alone in a Crowd: Women in the Trades Tell Their Stories*. Philadelphia: Temple University Press.

Schultz, V. (1998), 'Reconceptualizing Sexual Harassment'. *Yale Law Journal* 107: 1683–1805.

—— (2001), 'Sex is the Least of it: Let's Focus Harassment Law on Work, not Sex'. In L. LeMoncheck and J. Sterba (eds.), *Sexual Harassment: Issues and Answers*. New York: Oxford University Press, 269–73.

—— (forthcoming), 'The Sanitized Workplace'.

Schwartz, R. (1988), 'A Question of Allegiance?' In G. Chester and J. Dickey (eds.), *Feminism and Censorship*. Bridport, Dorset: Prism, 11–16.

Segal, L. (1990), 'Pornography and Violence: What the "Experts" Really Say'. *Feminist Review* 36: 29–41.

Shelton, B. A., and John, D. (1996), 'The Division of Household Labour'. *Annual Review of Sociology* 22: 299–322.

Sher, G. (1987), 'Other Voices, Other Rooms? Women's Psychology and Moral Theory'. In E. F. Kittay and D. T. Meyers (eds.), *Women and Moral Theory*. Totowa, NJ: Rowman & Littlefield.

Shrage, L. (1994), *Moral Dilemmas of Feminism*. New York Routledge.

—— (2002), *Abortion and Social Responsibility: Depolarizing the Debate*. Oxford: Oxford University Press.

Silbert, M. (1989), 'The Effects on Juveniles of Being Used for Pornography and Prostitution'. In D. Zillman and J. Bryant (eds.), *Pornography: Research Advances and Policy Considerations*. Hillsdale, NJ: Erlbaum, 215–34.

Smith, D. (1996), 'Women's Perspective as a Radical Critique of Sociology'. In E. F. Keller, and H. Longino (eds.), *Feminism and Science*. Oxford University Press, 17–27.

Soble, A. (1981) 'Beyond the Miserable Vision of "Vs. Ms." '. In Vetterling-Braggin, (1981: 229–48).

Soueif, A. (2001), 'The Language of the Veil'. *Guardian* (8 Dec.). www.guardian.co.uk.weekend/story/0,3605,614360,00.html, consulted 21 Aug. 2002.

Spelman, E. (1988), *Inessential Woman*. Boston, Mass.: Beacon Press.

—— (2000), 'How Do They See You?' *London Review of Books* (16 Nov.). www.lrb.co.uk/v22/n22/spel01.html consulted 6 Sept. 2002.

Spender, D. (1985), *Man Made Language*, 2nd edn. New York: Routledge.

Stack, C. (1993) 'The Culture of Gender: Women and Men of Color'. In M. J. Larrabee (ed.), *An Ethic of Care: Feminist and Interdisciplinary Perspectives*. New York Routledge, 108–11.

Steinem, G. (1995), 'Erotica and Pornography: A Clear and Present Difference'. In S. Dwyer (ed.), *The Problem of Pornography*. Belmont, Caif. Wadsworth, 29–33.

—— (2002), 'Sex, Lies, and Advertising', *Ms.* 12 (2): 60–64.(Reprint of article initially published in *Ms.* in July/Aug. 1990.

Steinherr, A. (2001a), 'Stop the Clock: Invest in the Future of Your Skin'. *Cosmopolitan* (Oct.): 291.

(2001b), 'Pretty Damn Sexy'. *Cosmopolitan* (Oct.): 269–72.

Stericker, A. (1981), 'Does This "He" or "She" Business Really Make a Difference? The Effects of Masculine Pronouns as Generics on Job Attitudes', *Sex Roles* 7(6): 637–41.

Stoljar, N. (1995), 'Essence, Identity, and the Concept of Woman', *Philosophical Topics* 23: 261–93.

Stowasser, B. (1996), *Women in the Qur'an: Traditions, and Interpretation*. Oxford: Oxford University Press.

Strossen, N. (1995), *Defending Pornography*. New York: Anchor.

Strunk, W., and White, E. B. (1979), *The Elements of Style*, 3rd edn. New York: Macmillan.

Summerskill, S. (2000), 'Working Women Face Backlash from Firms Wary of Mothers: Childcare Policies Are Failing, Says New Report'. *Observer* (20 Aug.).

Talbot, M. (2002), 'Men Behaving Badly'. *New York Times* (13 Oct.). www.ny times.com/2002/10/13/magazine/13HARASSMENT.html?pagewanted =print&position=top

Tamir, Y. (1999), 'Siding with the Underdogs'. In Okin, (1999: 47–52).

Tanesini, A. (1999), *An Introduction to Feminist Epistemologies*. Oxford: Blackwell.

Tavris, C. (1992), *The Mismeasure of Woman*. New York: Touchstone.

Taylor, H. (1970 [1851]), 'The Enfranchisement of Women'. In A. Rossi (ed.), *Essays on Sex Equality*. Chicago: University of Chicago Press.

Thompson, L. (1999), *The Wandering Womb: A Cultural History of Outrageous Beliefs About Women*. Amherst, NY: Prometheus.

Thomson, J. (1971), 'A Defense of Abortion'. *Philosophy and Public Affairs* 1: 47–66.

Todd, H. (2001), 'Are Women Bound to House and Children by Ties of Evolution?' Unpublished.

Tong, R. (1998), *Feminist Thought: A More Comprehensive Introduction*. Boulder, Colo.: Westview.

Tooley, M. (1981), 'Abortion and Infanticide'. In J. Arthur (ed.), *Morality and Moral Controversies*. Englewood Cliffs, NJ: Prentice-Hall, 214–26.

Toyne, S. (2002), 'UK Women "Losing Out on Pay" '. BBCi. http://news.bbc.co.uk/1/hi/business/192036.stm, consulted 28 Nov. 2002.

Tronto, J. (1993), *Moral Boundaries: A Political Argument for an Ethic of Care*. New York: Routledge.

—— (2002), 'The "Nanny' Question in Feminism'. *Hypatia* 17(2): 34–51.

Valeska, L. (1983), 'If All Else Fails, I'm Still a Mother'. In J. Trebilcot (ed.), *Mothering*. Savage, Md.: Rowman & Littlefield, 70–8.

Vance, C. (1992), 'More Pleasure, More Danger: A Decade after the Barnard Sexuality Conference', in Vance (ed.), *Pleasure and Danger*. London: Pandora, xvi–xliii.

Vetterling-Braggin, M. (ed.) (1981), *Sexist Language*. Totowa, NJ: Littlefield & Adams.

Viner, K. (2002), 'Feminism as Imperialism'. *Guardian* (21 Sept.): 26.

Wadud, A. (1999), *Qur'an and Woman: Rereading the Sacred Text from a Woman's Perspective*. Oxford: Oxford University Press.

Walker, L. (1993), 'Sex Differences in the Development of Moral Reasoning'. In M. J. Larrabee (ed.), *An Ethic of Care*. New York: Routledge, 157–76.

—— de Vries. B., and Trevethan, S. (1987), 'Moral Stages and Moral Orientations in Real-Life and Hypothetical Dilemmas'. *Child Development* 58: 842–58.

Walter, N. (1998), *The New Feminism*. London: Little, Brown.

Warren, M. A. (1973), 'On the Moral and Legal Status of Abortion'. *Monist* 57(1): 43–60.

—— (1989), 'The Moral Significance of Birth'. *Hypatia* 4(3): 46–65.

Weaver, J. (1992), 'The Social Science and Psychological Research Evidence: Perceptual and Behavioural Consequences of Exposure to Pornography'. In C. Itzin (ed.), *Pornography: Women, Violence, and Civil Liberties*. New York: Oxford University Press, 284–309.

Weitzman, L. (1985), *The Divorce Revolution*. New York: Free Press.

Williams, J. (2000), *Unbending Gender: Why Family and Work Conflict and What to Do About It*. Oxford: Oxford University Press.

Williams, L. (1993), 'Second Thoughts on *Hard Core*'. In P. C. Gibson and R. Gibson (eds.), *Dirty Looks*. London: BFI, 46–61.

Willis, E. (1992), 'Abortion: Is a Woman a Person?' In J. A. Kourany, J. P. Sterba, and R. Tong (eds.), *Feminist Philosophies: Problems, Theories, and Applications*. Englewood Cliffs, NJ: Prentice-Hall, 83–6.

Wilson, E., and Ng, S. H. (1988), 'Sex Bias in Visual Images Evoked by Generics: A New Zealand Study'. *Sex Roles* 18(3/4): 159–68.

Wolf, N. (1991). *The Beauty Myth*. London: Vintage.

—— (2001), *Misconceptions*. London: Chatto & Windus.

Wylie, A. (2000), 'Feminism in Philosophy of Science: Making Sense of Contingency and Constraint'. In M. Fricker and J. Hornsby (eds.), *The Cambridge Companion to Feminism in Philosophy*. Cambridge: Cambridge University Press, 166–85.

Young, C. (2000), 'They're No Angels'. *Salon*. www.salon.com/news/sports/2000/08/26/wnba/index.html, consulted 18 Nov. 2002.

Young, I. M. (1990a), 'Throwing Like a Girl: A Phenomenology of Feminine Body Comportment, Mobility, and Spatiality'. In *Throwing Like A Girl and Other Essays in Feminist Philosophy and Social Theory*. Bloomington, Ind.: Indiana University Press 141–59.

—— (1990b), 'Women Recovering Our Clothes'. In *Throwing Like A Girl and Other Essays in Feminist Philosophy and Social Theory*. Bloomington, Ind.: Indiana University Press, 177–88.

—— (1997), 'Punishment, Treatment, Empowerment: Three Approaches to Policy for Pregnant Addicts'. In *Intersecting Voices: Dilemmas of Gender, Political Philosophy, and Policy*. Princeton, NJ: Princeton University Press, 75–94.

Zalesne, D. (1999a), 'Sexual Harassment Law: Has It Gone Too Far, or Has the Media?' *Temple Political and Civil Rights Law Review*, 8(2) 351–376.

—— (1999b), 'Workplace Paranoia: Media Propaganda'. *Women's International Net* 21 (May).

Zillman, D. (1989), 'Effects of Prolonged Consumption of Pornography'. In D. Zillman and J. Bryant (eds.), *Pornography: Research Advances and Policy Considerations*. Hillsdale, NJ: Erlbaum, 127–57.

Index